GRUNDY'S LONDON

GRUNDY'S LONDON

Bill Grundy

QUARTET BOOKS

LONDON MELBOURNE NEW YORK

First published by Quartet Books Limited 1979
A member of the Namara Group
27 Goodge Street, London W1P 1FD

Copyright © 1979 by Bill Grundy

Photographs by Pat Dyos

ISBN 0 7043 3286 8

Printed in Great Britain

Contents

Preface

I'm not sure when I first went to London. It was probably at
the age of five or six and we'd be passing through on our
holiday way from Manchester to Clacton-on-Sea (I'm told I
was always most insistent about the 'on-Sea' bit: I obviously
still am). As we travelled LNER, that being the line my
father worked for, our train would have come in at King's
Cross or St Pancras. For Clacton-on-Sea we would have left
by Liverpool Street station. Crammed into a taxi, our once-
a-year luxury, we might have travelled up Pentonville Road
as far as the Angel, and then along the City Road to Old
Street, swinging south there down to Liverpool Street. It
must have been something like that anyway, and if any
London cabbie reads this and laughs at me, let him
remember that it was fifty years ago, that there weren't
many one-way streets in those days, and that I'm talking
about London before the Blitz. The one thing that matters,
however, is that, going by that route, the five-year-old me
can't have seen very much out of the cab window to excite
him about London. Certainly, whatever I saw induced no
'Turn again Whittington' feelings.

I remember London much more clearly five years later when I was returning from a holiday in Eastleigh (not intended as a joke: Eastleigh was a railway town and we had friends there. I know it sounds a bit like holidaying in Crewe, but it was another world to a lad from Lancashire). On the way back we stopped for a few hours in London and, I don't know how or why, found ourselves in the National Gallery. I have a distinct memory of some paintings of saints – I was religious and in the church choir by this time – so wonderfully painted that I was tempted to put out my hand to see if they were three-dimensional or not. I have been back to the National Gallery many times since, but I have yet to re-discover those paintings, seen so clearly in my mind's eye even now, which amazed me so much forty-five years ago.

I remember little else of that visit, nor do I think there were many others before war broke out and I ultimately found myself, a young naval officer, stuck up on the extreme north-east coast of Scotland. By this time I had developed a taste for London, since I had earlier been posted to Watford of all places, which had meant two or three months in which I could make frequent visits to theatres and concerts and begin to learn something of what London had to offer. But I don't think I had, at that time, acquired a 'feel' for the place itself. And then I realized, one day far north in Scotland, that I had some leave coming up. I don't know why I decided that, this time, it wasn't going to be spent in the bosom of my family but was going to be spent in London.

I remember I travelled down on a night train, by which I mean it travelled through the night, even though it started out early in the day. I remember little of that journey apart from its boredom and discomfort. We got into London about five the next morning. The first breath of air was wonderful by comparison with the foetid atmosphere of the compartment. But it was wonderful for another reason, a reason which suddenly made itself clear in an involuntary shout of 'I'm in London for seven whole days', a shout which drew odd glances and was certainly taken to mean I was looking forward to a week of wining, wenching, and general wild oats.

I did not, however, leap into a taxi, even assuming one

was available, but set out instead to walk south. I walked and walked and eventually found myself, I know not why or how, on a bridge over the Thames. I can't even remember which bridge it was. Memory says Waterloo, but a since-acquired knowledge of that bridge's history suggests it was actually Blackfriars I was standing on, that distant summer morning.

The important thing is that, about 6 a.m., on a June day, in a year I'm not too sure of, leaning on the balustrade of a bridge I can't positively identify, I looked to the north-east. There, glistening against a porcelain-blue sky, was the dome of St Paul's. My heart lifted, I knew London would never go under, I knew this was the sort of thing the war was about (naïve, those sentiments sound now, but I'm still not ashamed of them), and from that moment on I was hooked on London for life. It would be nice to know the precise second this incident on my particular Road to Damascus took place, but memory fails me. I do remember, however, that, as I stared entranced at the spectacle, a V2, or it could have been a 'buzz-bomb', crunched somewhere in the distance. The thought that it may have just destroyed someone who had loved London far longer than I did, or could have done, never occurred to me. The explosion merely punctuated, and thereby emphasized, my determination to learn whatever I could about this wonderful city, come what may.

Oddly enough, demobilization, when it came, did not see me make straight for the Capital. It saw me back in the sooty old sights and smells of Manchester, a town as dear to me in its way as London. But each rare visit to the Great Wen was a joy; each trip I saw more of it; and then came the days when I actually found myself working in it! Even more, some years later, I was making television programmes about it! I wanted to learn more. I needed to learn more. I *had* to learn more. There has never been a more inexhaustible London Perambulator, to borrow the title of a lovely book by James Bone the one-time London Correspondent of the *Manchester Guardian*, whose artist brother, Muirhead Bone, had supplied it with some heart-stopping illustrations. There has never been a more voracious reader of London history and guide-books. I learnt a lot, but never

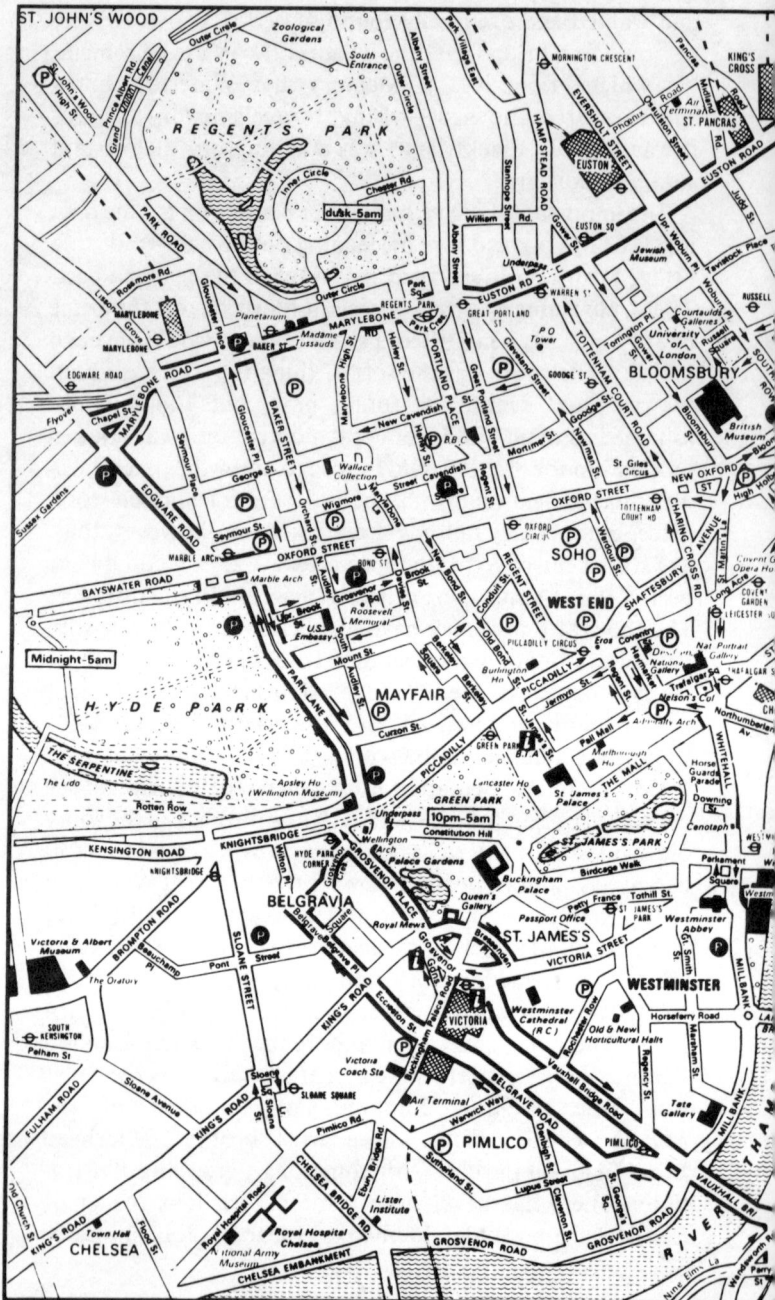

ST. JOHN'S WOOD

REGENTS PARK

Zoological Gardens

South Entrance

Outer Circle

Outer Circle

Inner Circle

dusk-5am

Chester Rd

MORNINGTON CRESCENT

KING'S CROSS

Air Terminal
ST. PANCRAS

EUSTON

EUSTON SQ

Jewish Museum

Underpass

WARREN ST

EUSTON RD

RUSSELL

Courtauld Galleries
University of London

BLOOMSBURY

British Museum

MARYLEBONE

Planetarium

Madame Tussauds

Baker St

REGENTS PARK

Park Crescent

GREAT PORTLAND

GOODGE ST

P O Tower

TOTTENHAM COURT RD

EDGWARE ROAD

Chapel St

MARYLEBONE ROAD

Rossmore Rd

PARK ROAD

Gloucester Pl

Seymour Place

George St

BAKER STREET

Wallace Collection

New Cavendish

Street

BBC

Mortimer St

St Giles Circus

NEW OXFORD ST

Covent Garden Opera Ho

Marble Arch

OXFORD STREET

BOND ST

Cavendish

OXFORD CIRCUS

WEST END

SHAFTESBURY

CHARING CROSS RD

SOHO

BAYSWATER ROAD

Marble Arch

Brook

Grosvenor

Roosevelt Memorial

Mount St

U.S. Embassy

MAYFAIR

REGENT STREET

Conduit St

Old Bond St

PICCADILLY CIRCUS

Eros

Coventry

Burlington Ho

National Gallery

Nat Portrait Gallery

Nelson's Col

Leicester Sq

Midnight-5am

HYDE PARK

PARK LANE

Curzon St

PICCADILLY

Jermyn St

Pall Mall

B.I.A.

Marlborough Ho

Admiralty Arch

Northumberland Av

THE MALL

WHITEHALL

Horse Guards Parade

Downing

THE SERPENTINE

The Lido

Rotten Row

Apsley Ho (Wellington Museum)

Underpass

GREEN PARK

Lancaster House

St James's Palace

Constitution Hill

10pm-5am

ST. JAMES'S PARK

Cenotaph

KENSINGTON ROAD

KNIGHTSBRIDGE

Wellington Arch

HYDE PARK CORNER

GROSVENOR PLACE

Palace Gardens

St James's Park

Parliament Square

Westminster

KNIGHTSBRIDGE

Buckingham Palace

Birdcage Walk

BELGRAVIA

Queen's Gallery

Royal Mews

France

ST JAMES'S

Tothill St

Westminster Abbey

Victoria & Albert Museum

BROMPTON ROAD

Beauchamp

Pont Street

SLOANE STREET

Belgrave

Square

Passport Office

ST. JAMES'S

VICTORIA STREET

WESTMINSTER

Gt Smith St

Horseferry Road

The Oratory

SOUTH KENSINGTON

Pelham St

Eccleston St

KING'S ROAD

VICTORIA

Westminster Cathedral (R C)

Old & New Horticultural Halls

Regency St

FULHAM ROAD

Sloane Avenue

SLOANE SQUARE

Sloane

Victoria Coach Sta

Air Terminal

Warwick Way

BELGRAVE ROAD

Vauxhall Bridge Road

Marsham St

MILLBANK

Tate Gallery

Old Chelsea St

KING'S ROAD

Sloane

Pimlico Rd

Ebury Bridge Rd

Lister Institute

Lupus Street

Sutherland St

PIMLICO

PIMLICO

Clarendon St

St George's Sq

CHELSEA BRIDGE RD

Town Hall

Royal Hospital Road

Royal Hospital Chelsea

National Army Museum

CHELSEA EMBANKMENT

CHELSEA

GROSVENOR ROAD

GROSVENOR ROAD

VAUXHALL BRI

RIVER THAMES

Nine Elms La

Ferry

To BATTERSEA PLEASURE GARDENS

CENTRAL LONDON

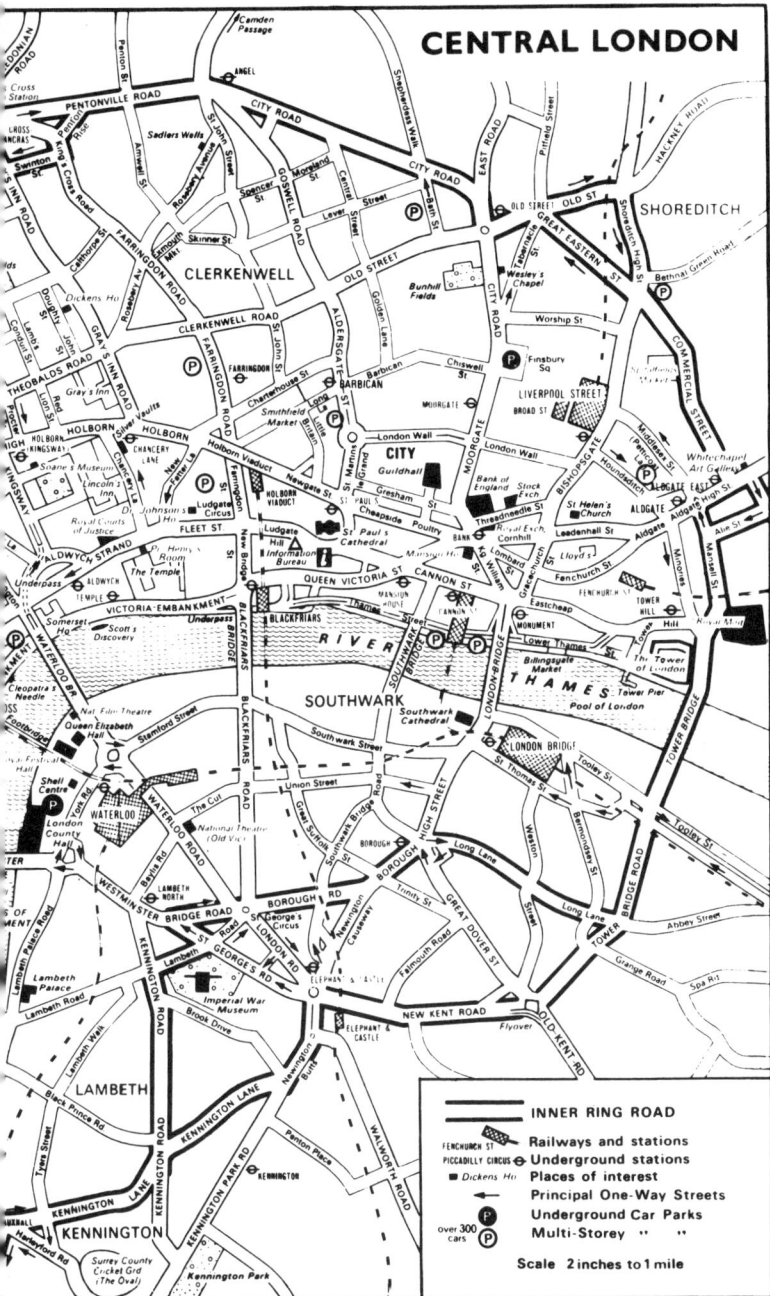

SHOREDITCH

CLERKENWELL

OLD STREET

CITY ROAD

Bunhill Fields

Wesley's Chapel

Worship St

Finsbury Sq

LIVERPOOL STREET

BROAD ST

CITY

Guildhall

Bank of England

Stock Exch

Royal Exch

St Paul's Cathedral

Ludgate Circus

HOLBORN VIADUCT

HOLBORN

CHANCERY LANE

Lincoln's Inn

Royal Courts of Justice

FLEET ST

STRAND

ALDWYCH

The Temple

VICTORIA EMBANKMENT

Cleopatra's Needle

BLACKFRIARS

RIVER THAMES

SOUTHWARK

Southwark Cathedral

LONDON BRIDGE

The Tower of London

Tower Pier

Pool of London

TOWER HILL

ALDGATE

Whitechapel Art Gallery

WATERLOO

Queen Elizabeth Hall

Shell Centre

London County Hall

National Theatre (Old Vic)

LAMBETH

Lambeth Palace

Imperial War Museum

ELEPHANT & CASTLE

NEW KENT ROAD

KENNINGTON

Kennington Park

Surrey County Cricket Grd (The Oval)

Legend

▬▬▬	INNER RING ROAD
FENCHURCH ST ▨	Railways and stations
PICCADILLY CIRCUS ⊖	Underground stations
■ Dickens Ho	Places of interest
←	Principal One-Way Streets
℗ over 300 cars	Underground Car Parks
℗	Multi-Storey " "

Scale 2 inches to 1 mile

enough. I walked everywhere. I sailed the river. I travelled the tube. I leapt on and off buses. I talked to cabbies. I made notes. I drew maps. And I started putting my impressions into words, words which were backed by film but which I hope could almost have stood by themselves, because they were so obviously full of my enjoyment of the place.

Altogether I made some forty or fifty of those (quite short) films, mostly, but not entirely, for Thames TV. When I was invited by my publishers to pull all the scripts together into a book, to re-write and expand them, in an attempt to reveal just what Grundy's London implies, I was more than delighted. Writing the book has been a labour, but a labour of love. I know, from the letters I received when those tv films were shown, that there is a large number of people who want to know more about London. I hope I need hardly say that, despite years of wandering around the place, and reading a lot of what has been written about it, I, too, am one of those people. Perhaps I can adjust the words of a popular song and say:

> Maybe it's because I'm *not* a Londoner
> That I love London so.

And if, like me, you, too, aren't a Londoner – and, dammit, even if you are – I hope I can make you love it as much as I do. That's why this book was written, anyway.

Begin here

There are certain things a visitor to London must do, as well as some he or she mustn't.

The musts are legion, but the most important one to remember is that you are a tourist. Do the touristy things. Many millions of Londoners have never seen the Crown jewels. Maybe it's because they are Londoners and they think it isn't quite the done thing to do what the tourists do. That way they miss a lot. Why do they think tourists come to London anyway? It isn't to see No. 15 Laurel Drive, Tooting. Nor is it to see the office where the owner/occupier of No. 15 Laurel Drive, Tooting, works. Even less is it to see the stretch of underground railway connecting the two places, however vital it may be to the continued gainful employment of the owner/occupier of the said No. 15.

People come to London to see the unique things it has to offer; its palaces, its parks, its museums, its masterpieces, its night life, its low life, Soho and Shaftesbury Avenue, Hampstead Heath and Clapham Common. In a word, its richness.

So...

First of all, spend a bob or two (a bit more, actually: it's £1.70 for an adult and £1.10 for a child at the time of writing) on the standard London Transport Round London Sightseeing Tour. It takes two hours, it covers about twenty miles of the City and the West End, and it runs every single day of the year with the exception of Christmas Day. You can get on it at Piccadilly Circus; at Marble Arch, near Speakers' Corner; or at Grosvenor Gardens, Victoria. The first bus out is at 10 a.m. During the summer they run until 9 p.m. (7 p.m. from Marble Arch). In the winter, naturally, they finish earlier: the last bus from each of these three starting points leaves at 4 p.m. You don't have to book, by the way. If you can't get on the first bus, they put another one on for you. Try and get on the top deck; you see more of London that way. There ought to be guides telling you what you're passing, or missing, but there aren't. Instead you get a free illustrated route diagram as you step on board. Inevitably, this means you will be consulting it just at the moment you are passing something absolutely splendid. But that is the only objection I have to these enormously enjoyable trips. If this is your first pleasure visit to London – or your hundredth – go straight away to one of those three boarding points. You'll see more and learn more in the next two hours than many Londoners have learnt in a lifetime.

The next thing to do is go to the Tower of London. In summer, go as early as you can in the morning and take your foreign phrase book with you: you may well find you are the only English-speaking person there, and you might have to do a bit of interpreting. If you go in the middle of the day, the crowds can be positively oppressive and you may feel an entirely irrational xenophobia rising within you. Don't forget to go and sit on the benches, or astride the cannons, on the walk overlooking the river: dockland may have moved downstream but there's still enough traffic on the Thames to make it a marvellous way to pass the time as you eat your sandwiches and unscrew your vacuum flask. The Tower opens at 9.30 a.m. each day of the year except Good Friday and Christmas Day, and at 2 p.m. on Sundays from mid-March to the last Sunday in October. It closes at 5 p.m. from 1 March to 31 October and at 4 p.m. for the rest of the year, but you are allowed one hour after closing time to finish your visit and get clear of the Tower. Nearest tube station is Tower Hill, which is on the Circle and District lines.

Go and visit the Houses of Parliament. You can do that by queueing up at the St Stephen's entrance – that's the one opposite Westminster Abbey – or by walking boldly in, going up to the policeman in the Central Lobby, and putting in a 'green card' for your Member of Parliament (make sure you know his name: the bobbies on the desk are friendly but busy). When the House isn't sitting, it's much easier. The Palace of Westminster, as it is officially called, is then open to the public from 10 a.m. to 4.30 p.m. on Saturdays, Mondays, Tuesdays, and Spring and Summer Bank Holidays. The Westminster underground station is on the Circle and District lines. While you are in the Palace make sure you wander around Westminster Great Hall. It is one of the oldest buildings in London and the hammer-beamed roof is something to stare at until you tire of it, which you won't. William II built it. Richard II 'repaired' it. That must be London's greatest understatement: hundreds of the finest oaks standing in the Britain of the late fourteenth century were felled to make the roof, and the whole hall was transformed from a 'mere bedchamber' to the superb, if severe, work of art you see around you now.

Pop across the road to Westminster Abbey, but be prepared for a disappointment. Not with the Abbey itself, which is wonderful, but with the way you are 'processed' through it. Any feeling you may develop that you are a sausage passing through a machine is perfectly understandable. I suppose it is the only way to get so many people through such a splendid place in the time available, but it does rather detract from the impression the Abbey ought to make on you. As you come spilling out into Broad Sanctuary and Parliament Square you will be excused if you say 'Today is Thursday, so it must be London'.

If you are a Roman Catholic, and if you aren't, go to

Westminster Cathedral, along Victoria Street from the Abbey. It is in Ashley Place and you are hardly likely to miss it since its bell tower is 284 feet high. It is, of course, a baby compared with the Abbey. The building of the cathedral started in 1895 on the site of the Tothill Fields Prison (Tothill = tothill = stronghold), and was completed in 1903.

The style is a trifle bizarre for some tastes, being early Byzantine. The interior is disappointing, largely because it is still unfinished: the bare, rough bricks are one day to be covered by marble and mosaic. Nevertheless, the proportions of the cathedral are stunning. The nave is the widest in England, with the possible exception of that of Manchester Cathedral, and the length is an exhausting 360 feet. There is much to see, and more than adequate booklets and leaflets to describe it all. For some reason – lack of history, I suppose – it is never anywhere near as crowded as the Abbey, so whenever you go to visit it you will have time and space to appreciate the most important Roman Catholic building in Britain.

Go to Buckingham Palace, but please don't make mock of the men on guard. They do an extremely boring job and they do it with dignity and a fine sense of ceremony. They are Changing the Guard at Buckingham Palace, whether or not Christopher Robin is there with Alice, every morning at 11.30. Don't miss it, but get there early if you want a good view. Even if the Queen is in residence – you can tell that by looking to see if the Royal Standard is flying – I don't think she'll invite you in for a look round, but you can inspect the Royal Mews on Wednesdays and Thursday from 2 to 4 p.m. (except during Ascot Week). I doubt if you will fall down with excitement at what you see.

Do not miss Madame Tussaud's and the Planetarium. When you arrive there – *whenever* you arrive there – your heart will sink at the sight of the queue. Don't give up. Twenty million foreigners can't be wrong. If they are prepared to wait twenty minutes, which is the average time, no matter how busy they are, then you ought to be prepared as well. The fascination of waxworks is something I don't understand, but the magic of the Planetarium, and the Laserium, if it is the season, is something I can understand only too well. You sit back in your seat, the lights go out, the music starts, and slowly the whole firmament comes into view, twinkling against an invisible black velvet background. The sensation of lying out on Hampstead Heath on an absolutely clear summer night is hard to resist. But here you get the guide's voice telling you just what you are looking at, and it is all done supremely well. You get there by tube to Baker Street, which is on the Circle, the Metropolitan, and the Bakerloo lines. Madame Tussaud's and the Planetarium are separate institutions but you can buy a combined ticket which admits you to both. The waxworks is open from 10 a.m. to 6.30 p.m., although it closes an hour earlier during the winter months. The Planetarium opens at 11 a.m. and closes at 6 p.m., Sundays 1 p.m. to 5 p.m. Please go there.

Now you're up in the Marylebone Road – Euston Road area, you must go to the Post Office Tower. There are people, of whom I am one, who think it is an ugly piece of work. But it is a must, even if all you do is photograph it with your camera turned sideways, the only way you can get its massive length in shot. Wherever you look in London you can see it somewhere on the skyline. As a result it is now virtually impossible to get lost in the city. Just locate the Tower and walk towards it.

It is much more than an electronic communications tower. It is the very best viewpoint in London, with the possible exception of the Shell Building, overlooking the Thames, and the top of the new Natwest building in the City, overlooking everything else, including St Paul's, which is dwarfed by it. (This last is a fine example of the New Brutalism. How on earth the Natwest directors approved the construction, I shall never know. I think I will take my overdraft elsewhere. Where were we? Ah yes.)

You'll find the Post Office Tower, its minaret all a-gleam, in Cleveland Street–Howland Street, halfway between Euston Road and Oxford Street. Nearly six hundred feet above ground you can dine in the revolving restaurant, so that the whole panorama of London passes before you many times between aperitif and coffee. Since it does not revolve so quickly that your soup is hurled out of your plate by

5

centrifugal force, or your coffee flies out of the cup and drenches your neighbour, you will find the experience enjoyable, although settling the bill at the end of the meal is rather less so. There are non-revolving viewing platforms which at the moment are not open to the public, since they were damaged by a bomb blast some years ago. In the hope that they will soon be open to visitors again, you might find it useful to note that you can start queueing for the Tower any time before 9.30 a.m. (9 a.m. on Saturdays and Sundays) and it stays open until 9.30 p.m. Obviously the time you go there will depend on whether you want the daytime panorama or the night-time view of the lights of the town.

From the Tower you will see, just a little to the north, the green roundness of Regent's Park. It is called that after the Prince Regent, of course, who gave it to a grateful nation – one presumes they were grateful anyway. It was orginally planned by the architect Nash to become a sort of superior garden city, with thirty or forty luxurious villas hidden among the trees, but the scheme never got off the ground. Regent Street was planned by Nash as a splendid highway, linking the Prince Regent's official residence at Carlton House Terrace, down by St James's Park, with his 'country' villa in Regent's Park. The villa never got built, but the imposing street up to it did. The terraces around the park are some of the most beautiful houses to be seen in London.

But the Park has much more to offer than lovely houses, impressive as they are. It has a boating lake of some charm and considerable extent. It has the beautiful Queen Mary Rose Garden, almost overwhelming on a fine summer evening (or during the day, come to that). It has innumerable football and cricket pitches where the games are played with more exuberance than skill. It has the Open Air Theatre, now completely redesigned, with a steeply-raked amphitheatre, and built-in microphones, so that every player can be seen and every word can be heard. The plays presented there are almost always by Shakespeare, and the changes since the days when one sat in deck chairs and listened to Robert Atkins and his company performing great poetry on a most rudimentary stage are very much to my taste. To sit in that lovely, tree-hung bowl, and watch the twilight creeping over those last wonderful moments of *A Midsummer Night's Dream* is an experience which will stay long in your mind. The microphones, coupled with the fact that present-day aeroplanes fly higher over London than their predecessors did, mean that the actors no longer have to fight a running battle against engine noise (a battle which, in earlier days, they usually lost, so that if the wind was in the right direction, great chunks of the plays would go unheard). If the weather doesn't look too good, you can always ring up beforehand and check whether the play's afoot that night. If the day has been fine, ring up anyway: the theatre is very popular and the earlier you book the greater your chance of not being disappointed. The number is 01-486 2431.

The other great attraction in Regent's Park is, of course, the Zoo. It is one of the great zoos of the world. The aviary, designed by Lord Snowdon, is a masterpiece, the Aquarium is riveting, and there is a 'Moonlight Hall' so designed that normally nocturnal animals can be seen during the day. A day at the Zoo can be pretty pricey for a family party, so take your own sandwiches and flask. And if you're really short of money there are still animals you can see without having to pay to go in. They are at the top end of Broad Walk, just beyond Chester Road. And if you are a Muslim, there's a mosque for you, on the west side of the Park, all brand new, complete with gleaming dome and traditional minaret.

One piece of advice. Always keep a map of the Park in your pocket. The Inner Circle and Outer Circle roads can be very long if you happen to go round them the wrong way. The Park is big – 470 acres – which makes it bigger than Hyde Park, but not if you add on, as I suppose you must, Kensington Gardens: they add up to a total of about 600 acres.

Go and have a look at them, too. The Peter Pan statue up towards Malborough Gate on the Bayswater Road is a must for all children who have ever seen the play; the Round Pond over by Broad Walk is a paradise for model-boat fans; the Long Water and the Fountains and Gardens at its northern end are quite delightful; the Flower Walk at the back of the Albert Memorial is a little masterpiece as well as being virtually a wild life reserve; while the Albert Memorial itself

– well, it's the Albert Memorial, and it deserves very careful study. If it's summer time and you have got your trunks or your bikini with you you can go swimming in the Serpentine, which is merely the extension back into Hyde Park of the Long Water. If you've got your horse with you you can go riding in Rotten Row, and if you haven't you can always watch the others doing it. On Sunday mornings, go to Speakers' Corner at the Marble Arch end of Hyde Park. You won't hear too much sense, but you may hear some witty heckling – and some sharp responses, too.

Wander across to Green Park and St James's Park, but use the pedestrian underpasses: the traffic around Hyde Park Corner is positively murderous. Reflect on the fact that from the Palace of Westminster, you can walk on grass all the way to Notting Hill Gate, except for the Hyde Park Corner underpass. Don't go to Piccadilly Circus, one of the slums of the city, unless you like scruffiness, vulgarity, and the sight of drug addicts and pushers sitting around waiting for the time when they can go to the chemist and get their sustaining, but ultimately killing, fix. Avoid Leicester Square: it is, if anything, even less attractive than Piccadilly Circus. Go through to Trafalgar Square and have your photograph taken with a pigeon sitting on your head. Note the police station in the east corner. It is the smallest in the world, being no more than three feet in diameter.

Walk down to the Embankment, and then stroll east, past HMS *Discovery*, HMS *Wellington*, HMS *Chrysanthemum*, and HMS *President*. Climb up from the river through Temple Gardens, walk down Fleet Street to Ludgate Circus, and then up to St Paul's. Walk through the City during the day and marvel at the activity: walk back again at night and marvel at the silence. Where have all the people gone? To the suburbs, every one. But then, you see, they are not tourists. They are commuters. But you are a tourist, and you should behave like one. If you do all the things I've just mentioned you won't have seen the half of it, not even the hundredth of it, but you will have seen far more than most Londoners who race in by tube, bus, train or car, and race back out again in the evening, missing so much and so much. They, you will understand, have no time to stand and stare. You have. You are tourists, so make the most of it. Stroll, stand and stare. Get an eyeful of this most interesting of cities before it is too late. The rest of this book is designed to help you get the most out of your visit, and not just from the obvious tourist places alone. Buy yourself a copy of Nicholson's *Guide to London Town* and/or London Transport's *Visitors' London*. Either or both will slip into your pocket and they won't be too hard on it either, because they're very reasonably priced.

First, however, a look at London from the only proper place to start looking at it. The River Thames. And that is going to need a chapter to itself.

The river

Bridges and Tunnels – Westminster Bridge
Downstream from Westminster Pier to Greenwich
Upstream from Westminster to Richmond

If you are going to look at London in an organized sort of way, rather than in unrelated bits and pieces, then there's only one place to start, and that's with the river. As a matter of fact, even if you prefer the bits and pieces approach, it's still the best place, if for no other reason than that without a river there wouldn't have been a London. The river is where, and why, London started.

Nobody knows quite when: even before Julius Caesar invaded these islands in 55 and 54 BC, there were rumours in Rome of a trading settlement by a ford across the river Tamesis. Whether Caesar crossed the river by that ford in 54 BC, or whether he used one ten miles to the west at Brentford – the name is revealing – we shall never know. In his own account of the campaign, all Caesar says is that the Tamesis 'can only be forded at one place and that with difficulty'. In that, he was wrong, since there were several fords, the lowest of which was probably directly below the two small hills which today are crowned by St Paul's Cathedral on the west, and the buildings on Cornhill to the east.

The reason why the settlement was founded there is pretty obvious. The Thames in those days ran lower than it does today; the river bottom thereabouts was gravel, not mud, so the footing of the ford was safer, and the height of the little hills made them safe from flooding.

However, whether the settlement was there when Caesar arrived or whether it was founded later, it was most certainly there by the time of the first real invasion of Britain, by Aulus Plautius on behalf of the Emperor Claudius, just about one hundred years later. When his commander had beaten the British, Claudius was to appear on the scene with his elephants and show the British just how mighty was the power they had been beaten by. Well, Claudius *did* appear, and the place he appeared at was London, or Londinium. Since Roman emperors were not in the habit of making triumphal processions to places of no importance, especially so far from Rome, the conclusion is obvious: one hundred years after Julius Caesar, London was a place of great importance. There's another point: when the Romans built a wall around the city they had laid out on the two hills, that wall enclosed 330 acres, which made it the fifth largest city in the whole Roman empire, and that was only seventy years after Claudius' elephants had tramped up from the river. I think it is fair to say that London has been important, supremely important, ever since.

That importance depended on, and springs from, the Thames alone. Up it sailed the Celts, the Romans, the Angles, the Saxons, the Jutes, the Danes, the Vikings, and all the other invaders who have given the British race its uniquely mongrel character. Out of the river sailed those Elizabethan adventurers, some would say pirates, whose voyages signalled to the world that a new and great sea power was about to make its presence felt. They, in their turn, were followed by the more legitimate traders of the seventeenth, eighteenth, and nineteenth centuries, who sailed the wide world and carried British goods and the British flag to every corner of it. The Thames, by creating

London, changed the face of the world, or at least the map of it.

The continuity the river has provided can be a little mind-boggling. For instance, about eighteen miles east of London Bridge, at Swanscombe, near Gravesend, they found, in 1935, fossilized fragments of the bones of what may very well be the earliest known Europeans, and may very fairly be called the earliest Londoners, since Swanscombe is only just beyond the boundary of today's Greater London Council. The bones were lying in gravel beds laid down by the Thames a million or so years ago. About the same distance to the west of London Bridge is Heathrow Airport, whose concrete runways contain thousands of tons of that same river gravel. So there is the river, joining past and present, linking the time when elephants roamed through the tropic warmth of the Thames Valley with our time, when Jumbos lumber down through the evening air to London Airport. A continuity stretching over a period of a million years isn't to be found everywhere.

But one doesn't have to go to the very distant past to find examples of it. The same wide estuary that funnelled the first raiders up the river many centuries ago also served as a flight path for the German bombers intent on destroying London in the First and Second World Wars. The river that saw the triumphal processions of the Tudor monarchs also saw the last sad journey of the body of Sir Winston Churchill. The river a handful of Romans crossed in the years after the Conquest is now crossed by millions every day on their way to and from work. The river that provided Swanscombe Man with his water in the days when mammoth and rhinoceros roamed the valley, still provides water, admittedly heavily processed, for today's Londoner, to whom the word 'mammoth' might only suggest a large packet of cornflakes or washing powder, and whose only encounter with a rhinoceros is likely to be in the safe preserves of the Regent's Park Zoo.

The Thames has changed, however, and changed in my lifetime. The Pool of London – that's the stretch between the London and Tower Bridges – was once a forest of masts. Now it is deserted. That shows what has changed. What goes across the river is now more, far more, important than what goes up and down it. The bridges across the Thames are what matter today. The bridges – and the tunnels. For while the road and rail bridges are obvious (and just in case they're not all that obvious, let me tell you there are twenty-seven of them between Teddington and the Tower), the tunnels are out of sight and sometimes, therefore, out of mind. To bring them back to mind, learn now that there are eleven of them: three, at Dartford, Blackwall and Rotherhithe, for road traffic; three, at Woolwich, Greenwich, and a disused one by the side of Tower Bridge, for foot passengers; and five which are part of the London Underground system. Together they enable more people to get from one side of the river to the other in a month than can ever have floated across its waters in the whole two thousand years of its recorded history. That is the measure of the decline in the river's importance.

But, changing or not, the Thames is still London's river, the string on which this pearl of cities is threaded. It is, as the man said, liquid history. Actually, he didn't say quite that. He was, very appropriately, a London docker, a man who originally got his living from the river. His name was John Burns and he was Britain's first-ever working-class Cabinet Minister, in the Campbell-Bannerman Ministry of 1905–8; and what he said, to a party of visiting Americans on the Terrace of the House of Commons, was: 'Every drop of the Thames is liquid 'istory.' The missing aitch was reported by his Judas-friend, Sir Frederick Whyte, a snob and a bore to boot.

However, snobbishness and aitches apart, what John Burns said was true. It may now have become a cliché, but it is still true. Most clichés are, which is why they become clichés. And no cliché is truer than the one John Burns uttered seventy years ago.

What I have been trying to establish is that, if we are going to look at London, the Thames is worth looking at first. That, however, immediately brings up the question – where do we look at it from? One suggestion comes instantly to mind. Look at it from the same spot that William Wordsworth stood on when he was inspired by what he saw

13

to write a sonnet men still quote from more than 170 years later. Let us therefore go and stand on Westminster Bridge.

'Earth hath not anything to show more fair' he said about the view in 1803. Which shows that, though we may be standing on the same spot, we are not seeing the same thing. Today, the earth hath a lot to show more fair than the view from Westminster Bridge. And it isn't the same view anyway. It's still not bad, mind you, but it isn't what Wordsworth saw. Look down the river as it flows eastwards to the sea (although at Westminster the river is actually flowing north in one of its great meanders). Of the buildings our William saw, you will be able to see only a handful. Somerset House is that dark pile just visible beyond Waterloo Bridge. St Paul's still holds its head above a skyline apparently intent on devouring it. And there are those other pointers to Heaven, the remaining spires of Sir Christopher Wren and his contemporaries. Other than that, nothing. Now look upstream. Wordsworth would have been able to see Lambeth Palace, over there on the left, home of the Archbishops of Canterbury for centuries. He might just have been able to see the top of Westminster Hall and the towers of Westminster Abbey. And that would be all his view had in common with ours. The Houses of Parliament, for all their ancient look, are not the ones he saw. His was the old Parliament, the one that burnt down in 1834, thirty-one years after he wrote the famous sonnet. Even the bridge he stood on was not our bridge. His was built in 1750. From the moment of completion, the foundations gave trouble, but because of parliamentary indecision – some things clearly haven't changed – the bridge wasn't rebuilt until 1862, by which time Wordsworth had been dead twelve years.

There are other reasons why you might feel compelled to disagree not only with the opening line of the poem, but with its closing lines, too.

> Dear God! the very houses seem asleep
> And all that mighty heart is lying still.

For one thing, there aren't any houses to see. For another, whatever time of the day or night you choose to stand where Wordsworth stood, that mighty heart now never seems to lie still at all. If general, non-stop, noisy, busy-ness is anything to go by, it is clear that what you are looking at is one of the great cities of the world. At least two thousand years of history have accumulated here, running down the tributaries of time to join the main stream which 'still glideth at his own sweet will'.

It is also clear, I think you will admit, that this flower of cities all has changed a lot, and not necessarily for the better, since Wordsworth's day, so that whatever emotions it arouses in us are unlikely to be very much like those aroused in the poet's breast.

Nevertheless, Westminster is still a very good place to start to look at London. It is an even better place to start to look at the river, which is what we are supposed to be doing in this chapter. And that is because, just down those steps at the Big Ben end of the bridge, past the statue of Boadicea driving her reinless chariot, is Westminster Pier, and from that pier passenger boats ply both upstream and downstream. Upstream to lovely Richmond, downstream to Greenwich – 'London with a smell of the sea', as the travel posters call it. In those umpteen winding miles there are lots of places where you can get off and wander around before catching a boat back.

The trip downstream from Westminster Pier is probably the more interesting from the point of view of history, since you are heading towards where London started. Even today, with gigantic tower blocks ruining the skyline and trying (and failing) to make St Paul's look small, it is easy to get the feel of the two hills, Ludgate and Cornhill, on which the Romans built their first city. From the water they *look* like hills: floating past them you really do have to look up at them. But long before you reach them you have passed a stretch which is rich in history. The land running down from the Strand and Fleet Street was once covered with the houses of great noblemen: York House, Durham House, Russell House, the Savoy Palace, Somerset House, Arundel House, Leicester House. The names read like a passage from Shakespeare, but the houses have not lasted as long as the verse. All have gone now, with the exception of Somerset House, but some of the feel of those days can be obtained from the York Water Gate, still preserved at the bottom of York Buildings in the Victoria Embankment Gardens. Now marooned far from the river, it was built in the days when the grounds of the great houses swept down to a Thames still unembanked. Under such water gates the aristocratic barges would draw up, so the lords and their ladies could board their gilded craft without muddying their feet.

But you can rely on the guides on your boats to tell you all that. Their commentaries are as accurate as can be expected, or more so, and they make it quite clear that in the short sail down to Tower Bridge you are passing through a lot of history.

The right bank is far less rich in history. It was, of course, not part of the City. Rogues, vagabonds, harlots, pimps, and actors were to be found there: lords and ladies were not. However, at least one of the products of the Borough across the water has outlived the gentry, for it was on Bankside that the Globe Theatre stood; a certain Will Shakespeare was part-owner, player and resident playwright. If you can conjure up those Tudor–Stuart times as you sail past it, well and good. It might help you not to notice the dereliction that stares at you once the Festival Hall and the National Theatre are behind you.

From Tower Bridge on, you are still passing through history, but history of a much later period. This is dockland, and dockland is already dying. The feel of this area is positively Dickensian. Old, decaying stairs sag down to the water; dark, uninviting creeks, from which the sunlight is always excluded, run between gloomy warehouses. Over on the right bank, just beyond Tower Bridge, where a particularly sinister creek runs inland, was Jacob's Island, where Dickens placed his great set-piece on the death of Bill Sikes.

All the riverside pubs in this stretch have long histories: The Town of Ramsgate, the Prospect of Whitby, the Gun, and the Grapes, are on the left bank, the Angel and the Mayflower on the right. They all have balconies overlooking the river and if there is one thing more pleasant than sailing past them it is sitting there watching other people sail past you.

Gradually the river is broadening. The bends sweep wider

16

and it begins to be easy to see just what a waterway to the world the Thames was and still is. Greenwich, which is as far as the boat will take you, deserves a page to itself and will get it in its proper place. And if, after you have looked around – there is plenty to see – you don't feel like sailing back upstream, you can always catch the train and be in Charing Cross in a matter of minutes.

The upstream voyage from Westminster Pier has a lot of history about it, too, and a lot of beauty, but the first part is fairly unrelieved squalor, mostly of the industrial sort. The first sight on your right is, of course, the Houses of Parliament. Apart from enjoying the Gothic splendour of its waterfront, there is always the chance, if the House is in session, that you may catch sight of your MP on the Terrace, enjoying the cheapest beer in London. While he sits there, you can wave to him, or shout rude things, safe in the knowledge that you are out of reach and recognition.

There is little to see of Lambeth Palace on the other bank, except for the towers of the Elizabethan gateway and a stretch of the ancient wall. Almost opposite is the huge mass of the Vickers Building, a monster which destroys the balance of that side of the river and may make you miss the Tate Gallery next door to it.

For a considerable stretch now, there seems to be nothing but power stations, gasworks, lumberyards and breweries. Lots Road power station, which is typical, gets its name from the Common Lots, land where cattle were allowed to graze from August to February: you won't find much grazing going on round there these days. But for all the industry, there are also Battersea Park; the Royal Chelsea Hospital, home of the Pensioners; Hurlingham Park; Wandsworth Park; Fulham Palace, home of the Bishops of London, with its Bishop's Walk running pleasantly along the riverside; and Craven Cottage, Fulham Football Club's ground, surely the prettiest-sited stadium in the whole Football League.

As the bridges go by, Putney, Hammersmith, Chiswick and Kew, the banks become much more attractive. Not so long ago this was the countryside. It still is, at least along the stretch of Kew Gardens and Richmond Old Deer Park.

Richmond itself is delightful. The view from the river of Richmond Hill over Richmond Bridge is deservedly famous, as is the view of the river from the top of the Hill. This is as good a place as any to alight. There are boats to take you further on, to Hampton Court, or you can walk if you are feeling energetic – and have the time: it is a fair stretch. But Richmond will probably keep you happily occupied as you explore its beauties. After which, the train will run you back to Waterloo in no more than fifteen minutes.

Both the upstream and the downstream trips are well worth doing. They take up a lot of time, of course. Boats don't go very fast and the Thames does tend to meander like mad. Nevertheless there are few more worthwhile ways of spending a day and knowing, as you do it, that you are sailing along a very large part of this rough island's story. A word of warning. However warm the weather is on land, it will be cooler on the water. It always is. And if your boat is making only five knots against a headwind of ten mph, you are, in effect, standing in a pretty stiff draught. So be prepared: stick a woolly for everybody in your bag. If you don't want to be lugging vacuum flasks and sandwiches around with you, make sure your boat has refreshments aboard. Some do, some don't. You can find out by ringing 01-930 5947 (that's the Thames Passenger Federation Association at Richmond Pier), or 01-930 1661, which is the Westminster Pier number. Incidentally, there is another way to Greenwich. You can take the boat from Westminster to Tower Pier, and then transfer to the hydrofoil which whistles you to Greenwich Pier in no time. It is not, however, recommended as a way of viewing the Thames. Once it gets up on its foils, you can see absolutely nothing. Useful for commuters wanting to get to the City in a hurry, but no good at all to the likes of us.

One final thought to comfort you as you sail along this splendid river. As little as twenty years ago, if you fell in they wouldn't bother giving you the kiss of life after they'd fished you out. They'd have rushed you to the nearest hospital and stuck a stomach pump down your throat. That's how dirty the river was. Now, thanks to the work of a dedicated band of water engineers and others, the river is so clean that about one hundred separate species of fish are regularly caught in the tidal stretch downstream from Teddington Lock, and there are rumours, and more than rumours, that salmon might one day come back! So these days, if you fall in, all you'll need are fresh clothes, not a fresh stomach lining. And even if you don't fall in, which you won't, you will still notice the difference, because the Thames no longer smells. One of the reasons Parliament goes into recess in the summer is that the early Victorian legislators couldn't stand the pong of the river in the high summer. Nowadays they could work right through the year and not notice even the suspicion of a smell (it is, of course, permissible to hope they never do, on the ground that they do enough damage as it is during the months they actually work at present).

You have seen the river the city is threaded on, all the way from Richmond down to Greenwich. Now it is time to take a look at the city itself, using the word 'city' in its widest possible sense. You'll need time, a raincoat, sound wind, and a pair of stout shoes. Given those, and enthusiasm, you are in for one of the most pleasant experiences that can ever happen to anybody.

Good viewing!

The City

Breathes there a man with soul so dead, who never to himself hath said, as he looked at St Paul's, 'This great church is the cathedral of a great city'? Or something similar, at any rate. Up there, the crown of Ludgate Hill, it still has something awe-inspiring about it, still somehow manages to retain its centuries-old dignity, despite the horrible architecture with which it is now surrounded. It would be fitting if the man who designed it, Sir Christopher Wren, had also chosen its location. The fact is, however, that there has been a church there for at least 1,400 years and maybe nearer 2,000 years. Nor was Wren's magnificent building larger than its predecessors, fitting end to a story of ever-increasing size and magnificence. The church burnt down in the Great Fire of September 1666, which the present building replaces, was far bigger. Its spire soared 500 feet above the ground – Blackpool Tower is only a few feet higher – but it was continually being struck by lightning and in 1561 was destroyed by fire and never reconstructed. Five hundred feet high, at least to the top of its golden weather-vane; whereas the present dome is a mere 365 feet, a figure one should be able to remember every single day of the year.

Even at the lower, Wren, figure, St Paul's had always queened it over the City. Not anymore. The developers have done their worst to the City of London – usually, let it be said, with the connivance of the City – with the result that that wonderful skyline, once so impressive from the water or from Bankside, is now a nonsense, with enormous office blocks reaching above St Paul's, and the latest horror, the Natwest building near Leadenhall Street and Old Broad Street, showing every desire to make St Paul's look completely insignificant. It won't, however: Wren was a genius. Colonel Robert Seifert, who designed the Natwest horror, is not.

Seifert, although a serious offender when it comes to re-development, is not the only one. What has happened to the City since the war is a comment on the greed of developers and the willingness of architects to pander to their clients' desire for as much money as can be made, as quickly as possible, and to hell with aesthetics, history, sensitivity, and all those other effete qualities architects were once supposed to be in the business of preserving and creating.

Despite the battering the City took from German bombs during the Second World War (and just how big that was can scarcely be appreciated by those who didn't actually see the extent of the damage) there was still a surprisingly large amount of the old City left. One might have thought that re-development would have gone ahead on the principle that the new should harmonize with the old. Not so. Much of what had survived the bombing was pulled down as the property speculators clawed their way to the crock of gold at the end of the rainbow. The only trouble about this un-seemly avarice was that they very nearly destroyed the rain-bow, too, as they scrabbled for their ill-gotten gains.

However, enough remains to make it worth while to take a slow walk around the City and to enable us to rebuild in our minds the London that once was. It was, let us be clear, the

City of Dickens, rather than the City of Wren. Redevelopment is a continuing process throughout the intervening centuries. Usually, though, it had been done with some taste and restraint, and quite often out of necessity, as some buildings showed every sign that if they weren't pulled down they would fall down. Obviously, also, the growth of the City of London as the world's business centre meant that expansion upwards was essential, since more and more office space was needed within a more or less fixed area, but height restrictions ensured that there was still an homogeneity about the place. The only punctuations of the skyline were the spires of the City churches, of which more later, and they were designed as, and can be seen as, fingers pointing to St Paul's and then to Heaven. Today's skyline punctuations clearly point to a different place altogether.

Enough of protest. Let us start looking at this wonderful place called the City. Today, its area is much greater than it used to be. Temple Bar is not where the old west gate of the City used to be. It is right at the top of Fleet Street, where it becomes the Strand, and that is about half a mile farther west. Similarly with the Holborn Bars at the bottom of Gray's Inn Road, and the Bars on the Embankment. The City spread northwards, too, giving a plan-outline which today looks curiously irregular compared with the clean shape that once lay within the City walls. Only on the east, where the Tower of London marks where the walls ran down to the river, is today's boundary much the same as it was. It is the boundary as it was that we are going to explore first. We are going for a walk around the walls. The question – which walls? – luckily doesn't arise. The medieval walls were virtually built on the foundations of the Roman ones.

Start then at Ludgate Circus. It is tempting, but misleading, to think of the old Lud Gate as being immediately on the east side of the Circus, just about where the railway bridge crosses Ludgate Hill today. Not so. The old gate, of which there are unfortunately no traces left at all today, was higher up the hill. Before we climb up to it, remember that the walls which were ahead of us ran down to the river on our right. There they ended at Baynard's Castle, which served the same function at the west end of the City as the Tower did at the east: that is to say, it guarded the potentially weak spot where walls and water met.

Baynard's Castle, destroyed completely in the Great Fire, almost disappeared from memory, oddly enough. Nobody seemed to know very much about it, or care, but the fact that it had existed was undoubted: there is a strong reference to it in Shakespeare's *King Richard III*. It is where Richard receives the crown from the hands of the Lord Mayor and citizens, after a display of hypocritical modesty unequalled in English comic literature until the arrival on the scene of Mr Pecksniff almost 250 years later. Baynard's Castle is there, too, on all the early panoramic views of London, from Wyngaerde's (about 1545) to Visscher's magnificently detailed one of about 1616. It was a Royal palace; many (isn't that the correct word?) of Henry VIII's wives were lodged there at one time or another. Mary was proclaimed queen there, a proclamation which led to the immediate trial and execution of that pathetic figure, the nine-day queen, Lady Jane Grey.

Yet despite all that fame, men seemed to forget Baynard's Castle had ever existed. Then, not so long ago, excavations in the area to the east of Puddle Dock and the Mermaid Theatre revealed its foundations once again. There is, however, no point in making a pilgrimage to them. They are no longer visible. All that can be done, therefore, is to remember that it was there that the wall ended in the west.

Up Ludgate Hill now, as far as Old Bailey, whose very name suggest fortifications (it is from an old French word, baille, meaning palisade). Somewhere around here the wall came up from the river and ran on towards the New Gate. Newgate ultimately became the site of one of London's most infamous prisons, unbelievably not demolished until 1902. On its site rose the Central Criminal Courts, popularly called the Old Bailey. In the cells of the Old Bailey you can still see remains of the Roman and medieval walls which were incorporated in the prison's foundations. You will, however, have to take my word for it. The public is not allowed down in the dungeons. I was, because I was making a film about the Old Bailey. It is, of course, possible for you to see for yourself by getting yourself incarcerated there. As a way of examining London's Roman remains this is not, however, to be recommended.

Near the north-west corner of the rough rectangle enclosed by the Roman wall there was a fort which, in fact, preceded the building of the wall. When they started building the wall, the Romans naturally included the fort in it. The best place to see this is in Noble Street. From the Old Bailey go eastwards along Newgate Street and then turn north up King Edward Street. (You will, incidentally, be passing a section of the Newgate Bastion of the wall, Bastion XIX, which lies under the yard of the Post Office's King Edward Building. You can only see it by writing to the GPO, however. As an added bonus, it is, or was, until recently, washed by a trickle of water, the only tributary of the Fleet River you are ever likely to see in Central London.) Turn right at Angel Street, which leads very quickly to Noble Street, named after Thomas Le Noble, who lived there 600 years ago: he has, I suppose, thereby secured some sort of immortality. This area was almost completely flattened during the Blitz, which is why here you can see so much of the wall. Along the left-hand (western) side of Noble Street, a section of it is laid out for your inspection and edification.

There are two things particularly to notice. The first is the way, shown in the section nearest the Church of St Anne and St Agnes, the wall was joined to the fort. The second is the little culvert which was constructed to enable a small stream to pass under the wall without weakening it.

Not surprisingly, after all this, Noble Street ends in the thoroughfare called, for reasons which will soon become obvious, London Wall. Eastwards along it you will see a modern underground car park. Not at first sight a good place to look for Roman remains, but in fact it is a very good place indeed. Go down the entrance ramp. The section of wall exposed is very fine, and in a room near one of the exits you can see the foundations of a turret and the central piers of one of the fort gates. These weren't excavated until the late 1950s and probably never would have been had the area not been so flattened by bombing that extensive rebuilding was essential. High buildings require deep foundations: what those deep excavations revealed is one of the few benefits directly attributable to the topless towers of idiocy with which London has been pimpled in the last twenty or thirty years.

There are three churches in this area, each of which has something Roman to offer. St Giles, Cripplegate, now incongruously included in the Barbican complex, is where John Milton is buried and Oliver Cromwell was married, but that doesn't concern us here. What does concern us is the bastion, right up against the wall of the church. Feel yourself impressed by its massiveness, and ignore the concrete jungle surrounding you: it isn't worth looking at.

Make your way back from St Giles church, across Wood Street, into Fore Street, where the name 'Roman House' on a modern building should set a bell or two tinkling. Don't get too excited: all it has to offer is a mural inside the front door, showing what Roman London was like. I won't swear to its absolute accuracy, but I will say it might give you a very good idea of what London looked like in those days.

Turn down the side of Roman House towards St Alphage Gardens. They are what is left of St Alphage churchyard, and the gardens include some really impressive bits of wall. If you go down the steps to the base of the wall, and I advise you very strongly to do just that, you will see the wall towering above you. Imagine what a barrier it must have presented to any would-be invader. Go down there on an autumn evening, when the City has gone home, and use your imagination again. You will begin to see why the Anglo-Saxons, coming to these islands after the Romans had gone, wrote overawed poems about the race of giants who built such cities, with their massive walls, in times long past.

The name of All Hallows-on-the-Wall is an obvious giveaway. It is also accurate. The vestry is built on one of the wall bastions and one side of the church is actually built along the line of the wall itself.

I think you will have been able to spot which are the Roman and which the medieval parts of those sections of the wall you have already seen. If not, the identification is easy. There is a distinct change in the quality and size of the individual pieces of stone and – most importantly – the Romans used to employ distinctive thin red tiles as bonds.

25

Once you've worked out how to do it, you'll never forget how to do it again, probably the only resemblance the wall has to riding a bicycle.

There's nothing of the wall to be seen now until you get right over to the east, so you might as well board the Underground at Moorgate and travel by the Circle line to Tower Hill.

Here, you will immediately be taken back in time because there is actually a tiny section exposed by the side of platform 1 of the station. When you leave the station you are on Tower Hill. Here, within a few yards, are some of the finest sections of the wall now visible. The exit from the station leads you into Trinity Place. The gardens to the left are called the Wakefield Gardens. They contain a splendid stretch of wall. The bottom courses are Roman, as you will see from the red-tile bonding courses. Above them is the medieval wall, with a sentry's catwalk on top, about 25 feet above the ground. There is no knowing, of course, just what height the Roman part of the wall originally was: it could well have been the same as the medieval one. With look-outs posted as high in the air as that there was little chance of the city being surprised.

If you want to make a tour of the Tower of London – and why not? – you'll see Roman remains there, too, which probably gave rise to the old stories that the Tower was built by Julius Caesar. All that remains of what was a defensive fort at the eastern end of the wall is a few courses, again identifiable by the red bonding-tiles. You'll find them near the White Tower, that formidable central keep, and they were incorporated, as you will see, in the foundations of the now-ruined Wardrobe Tower. As part of the general tour of London's famous fortress, they are worth a look, but if you aren't taking the tour, you won't have missed much of Roman London.

Instead you could go up Tower Hill again and ask the Toc H Club headquarters if they'll let you see their Roman ruins. They will not show you any of their staff or their members. Instead, they will show you one end of their dining-room. Again, the section of wall you will see is magnificent. But be warned. Toc H, quite rightly, aren't at everybody's beck and call. It would be polite to give them a ring beforehand to find out if a visit would be convenient: they can only say 'No', although they probably won't. The number is 01-709 0472, and they're just to the north of Trinity Place.

So is another section of the wall. It is in the courtyard of Midland House in Cooper's Row, which you find simply by turning right out of Tower Hill station, and you're there. Here is a ruin with a difference. It's mainly medieval wall, but the bit at the bottom is Roman, of course. The windows cut in the wall are medieval, too. So far, nothing new. What makes it different is the way it has been incorporated into a pleasant court, with a fountain tinkling away. Cool in summer, but a shade chilly in winter.

The wall ran north from here, as you will deduce from its line. Then round about where Houndsditch is today – the derivation is uncertain, but judging by contemporary descriptions of the rubbish thrown into it, the ditch could very well have got its name from the number of dead dogs floating down to the Thames – the wall changed direction and ran north-west to just about the corner of Bishopsgate and Houndsditch, whence it ran west to the point on London Wall where we last left it. There is, however, as I said earlier, little or nothing to see along its line, although much has been found in the excavations which have taken place before and since the last war.

So now you have done the circuit of the wall of the City. Well, maybe you haven't, because it is possible – not certain, but possible – that the wall also ran along the river shore, joining Baynard's Castle to the Tower of London. If this wall existed, then it would have two watergates in it – Dowgate and Billingsgate. On the other hand, they may merely have been wharves at which goods were landed or embarked, or there may not have been a wall at all. It is quite true that excavations all along the line of Upper and Lower Thames Streets have produced lots of archaeological finds. That could, however, be explained by the existence of a line of Roman villas along the shore, rather as, centuries later, a line of great medieval palaces ran the length of the Strand, each one with gardens running down to the water's edge, each one with its private, and usually very ornate, landing stage or watergate.

With the circuit of the wall complete it is time to look at what is inside it: after all, that is what most people mean when they talk about 'The City'. And just what is in it? The short answer is everything. St Paul's obviously. Fifty-six Wren churches, not to mention those by other architects. The Royal Exchange; the Mansion House; the Bank of England; the Stock Exchange; Lloyd's; Guildhall; the Old Bailey; about two hundred pubs – don't blench: before the Great Fire there were over eleven hundred and in Dickens's day the number worked out at one for every sixty houses; the Tower of London; the Monument; the highest (at present) building in Britain; some good architecture, some bad, some very bad, and some downright awful; innumerable restaurants; a daily influx of about three-quarters of a million people; and a resident population of only a few thousand. It is an awful lot to be going on with. Much of it will, obviously, not get a look in, but the sooner I get round to tackling this impossible list the more I will be able to mention.

Where to start? Obvious, I think. We'll start at the queen of the City, the crown of 'the crown of cities all'. St Paul's, Dr Wren's masterpiece, surely one of the finest buildings of all time. Which is your first leisurely but breath-taking view of it depends on where you are, of course. The view up Ludgate Hill is the best known, but the one I prefer is from Queen Victoria Street, that modern thoroughfare which carves its way from Blackfriars station to the Mansion House.

Go eastwards from the station, past the deliciously-named church of St Andrew-by-the-Wardrobe and the equally deliciously-named Addle Hill. You will come to Peter's Hill. There up the steep slope, soaring above it all, is the wonderful south front of St Paul's. The climb up the steps might catch your breath a bit, but it is an eye-opener as well as a pipe-opener. The nearer one gets to St Paul's Churchyard – a churchyard no longer, of course – the more magnificent the cathedral becomes. You can sit down on the south side of the roaring City-bound traffic and gaze your fill. Remember, if you will, the old – and true – story about the start of the building of the new cathedral on the site of the burnt-out ruins of the old one. Wren asked a labourer to bring him a gravestone, any gravestone, from the churchyard, so that he could lay it down as a base-reference for his masons. The labourer brought back one bearing the single word 'Resurgam', meaning 'I shall rise again'. Since the labourer almost certainly couldn't read, there can have been few finer and more appropriate coincidences.

You must go inside the cathedral. When it is packed with tourists – what are we but tourists, anyway? – it can bear a strong resemblance to a particularly noisy market place. Ignore the noise and the people. Look at the Latin tag carved above Wren's tomb: 'Si monumentum requiris circumspice', which is to say 'If you seek his monument, look around you'. Then do just that. Reflect on the fact that new St Paul's was thirty-five years a-building and that by the time it was finished, Sir Christopher Wren was seventy-eight and too old to place the last stone on the summit of the lantern. Instead, the stone was placed in position by his son. Reflect on the fact that in 1718, after Wren had been architect to the cathedral for forty-nine years, and its servant for fifty-five years, he was suspended as a result of political intrigue. He was deeply upset at first, but he continued to make a once-a-year pilgrimage to St Paul's and sit beneath the dome, contemplating what he had created, 'cheerful in solitude', as his son put it, adding, in one of the most moving descriptions of philosophical acceptance that can ever have been penned, 'and as well-pleased to die in the shade as in the light'. Would that we could all bow out of the world as gracefully as that. Wren died in 1723, at the grand old age of ninety-one, his heart full of thanks that he had been granted the gifts he put to such superb use.

We are all used to the interior of St Paul's. Photographs, films, television programmes have familiarized us with it. We tend, therefore, to take it for granted. Remember, though, that old St Paul's was a Gothic church, all stern lines, and soaring, pointed arches. Here, in its place, was a great exotic dome, built in a vernacular completely different from that of its predecessor. Not until you have made the imaginative effort to see it as those eighteenth-century Londoners saw it for the first time, will you realize just how startling was Wren's creation. Nothing could be more unlike the crumbling old pile it replaced. Wren was not, of course, the only architect working in this new style, nor was he the first, but nobody in England had seen anything like it before, at least not on that scale.

There are many guides to the cathedral, so a comprehensive listing of its contents is hardly needed here. Look out, though, for Wren's simple tomb, and for the statue of John Donne, once Dean of St Paul's, the only piece of statuary to survive the Great Fire intact. The crypt contains several marvels, including the funeral coach of the Duke of Wellington, but perhaps the most interesting, in view of the remarks at the end of the last paragraph, is the model of old St Paul's. The Library is well worth a visit, since it contains documents signed by Wren himself, as well as others signed by Archbishops Laud and Cranmer. The Whispering Gallery is famous, of course: the guides will demonstrate its peculiar acoustics for you. You can climb right to the top of the lantern crowning the cathedral dome, but be warned: there are over 600 steps to it. If you take it easily, and pause frequently for rest, you might be able to make it without too much trouble. If the weather is fine, you will be rewarded by a wonderful view of London. Not quite as wonderful as it was, of course: the great towering office blocks around you cannot be said to improve the prospect in any way at all.

The picture of the dome of St Paul's, standing proudly above the fires of the war-time air-raids, is so familiar to us that it tends to obscure the fact that the cathedral did, in fact, suffer severe damage during the Blitz. The east end of the cathedral suffered most hurt and it took nearly eighteen years before the new High Altar was ready for consecration in 1958. There is no need for the splendours of the High Altar to be detailed: they are obvious. The altar is a place of pilgrimage for overseas visitors, since it contains the names of 324,000 members of the Commonwealth forces, men and women alike, who were killed during the war.

After St Paul's almost everything in the City would be an anticlimax, but a reasonable transition from its splendour to more human-scale treasures is by way of some of the many Wren churches, whose spires you will have seen if you made the exhausting ascent to the top of the lantern. There are over fifty of them, so you may be spoilt for choice. One church which I am always impressed by is one you may have noticed at the bottom of Ludgate Hill.

St Bride's has long been known as the parish church of Fleet Street. Its association with the Black Art of printing is long. It could hardly be longer, since it dates back right to the invention of the process. Wynkyn de Worde – oh, heavenly name! – was an assistant to William Caxton. In 1491 he took over his master's stock-in-trade and set up shop in Fleet Street, hard by St Bride's churchyard. There he practised his craft for more than forty years – his date of death isn't known precisely, but it *is* known that he was still alive and working as late as 1535. It is entirely appropriate that he should be buried in the yard of the church so long associated with the craft he pioneered. On the inside wall of the Old Bell pub, built by Wren in Bride Lane to accommodate and provide food and refreshment for his workmen when he began to rebuild St Bride's after the Great Fire, a plaque gives a short summary of Wynkyn's life and work.

St Bride's itself has always seemed to me to be one of the most beautiful of London's churches. Heavily damaged during the Second World War, it was painstakingly rebuilt and was re-dedicated in 1957. The interior is a blaze of white and gold. The whole church radiates light and seems to sing to the glory of God. Memorial services are not usually the happiest of events; Fleet Street has its share of them, just like anywhere else, and perhaps more than most, so St Bride's has been the scene of many, but to hear the St Bride's choir at such a ceremony is to be uplifted whatever your religious beliefs are, or aren't.

Samuel Pepys was born only a few yards away from St Bride's. Go out through the main, glass, door – not the one leading to Fleet Street – and you will come to Salisbury Court, where a tablet on the wall of the Reuter building records the great diarist's birth. It was, therefore, natural that the young Samuel should have been baptized in St Bride's. He was, and the fact is still noted there in a parish register which miraculously survived the almost total destruction of the body of the church during the Blitz. Richard

Lovelace, 'the cavalier poet', died just across Fleet Street, in Shoe Lane and in dire poverty. He is buried in St Bride's. So is Samuel Richardson, who has a pretty solid claim – shared possibly with Henry Fielding – to be called the father of the English novel, although I suspect that, outside university Eng. Lit. courses, his novels *Pamela*, *Clarissa*, *Joseph Andrews*, and *Sir Charles Grandison* are more remembered than read.

Richardson was himself a printer, having been apprenticed to the trade after attending Merchant Taylors'. He then did the thing so many London apprentices seemed to do, if the romantic tales are correct: he married his master's daughter and set up business on his own in Salisbury Court (hence, of course, the St Bride's connection). It would be nice to say they lived happily ever after. They do not appear to have done so. As Richardson became more and more famous, his circle of acquaintances widened to include such mighty ones as Dr Johnson, but his wife did not seem to be in the least interested in social climbing. She bore him three daughters and lived out what could very well have been a life of quiet desperation, but equally well could have been nothing of the sort. Richardson was buried in St Bride's in 1761: his wife's interment does not seem to be recorded.

One aspect of St Bride's which has a great attraction for American visitors to London is the canopied oak reredos. It remembers one Edward Winslow, yet another printer's apprentice, who was a regular attender at Fleet Street's parish church and who later sailed with the Pilgrim Fathers and became three times Governor of New Plymouth.

It is very hard to get your fill of the St Bride's interior: that blazing light is almost irresistible. There is, however, something even more impressive to see. The crypt is staggering to anyone with the slightest sense of history. When the body of the church was destroyed in the bombing, its reconstruction was preceded by much excavation. It soon became clear that the original church had been built on the site of a Roman cemetery: more than 5,000 burials were found. There were Anglo-Saxon interments, too, as well as Norman and later ones. The excavations revealed that there had been no fewer than seven churches on the site, spanning almost two thousand years.

With such a wealth of history, it was clear that something must be done to provide a worthy setting for the display of selected remains. That something was done by Sir Max Aitken, son of the first Lord Beaverbrook, chairman and driving force behind the *Daily Express*, *Sunday Express*, *Evening Standard*, and many other publications. When Lord Beaverbrook died, Sir Max disclaimed his new title, saying there could only be one Lord Beaverbrook (which most of those who had met him would say was undoubtedly true) and decided to have the crypt laid out to best advantage to commemorate his father.

It is fair to say that the result is a fitting tribute to a man who, whatever his faults, was one of the most fascinating characters the Black Art of journalism has ever produced. I do urge you, though, to take your time. There is a great deal of history in the cellars of St Bride's. It cannot be rushed round. On a hot day it is refreshingly cool, a quiet refuge from the glare of the sun. On cold days it is comfortingly warm, a welcome shelter from the stormy blast. In other words, at any time of the year the conditions in the crypt are ideal for a gentle browse through two thousand years of London.

The actual lay-out is, to this relatively inexperienced eye, one of the most imaginative that can ever have been devised. There is not too much clutter — in fact, there is absolutely no clutter at all. The exhibits have been chosen with care and displayed with taste. Efficient lighting means everything can be seen, every inscription can be read. The use of an inclined mirror at the east end of the crypt to show off the Roman tessellated pavement is a particularly ingenious device. The foundations of the Roman building are particularly interesting in that they are the only ones yet found outside the line of the Roman city wall which, you may remember, was a good 400 or 500 yards to the east, halfway up Ludgate Hill.

Before you leave St Bride's church — and you may find it hard to tear yourself away — make sure you get a view of the exterior. This is actually quite hard to do, since the surrounding buildings hem it in so. The outer walls still show signs of what the building suffered during the war, but that can be said about hundreds of other buildings. The chief glory of the exterior is its spire. Almost the best place to see it from is up towards the top of Ludgate Hill. The poet W.E. Henley called the spire a madrigal in stone. One can see what he meant. The original spire wasn't added to the church until 1703, almost a quarter of a century after Wren finished his work of reconstruction. It was struck by lightning in 1764 but was repaired soon after. It is 225 feet high and its tiered 'wedding cake' construction may not appeal to everybody, although it does to me – very much. I have heard it described as London's best-loved spire. I can see why the man said it, but I don't think it is true, largely because it is so hard to see, and so few people have therefore seen it. So take that walk up Ludgate Hill, keeping to the north, or left-hand, side. Somewhere between Old Bailey and Ave Maria Lane, turn and look back. There it is, aspiring to the heavens, yet another proof that the existence of Dr Wren at the time of the Great Fire indicates that 'cometh the hour, cometh the man' is a saying true as often as not.

After St Paul's, once again bulking above you, and St Bride's, most other churches, however much they are products of a genius, could come as an anticlimax. They do, although not excessively so. However, there is one other Wren church, generally thought to be worthy to rank with Paul's and Bride's. This is St Stephen, Walbrook, now the home of the Samaritans, the organization set up to help the desperate by the Revd Chad Varrah. Actually, the full name of the church is a bit of a mouthful: 'The Lord Mayor's Parish Church of St Stephen Walbrook, and St Swithin Londonstone, St Benet Sheerhogg, and St Mary Bothall with St Laurence Pountney.' Try saying that after you've had your communion wine.

I'm not sure about St Stephen Walbrook. Guide books say 'It is generally thought to be Wren's finest City church'. Not by me it isn't. Give me St Bride's any time. There is, however, no denying its beauty. One reason for the adulation the church has received could be that its dome is genuine; in other words it does not have, like St Paul's, an inner dome which bears little relationship to the size of the outer dome (nor, if it comes to that, to the dimensions of the in-between dome, which both separates and supports the inner and outer domes). 'It is generally thought,' says one guide-book, 'that here Wren was experimenting for the Cathedral.' Why that should automatically endow it with beauty is something I cannot explain.

The Walbrook part of the church's name is, of course, related to the name of that shy little stream, the Walbrook, which actually ran down to the river some 50 or so yards to the west. In doing so, it watered a Mithraic temple, revealed in the excavations for the foundations of Bucklersbury House. At least, we assume it did. Mithraic temples were commonly, if not invariably, underground and had running water with which the several ceremonies were carried out. There was certainly no other stream running down to the Thames in this neighbourhood, and there is a very slight depression in the ground which suggests where the Wall Brook ran. Its course leads almost directly to where the Mithraic temple was discovered. The Mithraic temple was lifted after the archaeologists had done all their measurements, diggings and appraisals, and relaid in a forecourt in Queen Victoria Street. It is worth going to see, but you may feel disappointed. Somehow it fails to communicate excitement, though why this should be so is something I have never been able to work out. Maybe it is because its carefully relaid stones have an undoubted resemblance to an ornamental garden, and ornamental gardens are not what Mithraic temples were about. They were dark, mysterious places where solemn rites were carried out, where a brotherhood similar to the freemasonry of Mozart's *Magic Flute* was forged. The forecourt of a modern office block in Queen Victoria Street doesn't seem to be the place to suggest that sort of mysticism.

I seem to have got a long way from Wren churches, so let us go back (I suppose I really mean forward) and look at one final example of the great architect's work. There are still some fifty more to go at within the City boundary, so this will have to be as typical as I can make it. Or perhaps not? One very different from the others might give a better idea of

35

the range of Wren's talents. On the assumption, then, that second thoughts are often better, let us go and have a look at St Benet's, Queen Victoria Street.

There were three churches by Wren, named after St Benet. One was St Benet Finke, off Threadneedle Street. It was so called because the first foundation (1216) was built by Robert Finke, who lived in Finke's Lane, now known as Finch Lane, just off Threadneedle Street. Wren's replacement of the original church was pulled down in 1842. The second St Benet's was in Gracechurch Street, which runs across the end of Threadneedle Street. Originally an eleventh-century foundation, it too was destroyed in the Great Fire and rebuilt by Sir Christopher. It survived until 1867, when it was demolished. A plaque in Gracechurch Street marks the site. So there were two St Benet's within one hundred yards of each other, a fact which could have caused confusion in the days when taverns were numerous, closing hours non-existent, and drinking water so chancy that ale, or stronger, was most people's morning mouth-wash. Many communions must have been celebrated with at least some of the communicants wondering why the church had changed so much since their last visit.

The third St Benet's, the one we are heading for, is just off Queen Victoria Street, a thoroughfare which wasn't built until some 700 years after the first twelfth-century foundation was constructed. It, and its Wren replacement, were on the corner of Paul's Wharf and Thames Street. Paul's Wharf has gone now, an 'Upper' has been added to the other street's name, and Queen Victoria Street has been driven through the decaying property overlooking the river, so the Wren church now stands squeezed in between the latter street and Upper Thames Street. If that all sounds confusing, don't worry. You will have no difficulty in finding this St Benet's. It is almost opposite the College of Heralds, and is quite unmistakable, since it is built in groined blue-and-red brick, with a very simple tower, as unlike the spires of St Bride's and St Stephen, Walbrook, as can be imagined.

Inside the church, one of the best preserved of Wren's City churches, eleven pillars support a quadrangular roof.

There are galleries (not a very common feature), a splendid reredos, and an especially fine Communion table with an inlaid top. A glance around will be quite enough for you to see how different it is from the other churches I have already mentioned. There is one other marked difference, and this one not architectural. Two services in Welsh are preached there every Sunday, as the notice board outside might have hinted: the singing tends to have a touch of 'hywel' not often found in other London churches.

Different or not though, this church, where Wren's great predecessor Inigo Jones was buried, is very fine, and is a quite worthy end to this look at what might be called the City – of God. It is now time to look at the other City – that of Mammon.

The City – of Mammon

*Cornhill – Mansion House – Royal Exchange
Bank of England – Stock Exchange – Lloyd's*

The richest square mile on earth, is what they usually call the City of London. They are wrong about the area, although not by very much, but they are certainly right about the richness. Not many wolves can be seen lurking around the doors of the City.

As far back as AD 64, Tacitus described the city of Londinium as 'a busy emporium for trade and traders'. You can say that again. In fact, people have been saying it ever since, and with very good reason. Tacitus's description came only four years after Boadicea had burned the place to the ground (the explanation of the layer of black ash you can see between ten and twenty feet below the street level in modern excavations), yet he thought of it as 'a busy emporium'. The City's power of recovery was clearly good even then. It showed just how good it was in later years, too. The Great Fire of London, in 1666, almost completely devastated the

City, yet within five years it was doing more business than ever. Finally, it demonstrated its phoenix ability even more impressively after the blitzes of the Second World War, when it had been reduced to a rubble, a desolation extending as far as the eye could see. The City got up, dusted itself down, and set about conducting business as usual, or even more than as usual. Here is an American who knew and loved London, describing what he saw when he came back immediately after the war:

> Eastwards of St Paul's there was not much point in going
> far along Cheapside, for most of Cheapside had
> disappeared . . . I went into what used to be Wood Street.
> 'Used to be' – for here I was at once in no-man's city.
> Here was a square mile of exposed and blackened cellars
> of the past, acres of jagged holes half-filled with rubble:
> bracken and willow-herb struggled to grow in crevices.
> Far and wide, it was a sea of desolation, with a surprising
> number of white church-spires, each like the mast of a
> wrecked ship standing above a burnt-out hulk. A dead
> sea, a dead land, a desert.

That was Frank Morley, in his magical book *The Great North Road* (Hutchinson, 1961), giving the best impression I have read of what the City suffered in the Blitz. And yet, less than a year after that disaster, people were once again ringing London from all over the world to transact business. A tough place, this 'busy emporium for trade and traders'.

The odd thing is that all this trade and trading is conducted on the most gentlemanly basis. 'My word is my bond' is the motto of the Stock Exchange. It could well be taken as the motto of the City as a whole. Bargains struck on the phone, with no contracts exchanged – nor could they possibly be exchanged – are as binding as if inscribed on vellum. Gazumphing may happen in the field of house sales. It doesn't happen in EC 1, EC 2 and EC 3. It may be that the City, as some people have said, has the morals of an alley cat. If that is the case, then alley cats are quite remarkably honest, and very good at making money.

It is probably this last which irritates some people. Where there's muck, there's money, was a philosophy they disliked, and quite naturally. However, a kind of sea-change seems to have come over the phrase. It now reads, for a lot of people, where there's no muck, there shouldn't be any money. I am sure that this is not what socialist idealists like Ruskin, Morris, and Edward Carpenter ever had in mind.

Once again, the question is where to start. This time, though, the answer is simple. It is enough to remember that Londinium was built on two hills. The hill to the east, higher than the westerly one, but by so little you would hardly notice, was called Cornhill. A street running through the financial heart of today's City of London is still called Cornhill. Let us start there.

There are reasons for this choice. At the point where Cornhill and Threadneedle Street join, there is a circus. Arranged round it you will find the Bank of England, the Mansion House, and the Royal Exchange. As symbols of what, and who, the City is, you could barely find better. The only major institutions missing are the Stock Exchange and Lloyd's and they are only about two hundred yards away, so we are clearly not too much off target if we start here.

Let us take the Mansion House first of all, if only because it is the 'home' of the Lord Mayor of London, his official residence during his year of office. It is a pleasant, but not overpowering, building. A sign on the wall says that here was the site of the ancient Stocksmarket. The reference is not to stocks and shares, but to livestock, particularly poultry (do not therefore be surprised to see that the street running west out of the circus is called Poultry).

The Mansion House was built by the celebrated architect, George Dance the Elder, between 1739 and 1752. Dance, who lived from 1700 to 1768, built many other London buildings as well as the Mansion House. His son, obviously also called George, was responsible for the rebuilding of the old Newgate Prison between 1770 and 1783, and was one of the founder-members of the Royal Academy.

What Dance the Elder did with the Mansion House was to produce a pedimented building with a portico from which the Lord Mayor and his acolytes can watch processions pass – if they are not taking part in them themselves, of course. The Mansion House contains private and official apartments and a banqueting room which is called the Egyptian Hall for reasons nobody knows, since there is nothing Egyptian about it. The style, if it is anything, is Renaissance, but Egyptian Hall it became known as, and Egyptian Hall it will presumably remain. One little curio is the Lord Mayor's Police Court. It is said to be the smallest in England, and is there because the Lord Mayor, by virtue of his office, is the Chief Magistrate of the City.

The Mansion House is not the easiest building to visit. It is only open on certain Saturday mornings in the year. Which Saturday mornings you can find out by writing to the Lord Mayor's private secretary well in advance, and even then you cannot be sure that permission will be granted. For the fleeting or on-the-spur-of-the-moment visitor, therefore, the Mansion House can be considered something of a dead loss. But you never know: you may be lucky. You can best get there by taking the underground to Bank, which is on both the Central line and the easterly branch of the Northern line.

If you are lucky and are given permission to visit the Mansion House, try another visit on a weekday. The difference between the roar of the traffic then, and the silence of the week-end, is positively eerie. The City at week-ends can give the impression that the Black Death has struck again: it is as quiet as the grave.

The Royal Exchange is the building on your right, as you look from the Mansion House portico. It lies between Threadneedle Street and Cornhill and is the third building to occupy the site. The two predecessors were both destroyed by fire, the first in the Great Fire, the second in 1838.

The first Royal Exchange was entirely due to the initiative of Sir Thomas Gresham. He had travelled a lot in the Low Countries, where Antwerp had become the great centre of trade. Sir Thomas thought he knew why. It was because in Antwerp there was a great Bourse, where traders from all over Europe could meet in comfort. He contrasted that with London, where he and his fellows had to walk in the rain: 'when it raineth, more like pedlars than merchants.'

He decided something must be done. With the help of several hundred other merchants, he bought the Threadneedle Street/Cornhill site and built the Exchange at his own expense. The style was rather like the Cloth Hall in Halifax, which served an exactly similar purpose for the woollen trade in the West Riding of Yorkshire. There was a huge open courtyard, surrounded by colonnades, and above the colonnades were offices, looking inwards, and shops. There was also a tall tower, with a bell which summoned merchants twice a day, and above the bell was a model of a grasshopper, the Gresham family emblem. If you look up above the roof at the east end of today's building you will see the sign of the grasshopper still there, although perhaps in a more modern style than was Gresham's original one.

In 1570, Queen Elizabeth I, who was always a lady for latching on to something which she thought would bring her money, deigned to appear, with trumpets and heralds, and according to Stow, the first and maybe the best of London's historians, 'caused the same Exchange to be proclaimed the Royal Exchange'. Which it has been ever since, to the constant advantage of the Royal Household.

The second Exchange, replacing the one burnt down in the Great Fire, is not actually mentioned in the Latin inscription on the frieze. Maybe it was so awful everybody wished to forget about it. I doubt it: the period immediately after the Great Fire was one of the very best for English architecture. The most obvious explanation is that nobody told the architect who built the present Exchange – his name, by the way, was Sir William Tite – that he need mention the man who built the fire-ruined building he was replacing. *His* name was Edward Jerman and he was the City Surveyor. The fact I've mentioned his name proves that, frieze or no frieze, he may be gone but is not forgotten. No architect who worked at the time the great Sir Christopher was rebuilding so much of the City could ever have been forgotten. But why no name on the frieze, I wonder?: just another of London's little unsolved mysteries?

The Royal Exchange is better than the Mansion House as far as visitors are concerned. It is open each day of the week, from 10 a.m. to 4 p.m. as well as Saturday mornings from 10 to 12. The underground station is still Bank, and the suggestion I made about visiting the Mansion House applies here too: the difference between week-ends and weekdays is quite staggering.

Before you go across Threadneedle Street, take a look at the statue of the Duke of Wellington slap-bang in front of the Royal Exchange. How wonderful the carving, both of man and beast! How full of life! And how they fit with the lines of Percy Bysshe Shelley – admittedly about a somewhat earlier commander – when he says that the artist's control of his medium:

> Tells how the sculptor well those pasions read
> Which yet survive, stamped on these lifeless things,
> The hand that mocked them and the heart that fed.

There is, however, one thing about the statue which by now will have been driving all horse-lovers mad. The Duke is riding with a saddle, but with no stirrups. Boadicea at Westminster with no chariot reins, Wellington in the City with no stirrups! Something is rotten in the state of English equestrian carving.

Along the north wall of the Royal Exchange (which is to say the Threadneedle Street wall) there are two moderately interesting statues of more than moderately interesting London worthies. The first is of a certain Richard Whittington, who, despite the legend, was never three times Lord Mayor of London. The rank of Lord Mayor didn't exist in his day, and it was four times, not three, that he took over the title of Mayor. A house where he lived can still be seen to this day, halfway down the hill from the Royal Exchange towards the Thames. The other statue is to Sir Hugh Myddleton, a Welshman, who, apprenticed to a goldsmith, made a fortune, became a banker, and decided, in 1609, that he was going to be the first man to give London a completely dependable water-supply. To do this he offered to cut, at his own expense, a new river, from springs at Amwell and Chadwell in Hertfordshire, down to Islington. He was after the profits this would bring, of course, but he miscalculated slightly. The New River had barely reached Enfield when Myddleton's money ran out. King James I, an odious little man, saw an opportunity. He offered to put up half the necessary money (screwed from the people, of course) in return for half the profits. Myddleton recognized an offer he couldn't refuse. The construction went ahead. Despite the monetary embarrassments, the New River was finished only nine months after Myddleton had said it would be. He had cut nearly forty miles of winding, canal-contoured, New River, ten feet wide and four feet deep, with a gradient of half an inch a mile, had built one hundred bridges at points where these were necessary, and had done it all at the rate of more than a mile a month, and this with no help other than muscle power.

The New River Company, as it happened, never made a penny profit in Myddleton's lifetime. He was knighted for his efforts, but not reimbursed. Nevertheless, the men who had made money at the Royal Exchange while he squandered his fortune for their benefit, albeit indirect, showed how much they respected him by erecting a statue to him. At least they thought of doing it, but they never got round to it. The one that stands there now wasn't put up until the middle of the nineteenth century, by which time the man who had done the work, and those who didn't quite manage to spare the time to honour him, were all dead and long gone.

If you care to ignore the group of carvings (one can scarcely call them statues) in the little square at the east end of the Royal Exchange, you will be in all the better mood to cross Threadneedle Street and take a look at the Bank of England. We had better accept now that there's not much to see. The great un-windowed wall, like a granite cliff, offers little promise of delight. Of delight there is, indeed, none. The Bank of England does not go out of its way to attract visitors. Indeed, it goes rather farther than you and I might to repel them. Each evening a squad of Guardsmen move across the City to spend a pointless night playing cards, drinking cocoa, and protecting our money, an activity which might mean more if any of our money were stashed there. But at least things are being modernized. It isn't very long since the Guardsmen used to march of an evening from the top of The Mall to the Bank, usually round about rush hour, thereby adding considerably to the traffic jams and increasing the incidence of high blood pressure, debilitating strokes, and fairly fatal heart attacks among the more impatient motorists they were impeding. Now they go by coach.

The Bank of England, as every schoolchild can tell, has existed since the year 1694, but has only been on its present site for two and a half centuries. It has been added to over the years, to the disadvantage of buildings which stood in its way. The first major modification was at the hands of Sir John Soane: this period of rebuilding extended from the end of the eighteenth century well into the early nineteenth century. This was the time, immediately after the Gordon Riots of 1780 (see Dickens's *Barnaby Rudge*), when the fortress-like ground floor outer walls were built, since which time Bank of England employees have always been recognizable by their somewhat maggoty colour: the sunlight never reaches their cheeks during working hours. Rebuilding became necessary in the 1930s. The outer walls had to be underpinned: the phrase 'as safe as the Bank of England' had clearly begun to lose some of its force. Within those outer walls, Sir Herbert Baker built a seven-storey block, all very different from Soane's ideas. Whether Baker was influenced in his design by the work he did in building New Delhi for the Indian Government is something I do not know, never having even been to Old Delhi. I can however say that Baker's Bank is heavy and charmless. If viewed, however, from the top of Princes Street, which runs up the west side, its curious domes and turrets give it a distinct look of a sort of capitalist Kremlin, something which is surely unlikely to have been in Baker's mind. In any case, they are part of the Soane structure. Known as The Temple, the feature was copied from the Temple of the Sybil at Tivoli. Quite what it is doing in the City of London is anybody's guess.

The Bank is always known as the Old Lady of Threadneedle Street, especially by people who cannot resist a cliché. There *is*, in fact, an Old Lady. She is one of the sculptures over the portico, sculptures which were added during Baker's reconstruction and which are by Sir Charles Wheeler. The sculptures are worth looking at: they are all symbolic, or allegoric, or something, and represent, variously, Britannia and several guardians of wealth. The Latin inscriptions on the bronze doors in Threadneedle Street tell the story of the foundation of the bank, but are barely worth puzzling your head over. Much more worthy of a few minutes' gazing are the Bank messengers, tall distinguished men in top hats, pink coats and scarlet waistcoats. Along with the scarlet-and-gold gowns worn on special occasions by the Bank gate-keepers, they are a reminder of the livery worn by the servants of Sir John Houblon, the first Governor of the Bank of England, back in 1694. On a cold grey day they add a much-needed warming touch of colour to a City which, as redevelopment proceeds unendingly, is becoming greyer every day. The chances of your getting into the Bank of England for a legal look-round, let alone an illegal one, are not very high. There are no public viewing facilities. If you know somebody in the Bank your chances might be a little higher, but only marginally. The Bank of England may be the custodian of the nation's gold: it clearly is not interested in letting any of us see it. Nevertheless, if you stand at the entrances and peer inside with no obvious loitering-with-intent look about you, you might just be able to get a glimpse of one of our more arcanely mysterious City buildings. Or a policeman might move you on: there's no telling.

If you are moved on, accept it with good heart and make the best of it. Wander eastwards along Threadneedle Street, marvelling at the names of the banks and merchant bankers which abound all over this central area of the City, and bear left into Old Broad Street. Ahead of you is the monstrous tower of the new Natwest building. The one virtue of this offending shaft is that it is so high that, on misty mornings, you can't see the top half at all. For this relief, much thanks.

The Natwest is, however, not what we are after in Old Broad Street. What we are after is the Stock Exchange, an institution which, along with similar exchanges in other capitalist countries, has suffered more vilification than most. There is surprisingly little evidence to suggest that much of this vilification is justified.

The Stock Exchange, known to those in the business as 'The House', was founded in 1801. The reasons for its foundations are interesting, even if already moderately well known. Every school child has heard of the South Sea Bubble, even if all they know about it is that it is a rather delightful name. In 1711 a company had been formed to trade in the Pacific Ocean – the South Seas – and for a variety of reasons the idea caught on. Speculators went merrily mad; the wildest schemes were mooted – one was to extract silver from lead, another was for importing jackasses from Spain, and the cheekiest of the lot was 'a company for carrying on an undertaking of Great Advantage, but no one to know what it is'.

Madness is clearly catching. Within a short time the whole country, or at least that part of it with money to 'invest', was in on the act. Share prices rose insanely high. The whole of the Cornhill–Threadneedle Street area was thronged with buyers and sellers of stock. Coffee houses became centres of stock trading: Jonathan's in Exchange Alley was one of the busiest and soon became the most famous.

It was inevitable that one day the bubble would burst, and it did. The autumn of 1720 saw Exchange Alley in a panic. Fortunes disappeared overnight – not in every case: Sir Robert Walpole made a nice little packet out of it all. Suicides were common, one of them being the Postmaster General; and there was a great cry to punish the guilty men. Society often seems to need a scapegoat. The guilt really lay with those whose greed had led them to gamble so wildly, but that didn't stop the Chancellor of the Exchequer being sent to the Tower of London, or prevent the confiscation of the estates of the directors of the South Sea Company.

From the shambles, some sharp lessons were learned. Gradually a stock exchange of a kind came into being, with rules to make sure that sort of thing didn't happen again. Jonathan's Coffee House remained the centre of trading in stocks and shares until the first Stock Exchange was built in 1801. Incidentally, if you want to know where Jonathan's was, and at the same time experience something of the atmosphere of those eighteenth-century days, go into Change Alley, as the little byway is now called. You'll find it by going down Birchin Court off Cornhill. There you will see Garraway's Coffee House, or at least a plaque to mark its site: Jonathan's was next to it. I do not know why there is not also a plaque to mark what was unquestionably the more famous coffee house.

That little digression has taken us quite a way from Old Broad Street and the present Stock Exchange. Not really: distances in this part of the City are tiny. It is, however, very easy to get lost in the maze of little alleys lying between Threadneedle Street and Lombard Street, that is to say on both sides of Cornhill. Lombard Street, by the way, is a reminder of the fact that here lodged the bankers of Lombardy in North Italy, and here they first started their lucrative business of lending out money. We should now, however, be back in Old Broad Street, off Threadneedle Street. You cannot miss the new Stock Exchange. It is a vast and modern building, opened in 1970, and situated right on the corner of Throgmorton Street, named after Sir Nicholas Throgmorton, Elizabeth I's ambassador to France, where he was most undiplomatically imprisoned for siding with the Huguenots (he doesn't seem to have been a lucky man: on his return to England he was sent to the Tower of London).

This was the site of the original building of 1801, a building which was replaced in 1853 by a design of Thomas Allason's, later enlarged by J.J. Cole. The Allason–Cole building was pulled down between 1967 and 1969 to be replaced by the present twenty-six storey tower block. Since the old building wasn't really very impressive, extreme grief over its demolition would be out of place, but the tower block which replaced it has an equal nothingness about it. It is, however, much more obviously there. How it relates to the maze of little alleys which still surround it is not clear to me: it may be that time will reveal it to be not so out-of-place after all.

The Stock Exchange is a much better bet for the visitor than the Mansion House or the Bank of England. It is open daily, Monday to Friday, from 10 a.m. to 3.15 p.m., and admission is free. As you gaze down on the vast floor, with jobbers at their stations, and brokers' men buzzing about the floor like aerosolled flies on a window pane, you will notice that you cannot hear what is being said. You are glassed in, presumably to prevent your getting carried away by the prices being quoted and rushing out to ask your own stockbroker to splurge all your savings on some share or other. You will, however, be given a very clear idea of what is going on by the guides, rather good-looking girls who are a mine of information about the place and its history. There is also an exhibition area, which is more than slightly interesting, and there are film shows, further to improve your understanding of all that apparently meaningless activity in front of you. One of the films has for a title the motto of the Stock Exchange, 'My word is my bond'; I am not going to swear the film says *everything* about that activity, but it is as honest and full of facts as anyone can expect. Few fishmongers cry stinking fish.

Before you visit the last of the great London financial institutions – Lloyd's – perhaps you might like to rest and refresh yourself. A very good place to do this will necessitate a return to the Change Alley area of little byways off Cornhill, for our target is a couple of eating-places there. I have chosen them especially for you to see whether or not you agree with the famous Scott Fitzgerald–Ernest Hemingway conversation: 'The rich are different from us': 'Yes, they have more money'. For the customers at either of the two places I recommend are undoubtedly something in the City. It is they who ring Zurich, or Geneva or Tokyo. It is they who move millions of hot or cold money around the world with icy coolness and no other help than a battery of telephones and a computerized calculating machine.

The two places can be found by aiming for St Michael's Church, Cornhill. By its side is St Michael's Alley, or there might be by the time you get there: things change so quickly in the City these days. Down St Michael's Alley you may notice a blue plaque indicating that here was the site of London's very first coffee shop, the Pasqua Rosee. Immediately ahead of you is the George and Vulture, a splendid hostelry where Somethings-in-the-City eat fine old English food in an atmosphere which looks as though it hasn't changed since Charles Dickens's day. We know he knew it, and patronized it, because he installed Mr Pickwick and Mr Sam Weller there just before they heard whether Mrs Bardell intended to go ahead with breach-of-promise action. (See the chapter on Dickens.)

Like so many London taverns, the George and Vulture claims to be the oldest in town. Actually, it goes further: it claims to be the oldest in the world! The basis for the claim is that it became an ale house in the twelfth century, when it was called the George. After the Great Fire it was merged with the tavern next door, whose name was the Lively Vulture. It is only fair to say there are other versions. It is, however, certain that the old house is indeed old, that it has barely changed since the seventeenth century, and not at all since the nineteenth, except that the heating and lighting systems are as modern and efficient as one would wish. There can be few more comfortable places to await the outcome of a breach-of-promise action, should you be contemplating getting involved in one.

Directly opposite is the Old Jamaica Wine House, on whose wall stands the Pasqua Rosee plaque already referred to. The Jamaica Wine House is another seventeenth-century gem. It is a stone-built building, with a most comfortably-panelled interior, downstairs you can get that most English of drinks, beer. As sandwiches and bar food of all kinds are available, this is the place to see Something-in-the-City men refreshing themselves before setting about another round of international buying and selling of just about everything, but especially money.

There are many other hostelries frequented by City folk, but this chapter isn't supposed to be about pubs; it is supposed to be about financial institutions. Nevertheless that apparent digression earlier on about coffee houses leads us most naturally to the last of our quintet of major financial establishments – Lloyd's of London, the centre of the entire world of insurance. One Edward Lloyd had a coffee house in Lombard Street. Gradually, and nobody knows, of course, exactly how it happened or how long it took, Lloyd's Coffee House became the place to go to if you wanted to pick up any shipping news. From there it was only a short step to shipping deals. Cargoes were bought and sold there: so were the ships they were carried in. As shipping is a notoriously risky business (see what happened to Antonio in *The Merchant of Venice*), shipping insurance was an obvious necessity. Lloyd's Coffee House became the place where you could get it. His waiters carried messages about the room as well as cups of coffee, which is why today's Lloyd's messengers are still called waiters.

As the range of activities centred on Lloyd's grew with the passage of time, it was obvious that the old Coffee House was no longer big enough. Somewhere else had to be found. Rooms in the Royal Exchange provided the answer. It was in those rooms that the Lutine Bell was hung. Salvaged from a vessel of that name, the Lutine Bell was struck once for bad news of a ship, twice for good news. It still is, even though it, and Lloyd's, moved fifty years ago to premises at the corner of Leadenhall Street and Lime Street (Edward Lloyd is not yet forgotten: the site of his Coffee House, the onlie begetter of this mighty institution, is marked by a plaque in Lombard Street).

Lloyd's moved into these premises in 1928, the architect being Sir Edwin Cooper. Cooper, or his clients, had big ideas. The Room, which is the central hall where business is transacted, is 340 feet long. It is said to be the biggest room in the world. It may very well be, although how people establish such things is, and always has been, beyond me.

The scene in Lloyd's is very different from that on The Floor of the Stock Exchange. There, all is usually madness and movement. Here, in The Room, everything is ordered. It is impossible, without help, to work out what is going on on The Floor. It is easy, even without help, to work out what is going on in The Room. The men sitting four in a row on benches are the underwriters. The men wandering amongst them, with long folded cards, are the Lloyd's brokers. Each card represents something to be insured, from a tanker to a film actress's legs. They are inviting the underwriters to take a share in the insurance. If they agree, the underwriters write their names under the proposition – which is why they are called underwriters – and indicate just what share – a tenth, a twentieth, and so on – of the risk they are prepared to take.

The whole rigmarole still bears a strong resemblance to the way things were conducted in the old coffee-house days. There are, however, some modern innovations. For instance, the man in the red cloak, standing below the Lutine Bell, now calls out the names of brokers with the aid of a microphone. Beside the Lutine Bell is an electronic notice board, showing their names. The waiters write the names of the brokers they have been asked to find on an electronic screen, whence they are electronically displayed in front of the town crier-like man below the Bell. The general impression given by The Room is of calm. The general impression given by The Floor in the Stock Exchange is of chaos. Oddly enough, both institutions seem to work rather well.

There's not much left of the City for the outsider to see. The various commodity markets still exist, and still have their own special areas of the City, as they have done for centuries. The furriers still operate in the streets off Lower Thames Street. The clothiers cluster around Houndsditch. The Wool Exchange is just north of Guildhall. The Metal Exchange is near Lloyd's. The Baltic Exchange is in St Mary Axe (the Axe part of the name comes from the fact that the old church used to house the axe with which St Ursula and her virgins were martyred). There is still a Hudson Bay Company, appropriately enough down by the river. The vintners are down there, too, as well as the fishmongers. The place for textiles is around Aldersgate. Hatton Garden, just off Holborn Circus, is still the diamond centre, despite the enormous redevelopment going on there. And so on. It has been like that for hundreds of years. Presumably it will be like that for hundreds of years more.

When you consider the immense amount of money all these institutions deal with – an amount quite beyond any human comprehension – it is quite clear just why the old tag about 'the richest square mile in the world' came into being. Take the advice I have already given you: wander around there at the week-end. You will then have time to stand and stare at the names on the doors, to marvel at the variety of firms and the variety of their transactions. You will have time to sit back, stunned, at the sheer complexity of it all, and at the fact that, despite that complexity, it works. People marvel at the number of factors which must have combined to produce the peacock's tail, the human eye, the massive dinosaur, the tiny shrew, the high-grazing giraffe, the low-grazing goat. Scientists laugh at the idea of The Great Designer sitting down one day and drawing up blueprints of each and every different, and differently-specialized, species. Time and fitness for purpose, they say, are all that is required for evolution to produce its bewildering variety of living forms.

The City has had time to evolve, too. The less efficient were gradually weeded out, as in the process of natural selection. The result is that the City is a great, complex, living thing and, for all its faults, it works.

Bankside and the Borough

Clink Street – Southwark Cathedral – Anchor Inn
The George, Borough High Street – Guy's Hospital
Trinity Church Square – Lambeth Palace
South Bank Arts Complex

The presence of those two small hills on the north side of the Thames – Ludgate and Cornhill – meant that for centuries London's life was concentrated there. They provided a guarantee against flooding from a Thames much wider and far less confined than it is today. They provided a measure of protection against attack, especially when they were surrounded by first the Roman and later the medieval perimeter wall, guarded at the east end by the Tower of London and at the west by Baynard's Castle (where Blackfriars Bridge is today). With only London Bridge crossing the river for nearly 600 years, it was therefore inevitable that the north bank should be the important one.

London Bridge, however, suggests a potential for growth on the south bank. The bridge didn't just span the Thames to connect with nothing. It connected, of course, with the old Roman roads from Richborough, Dover, Rye, Hastings,

Newhaven and Chichester, roads whose lines were later followed by the old coaching routes. As the bridgehead of that fan of roads, the south bank of the Thames would inevitably become the site of a settlement. That settlement became known as Bankside or, just as frequently, as the Borough. It is still known by both names today, with an official title of Southwark.

It had one great advantage. It was not part of the City of London and it was therefore out of the jurisdiction of that city's Mayor and Aldermen. As a result, it became the home of rogues, thieves and vagabonds, pimps and whores, rooks, crooks, and actors. Here there was bear baiting, here were brothels, alehouses, and theatres. Here, too, was the palace of the Bishop of Winchester. He owned so much of the south bank that the whores who lived in the stews built on his land became known as 'Winchester geese'. Shakespeare certainly knew the phrase. He used it in *King Henry VI, Part I*, where the Duke of Gloucester hurls it as an insult at, of all people, the Bishop of Winchester himself.

Naturally, if you have so many villains in such a small area, you have to have a prison to keep some of them in all the time, and perhaps all of them some of the time. There was such a prison. It was called The Clink and it has given its name to prisons all over the world. It was in Clink Street. The prison is long gone, but Clink Street is still there.

You can best get to it by walking over Blackfriars Bridge. At the southern end, just past the sign on Blackfriars railway bridge which tells you it was formerly the London, Chatham and Dover Railway, you will see a flight of steps on your left. They hairpin down to the river and, at the time of writing, to a shambles of a new building. But the public right of way is still open. This is Bankside itself. Walk along it to the east and don't miss – well, you can't really – the views across the river to St Paul's and the City grouped around it. The street twists and winds, passing under Southwark Bridge, and includes the surviving few of the excellent seventeenth- and eighteenth-century houses which used to front its whole length. It is also worth keeping an eye open for the street names on your right-hand side. Bear Gardens is self-explanatory. Rose Alley was where the Rose Theatre stood, one of the great rivals to Shakespeare's Globe.

As you approach Cannon Street railway bridge, more unattractive than most railway bridges across the river, you will come to the Anchor, one of the best pubs on the river, with its own drinking/viewing platform built out over the water. Round the corner of the Anchor, and passing underneath the railway line, is Clink Street. Follow it round through dark canyons of warehouses, and watch out for an absolute gem on the right-hand side. This is just about all that remains of Winchester Palace. It is fenced off, the key has to be gone for (a notice gives you the address), and there is a spiral viewing staircase thoughtfully provided by the Department of the Environment. If, however, you don't feel like going to the trouble of getting the key, you can still see as much as you want by standing in Clink Street and gazing through the chain-link fencing.

Follow Clink Street round its right angle and the first street you cross is Winchester Square, the original palace courtyard. Winchester Walk, following the line of one of the palace walls, is a few yards further on. Reflect a little on what this area must have been like, and what it is like now, and give a sad and gentle sigh. But don't get too depressed, for a real, surviving gem is only a minute away. Southwark Cathedral is just beyond the Borough Market (itself well worth a look at if you can get up in time for the 04.30 opening) and although much restored, it is still very much as it was in Shakespeare's time, when it was the cathedral church of St Mary Overie. 'Overie', despite its conjunction with the name of Mary, simply means 'over the water', i.e. from the City. Buy the guide, which you'll find just inside the door, and treat yourself to an impressive half hour or so. And do not forget to go into the retro-choir, where you will see a model of Winchester Palace and the surrounding area, all as it was in the sixteenth century.

Southwark Cathedral is still, despite the nineteenth-century additions, one of the finest Gothic buildings in London. Everywhere around the walls are monuments and effigies. And there are the inevitable references to Shakespeare. He lived in Southwark – that is certain – for some time; he must have attended the church – that is the uncertain part. It is true that his brother Edmund was buried here (as a modern tablet tells us) in 1607, and there is a statue of the poet himself, carved in translucent alabaster, with a memorial window above it. Look at it carefully and you will see that in the background to the figures, which are of characters in the plays, there is Winchester Palace and the Globe Theatre, that famous wooden O. If you want to see where the Globe stood, go out of the church, make your way to Park Street, at the back of the Anchor, and there you will see a plaque, put up in 1909 by the Shakespeare Reading Society, which marks the site and also gives you some further idea of what the area looked like in the days when Will and his fellows were packing them in.

Since you are so very near the Anchor Inn, you might as well go inside and refresh yourself. This is an absolutely splendid pub. It is also a splendid eating place, with three restaurants, as well as the usual bar snacks. Since Dr Johnson's friend, Mrs Thrale, lived nearby (her father owned the Barclay and Perkins brewery, now Courage), the Great Samuel is supposed to have used it often. He may have done, since the present building was erected in 1750 to replace a much older one which had been burned down. Will Shakespeare, too, is said to have used the Anchor – the older version of course – but a pinch of salt should be taken with this story, and even then you may find it hard to swallow. It hardly needs to be said that since Charles Dickens lived nearby when his father was in the Marshalsea Prison for debt, he, too, must have been a regular. It seems unlikely: Charles was not much more than twelve at the time. In any case, the number of pubs these three authors alone are said to have been frequenters of makes it very difficult to understand how they got through the enormous amount of work they did. After all, Shakespeare wrote 37 plays and 154 sonnets as well as *Venus and Adonis*, *The Rape of Lucrece*, *The Passionate Pilgrim*, *A Lover's Complaint*, and *The Phoenix and the Turtle*. Dickens managed to knock together sixteen very long novels and so many other articles, short stories, and miscellaneous pieces that a catalogue of them would take about four pages of this book. And Dr Johnson was not behind the door, either: the first dictionary in the English language, the *Lives of the Poets*, a never-ending stream of reviews and parliamentary reports, as well as novels, travel books, and poems measureless to man. In each case, we are asked to believe that they produced all this work while spending most of their time in pubs, inns, taverns, hostelries, coffee shops, and other places of idle chatter and good fellowship!

Nevertheless, forgetting all that, the Anchor, which is where that digression started, is well worth an extended visit. Try the Russian Imperial Stout, a dark bitter liquid, rather like Guinness with the addition of liquorice, and much more attractive than that sounds. It was first brewed for the Czar of All the Russias in the eighteenth century, is said to be the strongest bottled ale you can get, and will leave you feeling distinctly eighteenth century if you drink too much of it. The bar beer is, naturally, Courage's, since their brewery is only a few yards away, and you can buy it straight from the barrel, not even from a hand pump, but out of a brass tap, and very nice it is too. The restaurants are good, although pricey – but then what London restaurant isn't, these days? – and you really need to book. The Anchor is on every tourist's list, which is why it is now on yours, and you can very easily be disappointed if you don't ring up beforehand: the number is 01-407 1577.

Another nearby, and very well-worthwhile, hostelry is the George in Borough High Street, a couple of hundred yards down from Southwark Cathedral and on the opposite side. London's only remaining galleried inn, it provides good English food in an atmosphere which can hardly have changed since the day when young Tip Dorrit nipped across from the Marshalsea Prison to the George to write a begging letter. The bedrooms off the gallery are no longer in use but can be seen if the landlord isn't too busy. The four-poster beds are genuine, and the floors they stand on have enough of a slope on them to convince you that this really is the sort of coaching inn Mr Pickwick and his colleagues knew so well. The George is approached, naturally enough, through George Yard, under a gateway high enough to let a stage coach in without beheading the passengers sitting on top.

Although this is the sole survivor of those days, it is worth taking a short walk up and down Borough High Street to see just how important a coaching terminus the Borough was in the first part of the last century. The yard names are all the proof you'll need. From London Bridge station they are: King's Head Yard, White Hart Yard (where Mr Pickwick first met Mr Sam Weller), George Inn Yard, Talbot (or Tabard) Yard, Queen's Head Yard, and Spur Inn Yard. Six inn yards, and therefore six coaching inns, and all within a furlong. The Borough must have been a bustling place before the arrival of the railways took the inn trade away.

The George is interesting for reasons other than its food, drink and history. Every summer it is the scene of productions of Shakespearean plays in the yard, which is how the earliest plays were first presented. The productions are part of the Borough Festival, which runs from May to July each year. They start at 3 p.m. every Saturday afternoon, but you have to be there by about 2 p.m. You can book tickets from the Festival Box Office, 28 Peckham Road, SE 5, telephone number 01-703 2917, or get them from the George itself.

One way and another, the George has a lot going for it, but be warned: like the Anchor, it is on the tourist map. Do not therefore be surprised if you are suddenly surrounded by hordes of Japanese, each one bandoliered with cameras, or Germans, or Americans, or whatever. Wait a few moments, and they will disappear, on their way to 'do' some other place, leaving you free to enjoy the George in more congenial company. If you want to make sure of eating there, give the pub a ring before you go. The number is 01-407 2056.

At the back of the George is Guy's Hospital, now a vast modern temple of medicine, but still named after the man who founded it in 1722. Thomas Guy was a Southwark man, born at Horsleydown, just where Tower Bridge is today (it is, incidentally, an indication of the sort of goings-on the south bank was famous for, that Horsleydown is thought to be a corruption of Whores-lie-down, a reference to the activities carried on in that area: they were less mealy-mouthed in the Middle Ages at putting appropriate names to things). Thomas Guy, born in 1644, was the son of a lighterman. He was clearly more literary-minded than his father, since he began in business by importing Bibles from Holland. When that trade was stopped, he secured a contract from the University of Oxford to print Bibles himself, and prospered greatly. He bought a lot of South Sea shares and sold them before the Bubble burst. By 1707, therefore, he was in a position to build and furbish three wards at St Thomas's Hospital (not the present St Thomas's opposite the House of Commons: the one Guy helped stood in St Thomas Street, opposite Southwark Cathedral, to which it had long been attached). In 1722, St Thomas's, which began as a twelfth-century foundation, was proving inadequate, even though it had been constantly added to over the ages, so Thomas Guy decided to build a hospital himself, on the other side of St Thomas Street. He lived just long enough to see it finished. Why, in the circumstances, he was known in his day as a mean and avaricious man, I shall never know.

Incidentally, perhaps the most famous product of Guy's never became a doctor at all. John Keats, the poet, after serving an apprenticeship to a surgeon, became a dresser at Guy's around the turn of 1815–16, when he was twenty. Was it there that he learnt about the effects of narcotics?

> My heart aches, and a drowsy numbness pains
> My sense, as though of hemlock I had drunk,
> Or emptied some dull opiate to the drains
> One minute past, and Lethe-wards had sunk.

Whether it was or not, he certainly didn't learn a great deal about his own health from Guy's. On 23 February 1821, he died of consumption, not yet twenty-six years old.

The old operating theatre of St Thomas's Hospital, the only part which was not demolished in 1871, can still be inspected if you want a slightly incredulous shudder. It is located in the old chapel of St Thomas's Hospital, which is now the Chapter House of the Cathedral, St Thomas Street, and it is open on Mondays, Wednesdays, and Fridays, from 12.30 to 4 p.m. If your ideas of what operating theatres should be like have been conditioned by years of watching Dr Kildare and such-like films, you are in for a shock. If the shock is so great that you feel you have done enough tourism for the day, then London Bridge station is only a few yards off, providing an easy way to get anywhere you want to go.

If, on the other hand, you are strong-stomached enough to feel that if the Borough has any more to offer you would like to see it, you are in luck. The south bank, so unfairly neglected by so many visitors to London, does indeed have a lot more for you to see. The oldest statue in London, for example.

To get to it, walk down Borough High Street for about a quarter of a mile, to the point where it divides into Great Dover Street on the left, and the splendidly named Newington Causeway on the right. Take either fork: it doesn't matter which, because the street we are after joins them both, like the cross-bar of a letter A. It is Trinity Street. Walk along it to Trinity Church Square, through an area of distinguished, although still not expensive, late eighteenth- and early nineteenth-century houses. In the centre of Trinity Church Square is Trinity Church itself, the very same Trinity Church where music hall singer Fred Gilbert met his doom, in the old song. In front of the church is a statue which is generally supposed to be of Alfred the Great. It was brought to the square from the old Houses of Parliament, those burnt down in 1834, and is thought – on what evidence I know not – to date from about 1395. If it *is* a statue of Alfred the Great then it is entirely appropriate that it should now rest in Trinity Church Square, for the whole area was owned by and gets its name from Trinity House, that extraordinary body responsible for our lighthouses and lightships. Was not Alfred the Great the builder of the first real English navy? If our school history books are to be believed, he was, which is presumably why he was moved from Westminster to here. He's getting a bit old and decrepit now: the atmosphere of nineteenth-century London was hard on limestone. The acid in the air ate it away, so Alfred today does not have that fine definition of feature he may have had when he was leading the English against the Danes, or sitting in front of fires, absent-mindedly letting the cakes burn.

There's still a lot of things left to see on the south side of the river. There's the Imperial War Museum, another absolute must, whether you think war romantic or lunatic. There's what might be called the cultural side of the South

Bank – the National Theatre, the Festival Hall, the Hayward Gallery, the Queen Elizabeth Hall, the National Film Theatre, and other wonders too many to be told, which will also be dealt with in their proper place. And there is also Lambeth Palace, and its proper place is here and now.

It stands on the Albert Embankment, just across the Thames from the Houses of Parliament, which means it is quite a way from the last thing we were looking at, the Alfred statue. If you want to walk, it is about a mile, by way of Borough Road, St George's Circus, Lambeth Road (passing the Imperial War Museum on your left), continuing across Kennington Road, still on Lambeth Road, until you fetch up against the Palace just as you reach the river.

There was a manor house here before the Norman Conquest, when it was owned by Hardicanute (did he have a brother called Softicanute, one wonders?). The Palace itself, or at least the earliest part of it, was started towards the end of the twelfth century. It is certain that successive Archbishops of Canterbury have had their London homes here since that time. The north side of the cloisters date from this period, and the Undercroft of the Chapel was built a few years later. The Chapel was heavily damaged during the Second World War but has been restored so skilfully that you'd hardly notice. The Gatehouse, which is the bit you are most likely to see, since access to the Palace is restricted, was built by Bishop Morton – he of the famous Fork – in 1495. The rest of the building has been added to in bits and pieces ever since, with much restoration of just about everything after an especially severe hammering during the night bomber raids of autumn 1940.

Its earlier history was just as violent. In 1381, Wat Tyler, leading the Peasants' Revolt, took over the place; his followers burnt books and charters, and then set about the cellars, which they drank completely dry: the rude soldierly was clearly much the same then as now. As was common in those days, the Palace was used as a prison, for political as well as church prisoners. As a result, mobs were continually trying to storm it, with varying degrees of enthusiasm, the strength of their feeling presumably varying with their identification with the poor wretches held inside. The height of the surrounding walls and the solidity of the Gatehouse are therefore easily explained.

There is a great deal to see in the Palace, but you'll have to make an effort if you really are interested. Write a nice letter to the Archbishop's chaplain, asking for permission to go round the Palace, and you might be lucky. The Great Hall is now the Library, containing the books Wat Tyler's mob didn't get round to burning, with many later additions, including a first edition of Sir Thomas More's *Utopia* and a cake baked to a recipe Queen Anne liked. The cake, considered as a cake, is now as dead as her late lamented Majesty. The Library is at present open daily, except Sundays, from 10 a.m. to noon. But if you don't succeed in charming the Archbishop's Chaplain into letting you go round all the Palace, don't worry: the Garden opens for a few days each June (try ringing 01-730 0355 to find out when).

Strictly speaking, we shouldn't really be talking about Lambeth Palace in a chapter headed 'Bankside and the Borough' because it is in neither, so let's get back to somewhere near where we started. A long stroll along the Albert Embankment will take you past St Thomas's Hospital – the new one – and then, after an intricate bit of dodging across the approaches to Westminster Bridge, to the back (or front: how can one tell?) of County Hall, the headquarters of the Greater London Council. Assuming you are interested – I admit it may be unlikely – you can go round County Hall on a conducted tour any Saturday at 10.30 a.m. and 1.30 p.m. Make sure you are wearing stout boots: the corridors are very long and hard on the feet.

Belvedere Road, home of artist Feliks Topolski's railway arch studio, takes you ultimately to that cluster of culture now generally known as the South Bank, the capitals being essential to differentiate the usage from the simple geographical one. The Royal Festival Hall is quite straightforward: a clean, modern design, it was built by Robert Matthew and Leonard Martin, both later knighted for it, in 1951, as stage one in the brightening up of the then desolate area around the southern end of Waterloo Bridge. The Festival of Britain was the reason for this sudden surge of activity. The Royal Festival Hall, which is used for major recitals, and houses 3,400 people in its vast (and acoustically splendid) auditorium, was followed sixteen years later by a much smaller building, the Queen Elizabeth Hall, designed by Hubert Bennett, also knighted, and a year after that by his Hayward Gallery, where some of the more bewildering or outrightly rubbishy aspects of modern art can be seen. Or not, as the case may be, since the Hayward has a habit of closing during the summer season while it prepares for its next exhibition. Do not look at the crazy structure on top of the Gallery. It will make you think you are drunk even if you haven't touched a drop. The National Film Theatre is what it says, and is built in the same architectural style, one you will either love or hate. The most recent and controversial addition to the complex is, of course, the National Theatre, which deserves a paragraph to itself.

The idea of a National Theatre was first suggested in 1848. Then, like the Sleeping Beauty, it slept for a hundred years. Three foundation stones were laid between 1951 and 1969, when the GLC gave the present site to the theatre. It cost £17 million to build, consists of three theatres, each one named after a peer of the realm – truly, it is a theatre of the common people – and at the time of writing has just become fully operational. If you can get a ticket, think yourself lucky. There are seats available on the day of the performance, which is great if you want to spend your visit to London queueing up. If you have a credit card, try ringing 01-928 3052: you never know, you might be in luck. The Olivier is an open stage theatre, the Lyttelton is the more normal proscenium stage, and the Cottesloe is smaller and cosier than either of the others. You can sit on the terraces for the price of a cup of coffee and look out at one of the best views in London, across the river to St Paul's crowning its hill, so the complex obviously has advantages, and so it should have, at a cost of £17 million. There are so many tunnels, blind corners, dead ends, and what appear to be specially-designed wind tunnels, that you may get a feeling you have rather lost touch with the rest of humanity. Nevertheless, there are many people who rave about the National, so give it a try and make up your own mind. I wouldn't want to influence you for the world.

64

There is no doubt that the whole of the South Bank complex is on a quite magnificent site, but the best place to examine it from is the river or, of course, from the other side of the Thames. If modern architecture is not much to your taste, however, maybe the solution is to take advantage of the view the complex offers and sit somewhere in it, looking out at London across the water, thereby being in a position where you can't see the complex itself. Then, when you have had enough of the view, get down out of the complex – in itself quite a feat: people have been known to starve to death just trying to find the exit – and walk along Upper Ground. You will find little to cheer you during this stretch, either. It is nothing more than a long line of decrepitude. The *Daily Mail* building stares blankly across the water. London Weekend Television's Centre has marvellous views over the river but has nothing to commend it on the landward side. The tower of the Oxo warehouse is distinguished only by the ugliness of the noughts and crosses, blazoned on the tower, that tell the world what product the place houses. The other warehouses seem to be merely desperate in their depression, as though they know there is no hope for them. By comparison, the great hulk of Bankside power station, designed by Sir Giles Gilbert Scott in 1935, seems positively dynamic, even though it compares badly with the Battersea power station by the same architect a year or two earlier. Battersea is bold, Bankside is merely brutal.

So all in all, since we are now back where we started, perhaps the best thing is to go along Bankside itself once more, take delight from those lovely little seventeenth- and eighteenth-century houses, in one of which Sir Christopher Wren lived when he was designing St Paul's:

> Sir Christopher Wren
> Said to his men
> 'If anybody calls,
> Tell them I'm designing St Paul's'

and then wander along to the Anchor. Get yourself a nice cheering drink, go up on to the viewing platform over the water, ignoring the ugliness of the railway bridge alongside you, and sit looking reflectively at Southwark Bridge,

St Paul's, the huge pile of the City, and the history it all contains. By the time you have finished your drink you will be feeling fit and ready to go looking for what else London has to offer.

Dickens

London has inspired many writers: so have other cities, Arnold Bennett and the Five Towns being the obvious example. But surely no city belong to one man in the way London belongs to Charles Dickens (and he to it, come to that). He was two years old when he first arrived in the capital, and however far he travelled in later life, whether he was living in France and Italy, or touring America, he never really left London. It was with him wherever he went. He could never shake its influence off. He loved its joy, its bustle, its sadness, the muffled dankness of its fogs, even the noisome squalor of its slums.

Dickens's love of London brings us back to the opening of 'The river' (p.10) again because, above all else, that love was threaded on the line of the Thames, a river which represented for him all that was great and all that was evil in the city. For a description of the Thames as a symbol of the dark side of the city, nothing can beat the opening of *Our Mutual Friend*. The mud, the slime, the stench, the darkness, the cold rawness, the current that bears all away, however dreadful: they are all there. When poor Lizzie Hexam pulls her hood over her face so she will not see the body their boat has in tow, her father, Gaffer Hexam, orders her: 'Take that thing off your face', and then adds 'It's my belief you hate the very sight of the river'. Lizzie's hesitant reply 'I...I do not like it, father' brings from the Gaffer the chilling reply 'As if it wasn't your living! As if it wasn't meat and drink to you'. As a symbol of what the darker side of London meant to Charles Dickens, that retort can't be beaten. London was his meat and drink. It fed all his best work.

Of course the London of his day was very different from that of ours. The worst slums have gone, the 'rookeries' of Jacob's Island and St Giles long since swept away. Yet it is astonishing just how much of Dickens's city is left, and all of it available for anyone prepared to do what Dickens did so often – walk around the place. There is, of course, no need to go on those marathon rambles he was so fond of, but an hour's walk in most directions from the Dickens Museum in Doughty Street, W 1, will reveal scores of places which have a genuine connection with the great man.

The first hour must, however, be spent in the Museum itself. It is open from 10 a.m. to 5 p.m. on weekdays, Bank Holidays excepted (the nearest underground station is Russell Square, about five minutes' walk away). Dickens House, as 48 Doughty Street is now called, was bought by the Dickens Fellowship in 1925 and is governed by a board of trustees. A visit is absolutely essential for any Dickens lover. Maybe the Dingley Dell kitchen in the basement is a trifle artificial, but every other inch of the house breathes the genuine spirit of Dickens. The staff has been seriously depleted recently, with the death in 1976 of the Fellowship's Hon. Secretary, John Greaves, surely the most knowledge-able Dickens fan there ever was ('the only man who can answer any question on Dickens *without looking it up*', as Monica Dickens once said) and by the retirement early in 1978 of the Museum's Curator, Marjorie Pillers. Neverthe-less, the staff is still as devoted and helpful as ever, so it is im-

68

possible not to come away from Dickens House without feeling that you are already very near to getting inside the mind of the young genius. 'Young' because he was only twenty-five when he set up house here with his wife, their child, and his wife's sister, Mary. It was in this house that he finished *Pickwick Papers* and *Oliver Twist*, wrote the whole of *Nicholas Nickleby*, and started *Barnaby Rudge*. Not bad going in less than two years. The house contains his reading desk, his writing desk, manuscripts, locks of hair, letters, busts, portraits, even door knockers from his other homes; and the total effect is to make it hard to believe that The Master isn't actually still at work in one of the rooms.

When you can tear yourself away from No. 48, turn right out of the front door towards Guilford Street. A left turn there will bring you to Coram's Fields, the site of the famous Foundling Hospital. Set up in 1739 by the kindly Captain Coram, it was for 'exposed and deserted' children, of whom there were thousands in the London of that time. The hospital was later to provide a name for Tattycoram, the companion of Pet Meagles in *Little Dorrit*. It was also the inspiration for 'The Marchioness', the poor little half-starved slavey to Sampson Brass in *The Old Curiosity Shop*. She was undoubtedly modelled on some of the children Dickens took in from the hospital to help with the housework at No. 48. Today the site of the hospital is, most appropriately, a children's park and gardens. Theoretically, no adult is allowed in without a child, which is a nice reversal of the usual restriction, but the park-keepers are understanding, so try your luck. In any case, the remaining original buildings, with their exquisite Georgian arcades, are well worth examining, even if you have to do it through the railings.

From here there are several choices. You can continue along Guilford Street to Russell Square, called after the Dukes of Bedford, family name Russell, who laid out the area just before Dickens was born. Turn right up Woburn Place to Tavistock Square, where Dickens lived from 1851 to 1860 and where he wrote *Bleak House*, *Hard Times*, *Little Dorrit*, and *A Tale of Two Cities*. But this diversion isn't particularly worth the effort to any but the most devout Dickens fanciers, since the house he lived in is long since demolished. The site is now occupied by the headquarters of the British Medical Association, which, in view of the novelist's not very high opinion of the medical profession of his time, could be thought to be a shade ironical.

So a better way to leave Coram's Fields is to go back along Guilford Street, across the top of Doughty Street, to Gray's Inn Road. Turn right, and put your best foot forward, because this part of the road has very little to commend it. After crossing Theobald's Road (pronounced Tibbald's by those in the know), hurry on down to Holborn, with your steps hastened by the sight of some splendid half-timbered houses end-stopping the view.

From this stretch of Gray's Inn Road your choices are many. For instance, before you reach Holborn itself, you will see, on the right-hand side, the various entrances to Gray's Inn, one of London's famous Inns of Court. Apart from its calm, quiet beauty, it is notable as the place where the young Charles Dickens took up his first steady, respectable job. Oh yes, of course, I know he'd done a spell at the infamous Warren's Blacking Factory down by Hungerford Bridge (only three months by the way, but it must have felt like a lifetime, to judge by those near-autobiographical opening chapters of *David Copperfield*). This, in Gray's Inn, was the real thing. His father having once again become temporarily solvent, Charles had gone to school, at a private establishment just south of Mornington Crescent (the street, not the underground station), after which he was hired as an office boy with a firm in Symond's Inn and then, after only six weeks, at the age of fifteen, he transferred to a clerkship with Ellis and Blackmore of 1 Raymond's Buildings, Gray's Inn, at 15s. 6d. (75p) a week. The firm no longer exists, and the name of the building has been changed, but if you stand in the doorway of the building on the south side of South Square, nearest to the little tunnel leading to High Holborn, there is no doubt you will be standing on a threshold the young Dickens crossed every working day of his life for eighteen months.

When you've finished posing for your photograph, why not go through that little tunnel and turn right? If you do, you will see, a few yards ahead, Henekey's Long Bar. There is no real proof young Charles ever did go in there but it seems likely: a young blade on 15s. a week, in the days before there were rules about under-18s, was surely bound to pop in there for a glass of something warming from time to time? There's a huge three-sided stove, dated 1815, apparently with no chimney (there is one, actually, but the smoke goes *down* first, by a forced-draught system, and then passes under the floor before ascending via an outside flue. So, in the end, the smoke goes up the chimney just the same). There are huge barrels, alas no longer full of the real stuff, and there are cosy little alcoves for those who want to be alone, all precisely as it was in Dickens's day.

Across from Henekey's, on the other side of High Holborn, is that group of half-timbered buildings you caught sight of as you came down Gray's Inn Road. This is very definitely Dickens country, although in his time the half-timbering was plastered over. The buildings mask the front of Staple Inn, once another of the Inns of Court. Dickens makes specific reference to it in *The Mystery of Edwin Drood*. The little alleyway splitting the shops leads to a court with lawns, flowers, a fountain and even a fig tree, and all this only ten yards from the noise of Holborn! No wonder Dickens described it as 'one of those nooks, the turning into which, out of the clashing street, imparts to the relieved pedestrian the sensation of having put cotton in his ears and velvet soles on his boots. It is one of those nooks where a few smoky sparrows twitter in the smoky trees, as though they called to one another: "Let us play at country", and where a few feet of garden-mould, and a few yards of gravel enable them to do that refreshing violence to their tiny understandings.'

Today, because of Clean Air Acts, the sparrows, and the trees they twitter in, are no longer smoky. Today, thanks, surprisingly enough, to the Prudential Assurance Company, who took on the responsibility for the repair and maintenance of the Inn after it had been bombed in the Second World War, the garden is no longer mouldy and the gravel covers more than a few yards. It is the very place to sit and wonder, as did Mr Grewgious, the *Edwin Drood* lawyer who had chambers here, whether the engraved initials over the doorway, 'P J T 1747', meant Perhaps John Thomas, or Perhaps Joe Tyler, or even Pretty Jolly Too. In fact, as Dickens didn't know, they stand for Principal John Thomson, who was President of the Inn of Court at the time of the inscription.

Mention of a certain insurance company a few lines back is a reminder that there is another Dickens connection only fifty yards away. On the other side of Gray's Inn Road, and you will certainly not be able to miss it however hard you try, is the massive red pile that is the home of the Prudential Assurance Company. A blue glazed tile by the side of the courtyard entrance tells us that this was the site of Furnivall's Inn, yet another of the Inns of Court which clustered round this area. Inside the entrance arch is a bust of Dickens. For it was here that the young writer lived with his brother Fred in bachelor chambers at No. 13. When he married Catherine Hogarth he took bigger chambers on the third floor, before moving to Doughty Street.

His first days in Furnivall's Inn were hard, but things soon began to look up. In 1835, when our hero was twenty-three, the publisher Macrone suggested that 'Sketches by Boz', which had been appearing regularly in his magazines, should be collected together in a volume. Dickens was on his way. That is a cue for us to be on ours. So carry on down Holborn, across the Circus, to Holborn Viaduct. The viaduct is only evident as a slight flattening of the dip down from Gray's Inn Road. The word 'dip' is significant. In Dickens's day there was no viaduct and the dip was much steeper. How much steeper, let one of the novels show you. In Chapter 21 of *Oliver Twist*, Bill Sikes drags the young Oliver along on their way to break into a rich house in Chertsey. As they reach Holborn, we read: '"Now, young 'un!" said Sikes, looking up at the clock of St Andrew's Church, "hard upon seven! You must step out. Come on, don't lag behind already, Lazylegs".'

It is the phrase 'looking up' that is revealing, for if you stand at the beginning of Holborn Viaduct and look at St Andrew's Church, with its statues of the little foundling boy and girl, you will find that you are looking *down* at it. What the viaduct spans, as it crosses over Farringdon Street a few yards ahead, is the valley of the River Fleet, long since covered over, on its way down to the Thames, just visible there to the south beyond Ludgate Circus. As the viaduct didn't exist in their day – it wasn't built till the 1860s – Sikes and Oliver would have rushed down Snow Hill and then had the steep climb up again to what naturally came to be called *High* Holborn.

Having gazed your fill over the Farringdon Street parapet, and wondered what it must have looked like when there were wharves on both sides of a busy river, instead of the present-day street, carry on along Holborn Viaduct in the direction of the City. (It may seem odd to call it a viaduct still when it is so clearly an ordinary street. But that is just what it is not. It really is a viaduct all the way to Newgate: it is only the modern buildings crowding in on either side which disguise the fact that you are still way up in the air.)

Newgate itself, that most notorious of prisons, is no longer there. It was demolished in 1902 and the Old Bailey now stands on the site. The blue glazed tile on the wall of the Old Bailey at the corner of Newgate Street confirms that this evil building really did stand there well within living memory.

Dickens had no love for it, either in his novels or in real life. In 1849, when he was thirty-seven and famous, he wrote a letter to *The Times* about the disgusting behaviour of the crowds watching a public execution outside the gaol. He had to wait another nineteen years, only two years before his death, for those nauseating spectacles to be abolished. Nevertheless, he could claim that his writings over the years had helped to reduce the number of crimes for which the sentence was death. When he was a boy they numbered more than two hundred. After one of the 'Sketches by Boz' about a hanging outside Newgate, the number was reduced to fourteen. By 1861 it was down to four, and after 1868, although the number remained unaltered, the executions were no longer held in public. I don't think you can say that was entirely due to the power of Dickens's pen, but there is no doubt that his fame, and his indignation, helped.

The horror Newgate inspired in Dickens is obvious from the novels. In *Great Expectations*, Pip, having time in hand before Mr Jaggers returns to his office, takes a little walk to Newgate. He meets a man who acts as his guide: 'he showed me the Debtors' Door, out of which culprits came to be hanged: heightening the interest of that dreadful portal by giving me to understand that "four on em" would come out of that door the day after tomorrow at eight in the morning, to be killed in a row. This was horrible and gave me a sickening idea of London.'

Only a sentence or so before, Pip had passed through another horrible place: 'So I came into Smithfield; and the shameful place, being all asmear with filth and fat and blood and foam, seemed to stick to me.'

Well, you can go to both places these days without having to be as disgusted as Pip. You won't see any hangings outside the Old Bailey; and Smithfield, which is just up Giltspur Street, across Newgate Street, is as hygienic as such places can be; a nice square which, in the best British tradition, isn't square at all; a nice central garden; two nice streets. Little Britain, where Mr Jaggers had his office, and Cloth Fair with its splendid medieval houses; the oldest hospital in London, St Bartholomew's; and the church after which it is named, surely one of the finest Norman churches in the land, with an atmosphere all its own, an atmosphere which would certainly have eased Pip's mind had he bothered to go inside, as I hope you will while you are there. The guide leaflet is most helpful and cheap, and the proceeds go to the upkeep of the fabric, so you couldn't wish for a better cause.

After you've toured St Bart's, go back down Giltspur Street, cross over and carry on down Old Bailey (which is, of course, the name of the street, not the name of the courts. They are properly called the Central Criminal Courts, and you can view them on Saturdays at 10 a.m.). Halfway down on the right-hand side is Fleet Lane. Go down it towards Farringdon Street, which covers over the Fleet River or Ditch. On your left, as you approach Farringdon Street, was the infamous Fleet Prison, where Mr Pickwick was incarcerated when he refused to pay the damages awarded against him in the case of Bardell v. Pickwick.

It is in the chapters describing his stay there that *Pickwick Papers* suddenly changes from a great comic novel into a serious one, a change which produced some of Dickens's most searing writing. But the Fleet could be moderately comfortable – if you were able to afford it. Mr Pickwick was, of course, which is why, when his friends came to visit him, a messenger was sent out to bring in 'a bottle or two of very good wine'. As Dickens goes on to say: 'The bottle or two, indeed, might be more properly described as a bottle or six, for by the time it was drunk, and tea over, the bell began to ring for strangers to withdraw.'

Well, the Fleet Prison is pulled down now, but the 'coffee house' from which the wine was brought is, happily, still there. It is the Horn Tavern, in Knightrider Street, and as it is almost unchanged since Dickens's day, and as he most certainly used it when he was a reporter in nearby Doctor's Commons, a long-gone ecclesiastical court, we might as well walk up there and take a little rest and refreshment.

The easiest way to find it is to go up the right-hand side of Ludgate Hill towards St Paul's. Walk round the south side of the curve of St Paul's Churchyard. Immediately opposite the wonderful south side of the cathedral are two little streets aiming down to the river – Godliman Street and Peter's Hill. Knightrider Street runs between them, parallel with the Churchyard. The Horn Tavern is on the eastern corner. It is an eighteenth-century pub, not much changed since the young Charles – he was only sixteen when he started work in Doctors' Common – used to visit it for his mid-day bite to eat. The wood panelling is genuine enough, the bar counter is as old as any pub enthusiast could wish, the beer is good, and there is a ground-floor dining-room where you might well be advised to book if you want to sit down to eat. The partition that once separated the public bar from the saloon bar has now been pulled down, which enables the white bust of Dickens to stare down at all who use the place and not just at the better-off customers, as used to be the case.

Leaving the Horn, however reluctantly, turn up the steps towards St Paul's again and then turn right towards the City, and another *Pickwick Papers* reference. This is the George and Vulture, where Mr Pickwick and Sam Weller settled in when they arrived back in London to prepare for the famous Bardell *v.* Pickwick breach-of-promise case. It is in a tiny alley, called St Michael's, which connects Cornhill with Lombard Street. Dickens described the George and Vulture as 'very good, old-fashioned, and comfortable quarters'. He was right. It still is, though not as a hotel. It is now one of the most famous, and deservedly so, eating places in the City. The wooden partitions, the white napery, the olde-worlde courtesy of the staff, the good English food, all make it quite clear why Pickwick chose the place, and why visitors should do so, too, before those beastly creatures, the developers, destroy it and its associations for ever. At the time of writing, it is still there and in its marvellously comfortable atmosphere it is possible to imagine that you are Mr Pickwick who, after dinner there, had 'finished his second pint of particular port, pulled his silk handkerchief over his head and thrown himself back in an easy chair' to indulge in what Dickens called 'tranquil meditations'. I don't think they'll let you do that today at the George and Vulture: they're far too busy at lunch-time. But the place is well worth a visit. If you can manage it in a misty twilight, I think that, despite all the concrete monstrosities around you, you will get a definite feel of what it was like when Dickens was a regular there.

Go north now from the George and Vulture to Cornhill and turn east. Cornhill becomes Leadenhall Street, with its incredibly out-of-place Victorian market, all girders and glass. This street has lots of Dickens connections. It was at the Blue Boar, just off the street, that Sam Weller sat down to write his valentine to 'the pretty housemaid', Mary. You won't find the Blue Boar: it was a Dickens invention. You won't find the Green Dragon, either, even though that was the original of the Blue Boar, for it has been demolished. At 157 Leadenhall Street, also demolished, Mr Solomon Gills had his shop, the Wooden Midshipman, described so vividly in *Dombey and Son*. Somewhere along the street, too, was the counting house of Messrs Dombey and Son themselves, that great power in the City: you can make your own decision as to exactly where it was.

There is very little resemblance between the City of Dickens's time and the City of today: the bombers and the developers have seen to that. There is still enough left, however, to make this walk worth continuing. On the left-hand side of Leadenhall Street, going east, is St Mary Axe where, if *Our Mutual Friend* is to be believed, the firm of Pubsey and Co. had their offices. They were supervised by Riah the Jew, a figure so kind and gentle as to clear Dickens completely of any suspicion of anti-semitism that might have been incurred by his creation of Fagin. On the roof garden of the offices Lizzie Hexam and little Jenny Wren often used to sit and chat.

At the top of St Mary Axe is Bevis Marks, the street where the rascally attorney Sampson Brass had his office and his house – the address was No. 10, where the pavement was so narrow that as you walked past the place your elbow was likely to wipe some of the dirt from the window.

By now you may feel you have walked enough for one day, although it's nothing compared with the distances Dickens covered on his largely nocturnal rambles. So turn up towards Liverpool Street Underground, and get your feet up on the Circle line to Bank, then change there to the Northern line, bound for London Bridge and Borough. You are now heading south of the river, to territory Dickens knew like the back of his hand, for he lived there for some time and not always with very happy memories.

The moment you come out of Borough station you will know you are in Dickensland. Look at the names: Pickwick Street, Marshalsea Road, Sawyer Street, Quilp Street, Dorrit Street, Weller Street, Doyce Street (after the amiable inventor in *Little Dorrit*), Copperfield Street, and so on. Don't get too excited: you haven't suddenly stumbled on the secret of where Dickens got his characters' names from. The names are, of course, all taken from the books, not the other way round, but they do show just how strong was the Dickens connection in this area.

On the same side of Borough High Street is Lant Street. This is both real and fictional Dickens: the young Charles lodged here when his father was in the Marshalsea debtors' prison, and it was here that he housed that extraordinary medical student Bob Sawyer of *Pickwick Papers*, and that unusual young man David Copperfield. And just to complete the picture, the school in the street is the Charles Dickens school.

Dominating the Borough of Dickens must, of course, be the Marshalsea Prison. Not only did it figure unforgettably in Dickens's own life during those months in 1824 when his father was incarcerated there, but it overshadows the whole of that wonderful novel *Little Dorrit*. You can still see part of the wall of the prison, which was demolished in the 1840s. And as for Little Dorrit herself, she is commemorated by a stained glass window in St George's Church (within whose yard are remains of the Marshalsea), and most appropriately, too, since it was in that church she was both christened and married. It is no wonder that St George's is known to Dickens lovers the world over as the Little Dorrit church. A pilgrimage is a must.

Even now the Borough hasn't finished with you. The High Street is full of Dickensiana. It was in the yard of the White Hart Inn that Mr Pickwick first met up with his valet-to-be, the immortal Sam Weller. The inn has long since gone, but the yard is still there (called, not unnaturally, White Hart Yard), on the right-hand side of Borough High Street, as you walk up to London Bridge. If you want to see what the inn looked like when Mr Jingle and Rachael stayed there after their elopement, and Mr Pickwick and Mr Wardle, in hot pursuit, discovered them, with the help of Mr Weller, then come back to the next yard south, George Inn Yard. Whatever you do, take time off here, for the George, although much reduced in size from its former glory, still remains London's sole surviving galleried coaching inn. In the yard itself you can almost see Sam Weller cleaning boots and contemplating the results 'with evident satisfaction'. Inside the pub you can feel that you are Mr Pickwick or Mr Wardle, refreshing themselves after their hunt for the eloped couple, for the interior has changed little in the last two hundred years or so. The cubicles, the napery, the waitresses in their old-fashioned aprons and hats, the food itself, fine English fare, the beer, the bonhomie, all are pure Dickens. And though the George will never be able to claim the honour of having been the location of that famous Pickwick–Weller meeting, it can say that it, too, is mentioned in the canon, for it was from this inn that Edward 'Tip' Dorrit, that idle and spendthrift young man, wrote his begging letters.

By now you will be tired and I don't blame you. You have, however, merely scratched at the surface of Dickens's London. In the *Charles Dickens Encyclopedia* (Osprey, 1973), Michael and Molly Hardwick list more than 350 separate entries of places directly connected with Dickens's life and works. As most of the entries contain many references, that must mean a thousand or more places to see that Dickens knew intimately and either wrote about openly or used thinly disguised.

If you are still not exhausted; if the pilgrim spirit still drives you on; then cross London Bridge, drop down the steps at the northern end to Upper and Lower Thames Streets (the one becomes the other underneath the bridge), remembering that within the shadow of the Monument just ahead was where the incomparable Mrs Todgers had her boarding-house; where Mr Pecksniff stayed with his daughters; and where Bailey, the houseboy, helps, along with Mrs Gamp (who also visited the place), to make *Martin Chuzzlewit* one of the funniest of the novels.

Walk west along Upper Thames Street and try and work out where Mrs Clennam's appalling house in *Little Dorrit*, and Ralph Nickleby's equally dilapidated one in *Nicholas Nickleby*, were situated. By the time you get to Blackfriars you will have reached the point at which the Fleet River once discharged itself into the Thames. Cross over (or rather, for safety's sake, *under*) the Blackfriars Bridge approach, walk along the Victoria Embankment and turn up through the Temple. This area, along with the Inns of Court on the other side of Fleet Street and the Strand, is mentioned so often in the Dickens's novels that any attempt to list specific references would be impossible. Just enjoy it. Sit in Fountain Court, listen to the tinkle of the water, look at the amiably plump goldfish, and dream your dreams away. And when you awake, delight yourself with the thought that there's so much more of Dickens's London still to go at.

But some other day, perhaps?

Pubs

Ye Olde Cheshire Cheese – El Vino
Old Cock Tavern – Wig and Pen – The George
The Edgar Wallace – Devereux Arms
The Witness Box – White Swan – The Harrow
Old Bell – Punch Tavern – King Lud
Magpie and Stump – Fox and Anchor
The Sir Christopher Wren – Ye Olde Watling
Ye Olde Doctor Butler's Head – Simpson's Tavern
Hoop and Grapes

That great and good man, Doctor Samuel Johnson, loved London. For him it had everything: 'When a man is tired of London, he is tired of life.' What he especially loved about London was its taverns, a love which he expressed in that other, equally famous, remark of his: 'There is nothing which has yet been contrived by man, by which so much happiness is produced as by a good tavern or inn.'

Dr Johnson wouldn't be disappointed by today's tavern. Whatever the planners have done to London – and they've done a lot, most of it deplorable – they have at least left us our pubs. There are said to be more than 7,000 of them in London. A man cannot hope to drink in all of them, but a man might try.

In doing so, that man would experience a great deal of pleasure, for, despite juke boxes, pin tables and electronic tennis, most pubs remain what they have always been; places where you can get the weight off your feet and the dust out of your throat, places where you can eat good, cheap food, places where you can enjoy good company, sing good songs, have cheery conversations, and generally find yourself agreeing with Dr Johnson yet again, when he said: 'A tavern chair is the throne of human felicity.'

So we might as well start at a pub he used himself: at least, we can assume he did, although there is, oddly enough, no mention of it in Boswell's famous biography of him. But since his house in Gough Square was only a few yards away, and since his good friend Oliver Goldsmith lived only a couple of doors from it, it's a fairly safe assumption that the Doctor was a regular.

The pub is Ye Olde Cheshire Cheese. The Cheshire Cheese, which must be one of the best-known pubs in London and therefore in the world, is in Wine Office Court, a tiny alley on the right-hand side of Fleet Street as you climb up from Ludgate Circus (the nearest Tube station to the Circus is Blackfriars, on the Circle and District lines). It really is a tiny alley, so keep your eyes skinned. You'll pass the *Daily Express* and the *Daily Telegraph* buildings (the only two national newspapers, incidentally, which actually have their offices in the Street of Ink). Wine Office Court is no more than four of five feet wide and is arched over for the first few yards up from Fleet Street. The door to the 'Cheese' is on the right, where the arching ends.

Do yourself a favour: get there early or late. Fame unfortunately means crowds. The manager himself once described it to me in his broad Cockney as 'the most unconfortablest pub in London when it's crahded'. He was right. So arrange to arrive there as they open, which is 11.30 a.m. on weekdays. There'll be fresh sawdust on the floor of the room on the right. The beer is magnificent, Marston's from Burton-on-Trent, and you can drink it sitting in the chair in the far corner, a chair which is known as Dr Johnson's chair (he may have sat in it, but not here: it came from another Johnsonian pub, the nearby Mitre). There's another bar downstairs, but mind your head: that notice isn't there for nothing, as I hope you don't find out. Across from the bar you are sitting in is the dining-room, which hasn't been changed since the days of Charles Dickens. They serve splendid English food in portions big enough to make you want to sleep the afternoon away. There is, however, enough history in this pub to make you want to keep awake so you can take it all in.

Just look at the famous people who have drunk here, for example. Johnson and Goldsmith we've mentioned already. The poet Alexander Pope, the playwright William Congreve, the novelist William Makepeace Thackeray and his even more famous friend, Charles Dickens, all gave the place their custom. They are likely-sounding clients, but what about François Marie Arouet de Voltaire? The glorious roast-beefy, bitter-beery atmosphere of the Cheshire Cheese hardly seems right for the sharply-acid wit of the famous French writer, but it is a fact that he was a regular here during his three years of exile in London from 1726 to 1729. He was probably introduced to the place by Alexander Pope, with whom he had become very friendly. Likely or not, though, it shows that Voltaire knew when he was on to a good thing.

The pub you are in today is substantially the same as it was in Voltaire's time. It was rebuilt in 1667, after the Great Fire of London, but the cellars of the original establishment are still in use. Indeed, until very recently, their ceilings were yet blackened by smoke from the Fire, which destroyed the entire superstructure.

The Cheshire Cheese, first licensed in 1538, when it was known as the Horn Tavern, stands on land which was once part of the famous Whitefriars Priory (Whitefriars Street is immediately across Fleet Street from Wine Office Court), and the well in the vaulted cellar is undoubtedly the one from which the friars drew their water. Actually the cellar, although in full use, is more like a museum. It contains a death mask of Johnson, a very early copy of his Dictionary, old letters from him, and so on. The manager is usually willing to show you round, but remember what I said about the popularity of the place: wait until the crowds have gone, or get there before they arrive. There used to be an aged retainer in eighteenth-century uniform who took visitors around, but he has gone the way of all flesh. So, too, has

Polly, except that she still sits on the bar counter in all her feathered finery. Polly was a parrot famous for her bad language. One story says it took a turn for the worse when she saw ladies being admitted to her bar for the first time. Another version says Polly had been taught very unprintable phrases during the First World War, when soldiers and sailors on leave explained to her exactly what the Kaiser should go and do to himself. Dead and stuffed, her memory lingers on, and catching a glimpse of that beady eye looking at you is quite enough to make you think that one of those famous blood-curdling phrases is likely to be shrieked at you any second. Polly, by the way, was a male.

If you want lunch at the 'Cheese' (or dinner, because they do those as well) remember to book: the phone number is 01-353 6170. But make sure you are really hungry. The size of the portions is apt to be a trifle overwhelming to all but hearty trenchermen.

A hundred yards up Fleet Street, on the other side, is El Vino (not El Vino's: they get annoyed if you say that). This is a wine bar, which means wines and spirits, but no beer, not even bottled. The haunt of journalists and lawyers, it has changed hardly at all since it was first opened about a hundred years ago. They have electricity now, but the original gas fittings are still there, and they work, to the great satisfaction of everybody whenever there is an electricity power cut. Its rules of behaviour are also much as they were originally. Men must wear coats and ties (and that means in the hottest of heat waves as well); ladies are not allowed to stand at the bar, but must sit down, either around the two tables near the door, or in the large back room. The latter is probably the better bet. Famous figures of journalism can be seen holding daily court there, and you can drink your wine or whatever whilst actually sitting in a carver labelled 'Lord Northcliffe's Chair'. Furthermore, the front of the place, being long and narrow, can be intolerably uncomfortable, sometimes rather resembling standing in a crowded corridor train. The wines are excellent (they ship their own), although the price may make you blanch slightly: the quality, however, is such that the colour will soon come back to your face. For some reason the spirit measures are very moderately priced. The bar sandwiches are good, and there is a downstairs restaurant for which it is sensible to book beforehand (telephone no.: 01-353 6786). Opening time is the same as for the Cheshire Cheese, 11.30 a.m. until 3 p.m., (but not Sundays). The 11.30 rather than 11 a.m. start is because both establishments are inside the boundaries of the City of London. Note that El Vino, which opens again at 5 p.m. closes at 8 p.m. This isn't uncommon in the City, which tends to become deserted once the workers have gone home, and which, on Saturdays and Sundays, is so empty of people that you could be forgiven for imagining that the Bubonic plague is back.

Do not look for a pub atmosphere at El Vino. It isn't that at all. But it is an atmosphere worth sampling at least once. The dark wood, the gas mantles, the huge barrels behind the bar, the smoke-grimed ceiling, and the ancient engraved-glass and other advertisements are well worth studying. As with the Cheshire Cheese, getting there early gives you time and space to look at them at your leisure. And don't forget to spare more than a glance for the Fleet Street frontage. It is extremely elegant Edwardian and shows up a lot of the much more recent 'tat' with which it is surrounded.

A few feet farther up Fleet Street is Mitre Court. A few yards past the entrance to the Court you may notice a blue plaque which says this was the site of another of Dr Johnson's favourites, the Mitre. Its name was appropriated, on its demolition in 1829, by a pub in Mitre Court. That too, was demolished in its turn, to be replaced by the Clachan, a Younger's house of the sort London is rich in: clean, quick, with a choice of bar food or a sit-down meal. There's absolutely nothing special about it, except that it does give directly on to the Temple, that oasis of quiet between Fleet Street and the river. Despite the hundreds of parked cars – clearly, not all lawyers are impecunious – the courts and gardens of the Temple are extremely restful. If you don't have time to explore them, make time. Then you'll be rested enough to continue our pub crawl.

Regretting that the old Mitre isn't there anymore – Boswell described it as a place of 'frequent resort' where the good Doctor loved to sit up late – go back to Fleet street and

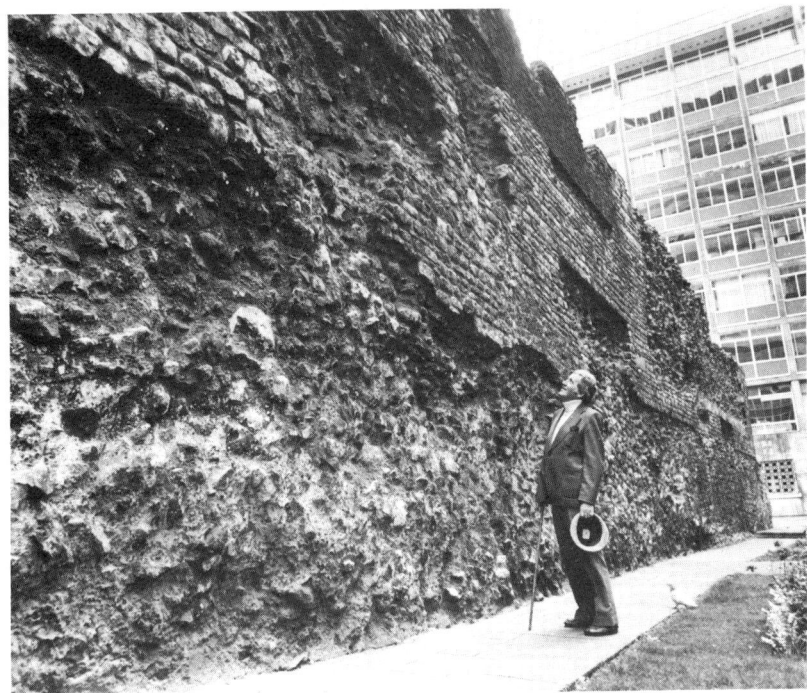

How impregnable the walls must have looked to an outsider

Old and new – Roman foundations, medieval bastion and modern Barbican

St Bride's wedding cake spire (p. 31)

The exquisite white and gold interior

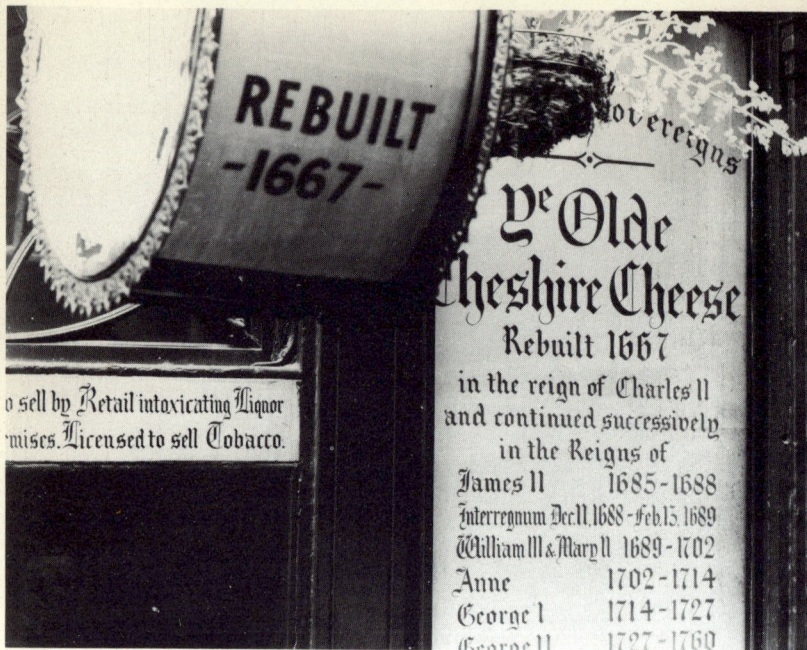

Ye Olde Cheshire Cheese (p. 81) proudly announcing it was re-built *in 1667*

The George, Borough High Street (p. 58), London's sole remaining galleried inn

Shepherd Market (p. 117) has a distinctly eighteenth-century feel

London's grim, grey guardian

St Paul's sailing high above the City

From the river you can abuse your MP on the Terrace, secure in the knowledge that you are out of reach and range

The river was once a busy place: a view from Tower Bridge

Petticoat Lane is actually called Middlesex Street (p. 107)

At Sermon Lane the Cathedral processions stopped to hear – a sermon

The Horn Tavern, Knightrider Street (p. 75), haunt of Mr Dickens and Mr Pickwick

The Edwardian façade of El Vino (p. 83) stands out from the tat that surrounds it

One of the topless towers of idiocy: the Natwest pile

The country comes to town – derelict Broad Street station (p. 142)

The doorway of the Natural History Museum (p. 186) should carry a Government health warning: 'This portal can damage your eyesight'

The Wig and Pen (p. 85), oldest Strand building to survive the Great Fire of 1666

The Anchor at Bankside (p. 57), where Dr Johnson certainly took his ease, and Shakespeare probably didn't

Put that Duke on a charge for riding without stirrups (p. 43)

The Hoop and Grapes (p. 93), fittingly for a vintner's, leans definitely to port

The George and Vulture (p. 49), tucked away in a corner of George Square

The Jamaica Wine House (p. 50), first famous for its coffee

The Welsh Church (p. 36), London home of hywel

Gresham's grasshopper (p. 42)

Boadicea riding reinless to eternity (p. 15)

turn left, which means that you're still going west. Not very far along you'll come to the Old Cock Tavern. Once again the great names of literature are associated with it – Pepys, Johnson, Dickens, Thackeray, and Tennyson, who dined there almost every day. Not quite 'there'. The present Old Cock is, in fact, fairly new. The original place was just across Fleet Street and when they pulled it down they rebuilt it on the south side using a lot of the beams, panelling, and so on: the room on the first floor is an exact reproduction of a room in the old building, the stone fireplace with its oak mantel being a survival from the seventeenth century. The pub is big, with a long bar, the food is good and the beer highly drinkable. It may be the 'antique' interior that does it, but the Old Cock seems to have developed an atmosphere and tradition of its own, despite the fact that it's no more than ninety years old.

Two more pubs on Fleet Street, and then we can turn towards the Thames. The first, the Wig and Pen, isn't a pub at all. It is a club, but it is one of the few buildings in the area which survived the Great Fire. As the name suggests, it is another haunt of lawyers and journalists, and if you can't manage to get inside to see its old upstairs rooms with their crazily-sloping floors, then simply cross the road to the Law Courts and enjoy the Wig and Pen's exterior, virtually unchanged to this day. If you can get inside, you may like to know that they serve lunch until 5 p.m. at which point they start serving dinner. The Wig and Pen is clearly a survival from more leisurely days.

The last pub in Fleet Street isn't in Fleet Street at all (neither was the Wig and Pen: Fleet Street has become the Strand by this time). The George looks old, but isn't, although most of the tourists who take pictures of its half-timbering clearly don't know that. It was re-built in the 1930s on the site of a much older pub, as you can see if you can persuade the manager to let you see the cellars (haunted, by the way, as we will be proving later). It is a Charrington house; the interior does have a feel of age about it. There's a good (and quite inexpensive) upstairs dining-room; and a range of snacks at the bar. Well worth a visit and an ideal start for a wander round the Temple, which is just behind you, or Lincoln's Inn and its Fields, which are across the road, behind the Law Courts.

Let's assume that you've decided to turn left out of the George and left again down to the river. It is a good decision, because there are some nice little pubs tucked away in this area.

The first you will come to, if you have gone down Essex Street, is the Edgar Wallace, once known as the Essex Head. The conversion hasn't improved the pub very much, but you can eat there and look at the relics of the crime novelist. This is one of the 'theme' pubs which have begun to appear in London. (A particularly good example, though not on this particular pub-crawl, is the Sherlock Holmes at the bottom of Northumberland Avenue, just down from Trafalgar Square. The bar is thick with exhibits from the more memorable cases of the Great Detective, including the head of the Hound of the Baskervilles; the upstairs room, a reconstruction of the famous chambers at 221B, Baker Street, is a masterpiece.) Here, at the Edgar Wallace, the more interesting attractions are the dining-room and the Whitbread beer, pulled on old hand-pumps. The notice board outside, just round the corner into Devereux Court, gives details of the novelist's life, but is a touch out of date, since it talks about Wallace as still living at Bourne End. I doubt it: he died in 1932.

A few yards along Devereux Court is the Devereux Arms. The name is derived from the fact that you have just turned out of Essex Street; the family name of the Essex's was Devereux. The pub is built on the site of a famous eighteenth-century coffee house, The Grecian, and is full of lawyers, something that may put you off. Don't let it. It is the sort of pub in which any sensible person (which may even include lawyers) can feel comfortable. It has, as all sensible London pubs have these days, an upstairs dining-room where the food is good. So are the bar snacks. So is the beer. So is everything about the place except that it is so near to the Temple, that haunt of lawyers, a breed of people you can begin to love if you live with them long enough, and let us hope to God that you never have to.

The gate into the Temple, which is only a yard or two from

the front door of the Devereux Arms, seems designed to keep you out, but ignore the signs and stroll through Fountain Court, Pump Court and Old Mitre Court to the Tudor Street exit. Immediately by the gate is another legal type pub, the Witness Box. Here the overwhelming presence of lawyers is less noticeable, largely because there is, instead, an overwhelming presence of journalists, since you are next door to the Associated Newspapers complex. Across Bouverie Street is the White Swan, universally known as the Mucky Duck. It is a great barn of a place, with all the charm of a railway waiting-room, but you will never feel alone there, simply because you never *will* be alone. Printers from the *Daily Mail* and the London *Evening News* can be found there at almost any hour of the day, and a noisy, cheerful lot they are, too. They run a darts team and until the mid-seventies even had their own soccer team, the Mucky Duck XI. Of all the pubs in the Fleet Street area, this is the one with the most definite feel of a 'local' about it.

Beyond the White Swan is Whitefriars Street. Turn left up it, towards Fleet Street and then immediately turn right up Primrose Hill. The daunting concrete of the massive new development surrounding you is relieved by The Harrow, a splendid little pub, again much used by journalists. In fact, you could have entered the Harrow by walking up Whitefriars Street instead of turning up Primrose Hill, because the pub has two entrances and two bars, on two levels. The lower, Whitefriars Street, bar is the haunt of the print workers; the upper, which must be the smallest in London, is used by the journalists: overalls downstairs, lounge suits upstairs. Up a twisty flight of stairs is the Micawber Room. The landlord, Alan Dove, says it is called that because anybody who runs a pub for journalists has got to be an optimist. The Micawber is much more of a cocktail lounge, and as such is the home of several of the redoubtable lady journalists Fleet Street seems to breed. Food is always available and if you stay there overnight – there are a few rooms – you will be served the biggest breakfast in London at about the smallest price.

The Harrow looks out over what used to be a gracious Georgian square. It is now a desert of office blocks and underground car parks, as soulless as it once was beautiful. If you want to see what has been destroyed, go out of the upper door of the Harrow, along Hutton Street, and turn left up Dorset Rise to Fleet Street. Opposite Dorset Court the Rise widens out into Salisbury Square. There is just one house left, a Georgian gem. The rest is concrete. You will need a drink to recover from the horror of it all. So turn through St Bride's Passage, which leads directly to the main door of St Bride's Church. A sharp jinking left-right will take you along the wall of St Bride's Graveyard to the back door of the Old Bell. This is an absolutely unassuming pub which has a tremendous amount of history attached to it. It was built by Sir Christopher Wren for the workmen who were re-building St Bride's after the Great Fire. No pub, no work, seems to have been their ultimatum. The site Wren chose had formerly accommodated a much older pub, variously known as the Swan, the Golden Bell, and the Twelve Bells. Just how old can be gathered from the fact that Wynkyn de Worde, Caxton's pupil and successor, issued many of his books from 'the signe of the Swan in Fletestrete', and that was around five hundred years ago.

The back bar of the Bell is all Victorian: not self-consciously so, but just naturally so. Have a look at the cast-iron tables. You are entitled to ask what the head of Dr W.G. Grace is doing on some of them. I wish I could tell you, but I can't. The beer will suit most tastes, since the Bell is a free house, and a pint plus a bar snack, served with crusty French bread, should make you feel a new man or woman.

If you leave by the back door, be sure not to fall down the steps leading to Bride Lane, but if you do, be comforted by the fact that you aren't the first. Just to your left is the side door of the Punch Tavern. Make sure you have time to spare, because there's a lot to see inside. The association with the famous humorous magazine is obvious and inevitable, for it was here that the founders of *Punch* used to meet for good wine and good fellowship. The walls are covered with prints, engravings, etchings, and photographs of the magazine and its contributors, and there is, or used to be, a gas lighter on the bar in the shape of Mr Punch, with the flame coming out of his mouth. Since there is so much to see, you will probably need sustenance during your stay. It's there for you. The beer is Bass Charrington, and the snack bar can provide just about anything you want, so, with all the cartoons on the walls, your stay in the Punch Tavern should be an occasion for eating well, drinking well, and laughing a lot.

And now we're back to Ludgate Circus, where this pub-crawl began. Before it ends, cross the Circus to the King Lud. You must, however, make sure you are sober before you enter since you are in for a shock. The bar is surely the oddest-shaped in London, a curious zig-zag affair designed to baffle the unwary. A further refinement is that every time a train goes over the railway bridge into which the pub is built, the whole place shakes. The sight of the hand trembling and the beer spilling has been known to un-nerve many. Let it be a signal to you that your pub-crawl is over for the day.

Having lived to crawl another day, though, you may just as well start at Ludgate Circus once again. Up Ludgate Hill, on the left, is Old Bailey. At the top is the Magpie and Stump, fittingly placed opposite the Central Criminal Courts. 'Fittingly' because, when Newgate stood on the site of the Courts, the best view of the public hangings held outside the jail was from the pub's first-floor rooms. High prices were paid for the privilege of eating and drinking while watching some poor wretch twitch his life away at the end of a rope. Since the last public execution, in 1868 – of a Fenian, Michael Barret, who tried, and failed, to blow up Clerkenwell Jail – the atmosphere of the Magpie and Stump has changed, and, I need hardly say, for the better. It is a Bass Charrington house, the beer is good, and so is the food. The clientele is as mixed a lot as you'll find anywhere. Postmen, refugees from the George next door, which was devastated in the Old Bailey bombing; witnesses with time on their hands, some of them looking as hard-nosed as some of the people in the dock; tourists, like yourself; and the usual lunch-time clutter of City clerks and secretaries. In the later evening, the pub is emptier and you will find it much more comfortable, giving you time and space to look at the many interesting notices, old cuttings, pictures, and advertisements framed on the walls. You may even find an explanation of why the name of the pub was once changed from the Magpie and Stump to the King of Denmark, before reverting to the name Londoners have always known it by.

While you are up at this north-western corner of the City, you may as well cross over Newgate Street and go up to West Smithfield. You can read a lot more about this area and what to see there in the chapter on Dickens's London, but at the moment it's pubs we're after, so aim for the Fox and Anchor, near Charterhouse Square (it is useless giving precise directions: what they are doing to this area at the moment passes all description. It is horrible enough to have driven Sir John Betjeman, who used to live in nearby Cloth Fair, out of his lovely house before it could drive him out of his equally lovely mind). Here you can drink reasonably well and eat superbly, particularly steaks: you are, after all, only a few yards from the best-known meat market in Britain.

Cut down Little Britain and King Edward Street towards the great dome of St Paul's. All this area was flattened during the Second World War, so few pubs of any historic interest remain – or so one might think. The odd thing is that quite a few came through more or less unscathed, or at least not wounded so seriously that they couldn't be bandaged up and later fully restored to licence and good health. You must, however, try one completely modern one before going on to the tough old survivors, if only because its name, the Sir Christopher Wren, ought to be enough to attract any-body who loves London.

You'll find it in Paternoster Square (incidentally, see the chapter on Ghosts: Amen Corner, Ave Maria Lane, Creed Lane, and now Paternoster Square. They all remind us – as if we needed it with that beautiful dome looming over us – just how near we are to the Cathedral). The ground floor bar is a replica of that splendid eighteenth-century institution, the coffee house, complete with those delicious private alcoves; the restaurant is a 'genuine' replica of Paternoster Row in 1750: 'genuine' because the designer used genuine articles when he was reconstructing it. The Wren has a special bonus. The Barrow Poets perform there regularly, singing songs and reciting poetry. Don't shy away like a

Philistine. There is nothing the least bit 'arty' about their work. There is, however, much that is beautiful, much that is moving, and much that is funny. I can't, unfortunately, tell you when they are there. You'll have to ring up and find out for yourself: the number is 01-248 1708.

Broadly speaking, all the pubs of the City now lie to the east of you. They are too numerous, too different, too local to be dealt with here. Try them by all means, but don't blame me if, after having done so, you are incapable of handling the two I have chosen as decent, representative samples.

Carry along Newgate Street, negotiate the big slalom which gets you from the bottom of St Martin-le-Grand to the start of Cheapside, and keep your eyes skinned. On the right you will see Bow Lane. Go down it to Watling Street. It is called that because it follows the line of the old Roman road from London Bridge, the Watling Street which, in the disguise of A5, runs all the way to Holyhead. The pub is called, not surprisingly, Ye Olde Watling. It is a Charrington house and goes in for nothing fancy. I choose it out of the hundreds simply because it is what all City pubs should be – warm, inviting, darkly comfortable – and because of its historical associations. You'll find the pub easily enough. Although the address is 29 Bow Lane, it is actually on the corner of that lane and Watling Street. It is very old, having been rebuilt after the Great Fire (Wren had his priorities right: first build your pub, then set about your Cathedral), and then restored at the turn of this century and again after the Second World War. They used as many of the original materials as were available: the result is a pub that feels old, even if it isn't.

If you want to come with me to the next pub I've chosen, you had better keep your wits about you, because the route is more than a little complicated. The simplest, though not the shortest, way is to go along Watling Street to the east until you reach Queen Victoria Street. A very few yards along on the left you will see Bucklersbury, a narrow alley hair-pinning back towards Poultry. Pop in the Green Man if you wish, an extraordinary mixture of pub, snack bar, gin palace and oldey-worldey something or other. Carry on to Poultry, cross that curiously-named street and go up one with just as odd a moniker, Old Jewry. This becomes Coleman Street. On the left you will see Mason's Avenue. In that tiny thoroughfare is the pub we are after. It is called Ye Olde Doctor Butler's Head, and I must confess to recommending it as much for its history as for what it provides – which, admittedly, is splendid: good food and good beer.

The Doctor Butler is, in fact, as much a restaurant as a pub, but don't let that put you off. However, whether you are eating, or drinking, or both, your palate cannot fail but be sharpened by the tale of the Doctor himself. He cured King James I's sciatica by prescribing a barrel of his ale, whereupon that odd little monarch, forever scratching in his codpiece, made him a Court physician, and this though he had no medical qualifications whatsoever. The 'Doctor' then became a general practitioner, using some highly unorthodox methods. Epileptics were cured, for example, by his unexpectedly firing off a pistol below his desk. He is not recorded as ever shooting himself in the foot. Another cure was for the ague, that curiously Jacobean fit of the shakes: Dr Butler's solution was to throw the patient into the Thames. The pub is old, having been founded by the good Doctor himself in 1616. It has, however, been much gone over in the intervening years. Nevertheless, the pub's interior and its exterior, set as it is in the narrow walk of Mason's Avenue, gives a very accurate idea of what a City pub was like in the good old days (good, that is, if doctors weren't firing pistols at you or throwing you in the Thames).

There are two City pubs I'd particularly like you to visit, the George and Vulture and the Horn Tavern, but as I've dealt with them in the chapter on Dickens's London – he was a great pub man – there's no need to deal with them here. Three more pubs then, and we can all go home. The first two, oddly enough, aren't really pubs at all. The Jamaica Wine House is exactly what it says. It merits mention here simply because it is so splendid, and because it was London's first coffee house, as you can read on the blue plaque outside, opened in 1652 by a merchant called Daniel Edwards and a young Levantine named Pasqua Rosee. The coffee they served apparently cured distempers, defluxions of rheums, dropsy, gout, scurvy, king's-evil, and the spleen.

Would that modern coffee were so efficacious. Never mind the coffee, though: the Jamaica also serves beer and splendid food. Try the atmosphere of the place, whatever you do. If you don't come out wearing a full-bottomed wig, my name isn't Samuel Pepys.

Only just round the corner is an establishment one would want to mention if only because of its address: 38½ Cornhill. It is Simpson's Tavern, in Ball Court Passage. If you were having only one bite to eat and one mouthful to drink in London, you ought to have it here. Simpson's is a positive delight on just about any count you care to think of. The pub part is tiny, but big enough to qualify it for a mention in this chapter. It was a chop-house when it opened in 1757 and it still serves magnificent food: the stewed cheese is a speciality. It goes with beer like a dream goes with sleep. Don't take my word for the place. Just go there.

Having done that, head eastwards again, along Cornhill, which changes into Leadenhall Street before you have gone very far. Not all that many yards ahead you will find Aldgate High Street running across your bows in a near-T junction. If the traffic allows it, cross over and walk up the street (that is, in a north-easterly direction). At the junction of the High Street with Middlesex Street, a junction much disguised by the accidents of modern development, you will feel a sudden urge to stand up straight. That will be because the pub you are near to isn't standing up straight at all. It is leaning alarmingly. There is every excuse for that, since this is London's oldest licensed premise, although not its oldest pub. The Hoop and Grapes, as the name suggests, was once a vintner's – the hoop went round the barrel that contained the grapes – and it only became a pub a hundred or so years ago. But the building stands on cellars that go back to the thirteenth century. The superstructure itself goes back quite a long way, too. It escaped the Great Fire of 1666 by a mere 50 yards: the wind changed just as matters were getting crucial, which is why we can eat and drink there to this day. If you want to sit down to eat, there are cubicles at the back where you can satiate yourself in comfort. But don't get too sleepy; the pub has a lot else to offer you. Take a look at the stairs as you climb up to the Micawber Restaurant. They are Elizabethan. Go into the cellar and listen at the lug-hole, by means of which the landlord could hear what his customers were saying about him when he was down drawing them a pint of the best. And do not believe the story that the blocked-up tunnel leads to the Tower of London: you don't believe that all roads lead to Rome, do you? But go to the Hoop and Grapes whatever you do. It is in the middle of a most horrendous development area and nobody knows just how long it will be before it goes the way of the rest of the buildings in the vicinity.

There are thousands more pubs in London. You must find them out for yourself. This chapter may have given you a taste for them. You may also have noticed that it is almost the longest chapter in the book. Ask me why. I will reply in the words of a poet, Hilaire Belloc, who was as English as his name was French:

When you have lost your inns, drown your empty selves, for you will have lost the last of England.

P.S. The Belloc quotation adds point to the fact that the Hoop and Grapes has, since the above was written, now apparently gone the way of so many pubs. We have lost a piece of England.

The market place

This chapter is about London's markets. In a sense it is silly to talk about London's markets, since London itself is one huge market. That is how it started, as a great trading post: that is how it is today: and that, presumably, is how it will stay for as long as matters to most of us. Nevertheless, the phrase does have some meaning. It stands, in everyone's usage, for the street markets known the world over, by name at least. It stands for two of London's covered markets, just as widely known. And it stands for the many little street markets, not at all widely known, but much appreciated by those who stumble across them or live or work near them. Strictly, it also ought to stand for the huge commodity markets for which London is world famous, and for that most mysterious of markets, the Stock Exchange, where every day, by a process that passeth human understanding, the number of shares that people want to sell always equals the number of shares that people want to buy. I have, however, discussed these 'markets' in another chapter.

The problem is where to start. The street markets themselves are scattered all over London from Shepherd's Bush in the west to Spitalfields in the east, from Islington in the north to Brixton in the south. Another problem is *when* to start, for the markets open at different times. Some are open on weekdays only, some only at week-ends. Some are open all day, some only in the very early morning.

Alphabetically seems the only way to tackle the problem, although it looks at first, and even at second and third sight, to have little or no logic about it. It does, however, have the advantage of starting with my own favourite, favourite simply because I've known it for a very long time and because it is near to where I've spent a great deal of my working London life.

Berwick Street – long, straight, narrow, one-way – runs south from Oxford Street, parallel to Wardour Street, until it bumps into Broadwick Street. The market starts here and runs south for a couple of hundred yards or so, across Brewer Street, into Rupert Street, down almost to Shaftesbury Avenue. In other words it is in the heart of Soho, about which much more later. You can buy an awful lot of stuff here. You can also – in this Berwick Market is no different from any other – buy a lot of awful stuff.

Berwick Market is particularly good for fruit, vegetables and flowers. The stallholders are pushy, but then if they weren't they wouldn't survive in this brash little world of theirs. Don't fall for everything they say, but on the other hand don't assume everything they are selling you is rubbish, because it isn't. Despite the fruit and vegetable emphasis, you'll find that the market sells a lot of other things. Jumpers, blouses, household goods like soap powders, pan scrubbers, pots, pans, and kettles. Because it is so near to Wardour Street you are likely to see quite a few famous faces buying or looking before they go into the preview theatres, dubbing suites, and film-cutting rooms which abound in this area. You are also likely to rub shoulders with the girls – strippers, dancers, singers – who work the various clubs and cellars round about. Raymond's Revuebar, which is really an extremely pleasant way of relieving you of your money, is at the bottom of Berwick Street, and with its general glossy air makes a refreshing change from the seediness of so many of the other so-called clubs which are thick on the Soho ground. Broadly speaking, therefore, you can say that you meet a good class of goods and a good class of person at Berwick Market. Highly recommended, particularly as it is so small. You can wander round it, comparing prices and never feel that it is too far to go back to that stall where you saw what has turned out to be the day's best buy. Like all marketeers, the Berwick people are up early and are already shouting their wares by 8 a.m. How they keep it up, without losing their voices, until 6 and 7 p.m., is beyond me. Perhaps it is because there is a little pub on the corner of Berwick Street and Broadwick Street (the Blue Posts) as well as another one tucked away on the right-hand side, just about halfway between Broadwick Street and the Revuebar (the King of Sardinia); market stall-holders have been known to slip away to gargle occasionally so that the piercing quality of their dulcet tones may be preserved. The nearest Underground station to Berwick Market is Piccadilly Circus, which is on the Piccadilly and Bakerloo lines, and the Berwick Street area is served by more nearby buses than you'll ever need to know about. The market is closed on Thursday afternoons and on Sundays, and remember that when it is wet or towards the end of the day prices tend to drop sharply – of the perishables, that is.

Alphabetically, the next market is Billingsgate, but you won't be able to buy anything there, since it is a wholesale fish market. On the face of it, it is not a good place for the tourist for another reason: they start selling about 5 a.m., most of them having been there hours before. If you go when the streets are properly aired you'll find everything finished, and the only signs of life will be a few chaps hosing things down. But despite having to get up so early – which means that summer is definitely the best time for the tourist to do Billingsgate – and despite the fact that you won't be able to buy anything when you get there, Billingsgate really is a must.

There has been a market here since the very earliest times.

The name tells you quite clearly that this was one of the water gates of the City (the other, Dowgate, was further west, just about where Cannon Street station is now). There is a reference to Billingsgate as a fish market as far back as the late ninth century. Eight hundred years ago a statute was made establishing it as an open fish market, but, oddly enough, despite that, they continued to sell coal and corn there until the middle of the eighteenth century. Nothing wrong with that, as long as you don't mind your fish covered in coal dust or your cornflakes tasting of fish.

Billingsgate is in decline. In a normal working day they now only handle about 300 tons of fish (only!). In the past the figure was very much higher: fish fingers must have something to do with that. Nevertheless, it is still an impressive sight – and smell. Even if you get there too late in the morning for the sight, you will still notice the smell. And why not? If they've been landing fish here for more than a thousand years, and perhaps for nearly two thousand, isn't the place entitled to its pong?

The market itself is that Victorian building on the south side of Lower Thames Street. It was built by Sir Horace Jones in 1875, and looks like it, but to everybody who knows it, Billingsgate means all of the surrounding area, almost up to Eastcheap, and from London Bridge (is not the street immediately below the bridge approach still called Fish Street?) to the Custom House, the Billingsgate building's eastward neighbour. It has long had a reputation for bad language, though I could never understand why: I've heard just as bad from so-called debs. And if, like the fish porters, you have spent the five hours from 5 a.m. to 10 a.m. carrying above a hundredweight of fish on top of your head, aren't you entitled to swear a little to help you forget the pain in your neck? To help them carry that weight of fish, by the way, the porters still wear odd-shaped leather hats called bobbing hats. To see two porters talking, each with maybe ten wicker baskets of fish towering above his head, is quite an experience, bad language apart.

One of the nice things about Billingsgate, and it applies to the other food markets as well, is that the local pubs open just as early as the market, and so do the local cafés. The pub across the way from Billingsgate Market starts serving very early (not really: the workers have just about finished their gruelling stints by the time the doors open, so you could say the boozer is opening late). There are, however, warning notices everywhere saying that alcoholic drinks can only be served to those going about their lawful business in the market. Do not be deterred. Your lawful business might be doing some research on market conditions for a paper you are writing: anyway, it's worth a try, but don't blame me if the landlord refuses you. If he does, try one of the cafés for a – for you – early breakfast. The odd thing is that none of them seems to serve fish. Perhaps if you've been humping the stuff all through the small hours, fish is the very last thing you want to look at once the job is over.

When you've finished your egg and chips, or Welsh rarebit and chips, or whatever it is, wander around the area breathing in the rich, ripe, fishy smell until the Monument opens. It is only a couple of hundred yards away, and was, of course, erected to commemorate the Great Fire of London, which started in Pudding Lane, just halfway between the Market and London Bridge. The view from the top is very fine, although it may take some time before you are in a condition to appreciate it, since you get to the top by climbing – there is no lift – 311 steps. Once up on top, though, the breeze will blow away the smell of the fish and the effects of the Welsh rarebit and chips. To your left, as you face eastwards towards the Tower of London, is another famous covered market. To your right, across the river, is a third. Let's stay on the north side of the Thames for the time being, and forget all about that alphabetic nonsense.

Since going down is so much easier, you will not have to pause for breath when you get back to the bottom of the Monument, so immediately strike up the hill towards Leadenhall Market. The direct way is to walk straight up Gracechurch Street to its junction with Leadenhall Street. On the corner is Leadenhall Market, standing on exactly the same site it occupied when Ralph Agas drew his map-cum-panorama of the City in 1559, generally thought to be the very first reliable survey. It must have been there long before Agas's time, since he shows it as a battlemented stone building, four-sided round a courtyard in which can be seen a huge pair of scales. Leadenhall was clearly an old mansion converted into a market. The name may derive from the fact that, unlike so many buildings of the time, the roof was leaded, not tiled or thatched. It survived the Great Fire of London in 1666, largely because of the initiative of a City alderman, who went round with a hatful of coins which he used to encourage the volunteers to work even harder in fighting the fire.

Originally, Leadenhall was the place where all poultry brought into the City had to be taken to be sold. So why is Poultry, further west beyond Cornhill, so called? Because it took over Leadenhall's poultry market function years later. Leadenhall was also the place where cattle were bought and sold, which must have made for some mucky highways and byways in the surrounding area, and also accounts for those scales in the courtyard, since the grain, meal, and so on for feeding the cattle had to be weighed somewhere.

The present building is, of course, a young one compared with that shown in Agas's Survey. It is a Victorian master-piece of ironwork and glass and gives off a curious feeling of a railway station crossed with a cathedral. How it has survived the developers who have succeeded in making today's City look as though it was built out of giant Lego is beyond me. But it has, and we should rejoice in it.

You will, incidentally, be able to pay it homage *after* doing the rounds of Billingsgate, because Leadenhall keeps more civilized hours. It opens at 9 a.m. and closes at 5 p.m. These days it sells vegetables, fruit, plants, poultry, and a lot of other things as well, and it will sell them to *you*, because it is a retail market. Slap in the centre of the City, its lunch-time crowds have a strong tendency to be wearing dark suits or smart dresses, having swarmed out of the surrounding hundreds of thousands of offices, to buy provisions to carry back to their homes in the Home Counties. It may be, therefore, that a chicken born and bred in Chalfont St Giles would make its first and only (because fatal) trip to London merely to be taken back to its birthplace and eaten at some stockbroker's dinner table on the very day it departed both this life and Chalfont St Giles. And to think that on its only excursion to the Great Wen it had, unlike you and me, no time to stand and stare! Life can be cruel, can it not?

Despite its normal opening hours, Leadenhall Market has the usual array of cheap and tasty (and some which are cheap and nasty) cafés scattered around it: try Whittington Avenue and Ship Tavern Passage. You'll get filled without getting fleeced. Do remember, though, that since the City is dead on Saturdays, and this is a retail market, you'll find the market closed that day, too, as well as most of the nearby pubs and eating places.

If by now, because of your early start, you are feeling too tired to walk anywhere else, then your nearest underground station is not far away. It is Bank, and you get to it by simply walking along Cornhill. Bank is on the Central and Northern lines, which means you can get to almost anywhere on the underground system with very little bother, so you will soon be catching up on your sleep in no time at all.

Smithfield Market is another of the great wholesale markets, with its accompanying early start, in this case 6 a.m. As in the case of Billingsgate, the surrounding pubs and cafés open correspondingly early. The nearest underground stations are Barbican and St Paul's, the former on the Circle and Metropolitan lines, the latter on the Central line. Out of Barbican turn right and right again, down Long Lane: out of St Paul's turn left along Newgate Street and then turn right up Giltspur Street.

Smithfield, its full name being West Smithfield (there is an East Smithfield, just beyond the Tower of London, behind what used to be St Katharine Docks), was once a jousting ground. Its name, as that of the eastern one, has nothing to do with blacksmiths, but means simply 'a smooth field'. The fourteenth century was its heyday. Both Edward III and Richard II threw the most magnificent shows there, tournaments which involved heralds going throughout the length and breadth of this island and as far as France, Flanders, and the lands beyond the Rhine. Richard's tourney lasted for a whole week, starting on the first Sunday after Michaelmas in the year of our Lord 1394. One wonders whether the blood oozing from the joints in the knights' armour put King Richard in mind of that day in 1381 when, as a boy-king of fourteen, he treated with Wat Tyler and his men in an attempt to bring the Peasants' Revolt to an end. The meeting was at Smithfield: during the negotiations William Walworth, the Lord Mayor of London, suddenly and quite treacherously stabbed Tyler to death. At this the boy-king rode up to the mob, unafraid, asked them would they murder their king, and offered to be their leader himself. It was virtually the end of the revolt, although not of the revenge that followed.

Smithfield was also the site of Bartholomew Fair, one of the most famous of all the great English Fairs. Bartholomew Fair, held on St Bartholomew's Day (and for at least two weeks afterwards) in front of St Bartholomew's Church – that is the gateway on the eastern side of the square – endured, incredibly, until the middle of the nineteenth century. It was famous enough for Ben Jonson to write a play about it – a play perhaps more spoken of than performed – and for people to come from all over the country to enjoy the proceedings, if one can use so prim a word for what must have been one of the most uninhibited gatherings this country has ever seen.

As Smithfield lay to the north-west of the medieval city, at the junction of a whole fan of roads leading in from the north-west, the north, and the rich lands of East Anglia to the north-east, it soon became the target of the cattle droves making their slow way to the capital to feed its hungry thousands. In those days, and right up to the middle of the nineteenth century, Smithfield was a live meat market. It was here that the animals came, it was here that they were slaughtered, and it was here that their offal and their blood were allowed to pollute the streets. No wonder Pip, in *Great Expectations*, on his first visit to London found it a 'shameful place, being all asmear with filth and fat and foam and blood', and left it at once.

Smithfield had a reputation for killing long before Pip saw it, of course. It was the site of many religious burnings during the mad days of Mary and Elizabeth, and excavations in 1849 actually turned up some charred human bones, some partly-burnt oak posts, presumably stakes, and some of the rings by which the poor unfortunates were fastened to them.

It is perhaps fitting that Smithfield became a meat market.

In 1855, Prince Albert opened a new live meat market further north, on the Caledonian Road, between where Pentonville and Holloway prisons stand today, and Smithfield became the 'dead' meat market it still is. Infinitely more hygienic than the old market, it is nevertheless not a place for the squeamish, nor for those who, though they like meat, don't want to face up to the reality that provides them with their fillet or rump steaks.

West Smithfield, despite all that, has its own charm. The square, which isn't square, but more or less kite-shaped, has a pleasant little circular garden in the centre, and the market buildings, designed by Hubert Jones, are pleasantly Italian in style. They were erected throughout the last quarter of the nineteenth century and are undoubtedly out of date now. Whether this means that Smithfield is doomed to be moved away from the centre, as has happened to Covent Garden, remains to be seen. It is as well to remember, though, that the Caledonian Road Meat Market has long since been demolished and converted to a housing estate. The pleasantness of Jones's buildings is no guarantee that they will be there much longer.

After all that history, you will be in need of food and drink. Look around you. Try as far afield as Cowcross Street. Experiment in the area near Charterhouse Square. Remember that the Smithfield meat market is said to be the biggest in the world, covering some ten acres. In that area there are many places worth patronizing and, unlike Billingsgate, they do their own product very well. If you can face a fillet steak at that time in the morning, good luck to you. You won't be disappointed. If you want something a little lighter, try the Cock Tavern, the Coffee House in Cowcross Street (that's got to be a meat market name, hasn't it?), or the suitably-named Bartholomew's in the square itself. If it's the hard stuff you're after, or even the long stuff, then the same applies as at Billingsgate: theoretically you're not entitled to any unless you are going about your genuine employment in the market. Nevertheless, have a go. You never know your luck.

Covent Garden is no more. Correction: the planners

thought they had made sure Covent Garden was no more by moving it out to Nine Elms, near Battersea power station. But just as a demolished site is soon covered by plants, so the old Garden piazza is again the site of a market. Nothing like the old one, of course, but still a market, with stalls and the sort of stallholder you can find in any street market in London. So far the lovely buildings of Inigo Jones, Charles Foster, and Edward Middleton Barry (son of the Sir Charles Barry who designed the Reform Club, the Travellers' Club, and, with the young Pugin, the Houses of Parliament) are all there. Don't take it for granted they'll survive though: go and see them while they still exist.

The moving of the market has meant, of course, that a lot of the character of the place left with the departure of the characters who peopled the place. Nevertheless, you can still get a whiff of the old days in the Nag's Head, on the corner of Floral Street and James Street (nearest underground station Covent Garden on the Piccadilly line). You won't, however, get an early morning drink there now. The pub still has its special licence, but the landlord, very understandably, can't see the point of opening up for the sake of a few early-morning rubberneckers like you and me. You may, however, still think it worth while sampling the area despite everything. The Royal Opera House is still there. So are its musicians and singers, who are as fond of a jar as the next one. The church of St Paul's, Covent Garden, 'the actors' church', is as beautiful as when Inigo Jones designed it. The Duke of Bedford, who owned the Covent Garden area, had to have a church in the grand design, but because it wouldn't produce any revenue he told Jones to make it simple, as simple as a barn. To which Jones replied 'Very well, I will design a barn, but it will be the handsomest barn in Europe'. It is.

I do not recommend you to take the trip out to Nine Elms to see what the transplanted Covent Garden market is like. Like a lot of transplants, this one is going to need time to put down any roots. The usual early morning facilities are there, of course, but is it really worth while walking from Vauxhall underground station (Victoria line) or Battersea Park railway station just to get a little alcoholic refreshment an hour or so before the rest of the pubs open? I leave it to you.

104

There is really only one major fruit and vegetable market left to look at and if you are a banana lover it is yet another must. For at Spitalfields, under five acres of covered market, is the biggest banana ripening centre in Britain. Banana maniacs have a choice of three underground stations, which together make a triangle with Spitalfields Market at its centre of gravity. The stations are Liverpool Street, Shoreditch and Aldgate East. None is more than a quarter of a mile away and Liverpool Street is much nearer. As it is on three lines – the Central, the Metropolitan, and the Circle – Liverpool Street is your obvious bet.

Spitalfields practises the same infernal hours as do the other markets for perishables, except that in this case it is slightly worse. They start operations at 04.30, a time when some of us have not yet got our hearts started. Even more than in Billingsgate, Smithfield and the old Covent Garden, you will feel here that you are in the real London. This is genuine East End, outside the old city walls and proud of it.

An awful lot of sentimental guff is talked about the golden-hearted East Ender. It is as well to remember that some of the world's biggest villains have come from here. You'll see no villainy at Spitalfields, though. They are much too busy working hard to make a living. Although it is essentially fruit and vegetables, it does sell other things as well. Nevertheless, remember that specialist markets have grown up over the years simply because they got very good at dealing with certain things. Spitalfields's position, on the extreme eastern edge of the City, means that it is the natural centre for all the produce of East Anglia, Hertfordshire, Bedfordshire and Cambridgeshire. Not that you'll be able to buy. It's wholesale.

Spitalfields grew up as the East End grew, in that tremendous population explosion and geographical expansion that went on through the whole of the nineteenth century. It retains the feel of those hectic and heady days of development. It is not a pretty place, but it is a very friendly one, and if you want to experience something of what London was like at, say, the times of Dickens, this is the place for you.

By now you may have seen, or at least read about, enough food markets to put you off the stuff for life. Do not despair.

We are now going to turn to some of the other, non-food, markets famous far outside London.

The Caledonian Market, for example. Just to confuse you, it isn't in the Caledonian Road, which runs north from the side of King's Cross station. No, it is on the other side of the river, in Bermondsey Street SE 1, to be precise. Just to confuse you further, Bermondsey Street isn't in Bermondsey: it is in the Borough. The nearest underground station is London Bridge. Here's a comforting fact, though. You couldn't get any nearer, since Bermondsey Street actually runs down the east side of the station. So getting there and back isn't going to be a problem. Except for one thing. Although they sell antiques in the Caledonian Market, and not perishables, they still insist on a diabolically early start. Trading doesn't officially begin until about 06.30, but there are always some insomniacs there from 05.00 and even earlier. The market is really the main antique market for dealers, but you'll find the traders are quite friendly and willing to sell to you, even though you're not a professional. Which brings up another point. They *are* professionals. Don't think you're going to get a bargain they haven't spotted, because you won't. But it's a nice place to potter around. Incidentally, it's only active one day a week, Friday, so if you do exhaust yourself getting up very early, you've got six days to sleep your weariness away.

Another well-known antique market is in Camden Passage, and to confuse you even further, that isn't in Camden. It's in Islington. The quickest way there is by underground to Angel (the next stop eastwards on the Northern line from King's Cross and St Pancras). Turn right out of the station into Islington High Street. As it bends round to the right a much narrower street slivers off to the right. This is High Street and within yards it becomes Camden Passage. Be warned about this one. Camden Passage is fashionable – even trendy – and the prices are high. That is not to say the stuff there is worthless: it isn't. It is just to say that you may have to pay higher prices in the Passage than you might somewhere else. If you want to see and be seen, Camden Passage is the place for you. You could, for example, eat at Robert Carrier's place: you're bound to see a famous face or two, but don't forget to take your wallet: you'll need it.

Two more famous street markets, perhaps the most famous of the lot – Petticoat Lane and the Portobello Road. Let's take Petticoat Lane first. It isn't in Petticoat Lane at all (well, a tiny bit of it is). The main part is actually strung along, and in the streets off, Middlesex Street, that street which hairpins back south-east from Bishopsgate, immediately opposite Liverpool Street station. Because Liverpool Street is on three underground lines – Central, Metropolitan, and Circle – access is easy, just as it was in the case of nearby Spitalfields. In fact, to save time you could do both markets in the same trip, were it not for the fact that Spitalfields doesn't open on Sunday, and that's the only day Petticoat Lane does.

The market starts at 8 a.m., but there's nothing to stop you getting there earlier, to see if you can pick up anything cheap before the crowds come pouring in. There's very little you can't buy in Petticoat Lane, although I wouldn't like to guarantee it will all be of the highest quality. In fact, some of it will be pure tat. But there is such an atmosphere about the Lane, an atmosphere which has survived even these depressed times, that being there is probably more fun than buying there. Amble around, looking at everything, listening to everybody, and not buying very much, and you will have experienced one of London's cheapest enjoyments. Then, as lunch time approaches, you can keep on right down to the southern end of Middlesex Street, and there, opposite you, and leaning at an angle that will make you think you are drunk already, is the Hoop and Grapes, already mentioned in the chapter on pubs. If still there it is a splendid place to go and refresh yourself in after the exhaustions, enjoyable though they may be, of the Lane.

Portobello Road is on the opposite side of London, but has exactly the same air of enjoyment about it. The best underground station is Notting Hill Gate (Central, Circle and District lines). Pembridge Road runs north from Notting Hill Gate (the road, not the station) and Portobello Road runs north-west off Pembridge Road. It is a flea market of the very best kind. You never know what you are going to pick up there. Since the market is so popular, you're hardly likely to come across an hitherto unnoticed Rembrandt for a pound or so, but it's still a great deal of fun. There is, in fact, a market in the Portobello Road every weekday from about 7.00 in the morning to 6.00 at night, but the famous day, the day which really *is* Portobello Market day, is Saturday. This is the day to go.

You are quite likely, as you wander around, to see a face you last saw on the big cinema screen or the little tv screen. Or it may be a visiting politician, whose face you can't quite put a name to. There will also be thousands of other faces you've never seen in your life before and will probably never see again. They will have one thing in common. They will all look to be enjoying themselves. Portobello Road was always a happy market. These days the strong West Indian element in the area has added to the fun. Vegetables, fruit, flowers, antiques, tat of all kinds, an exuberant atmosphere, and all for nothing. What more do you want? Specialization is setting in: you'll notice that the antiquery-junkery stuff is more pronounced at the northern end, that is to say, up towards the Westway fly-over. Don't let that worry you. The whole long length of the market is a joy, so enjoy it.

Of course, street markets like Petticoat Lane and Portobello Road don't have the special drinking laws the wholesale food markets have, but there's nothing to stop you taking your own if you feel you'll be needing a drop before the law allows the pubs to open. And when they do open you've got as big a choice as anywhere in London, with a racial mix that may be equalled but certainly isn't surpassed anywhere else. And if the thought of that makes you nervous, forget it. Look happy and you'll be happy, and you'll help to make everybody around you that little bit happier too. Remember, people go to the Portobello Road to have fun. There are worse ways of spending a Saturday.

Quartiers

Soho – Mayfair – Kensington and Chelsea
Bloomsbury

It may seem odd, or even a trifle affected, to use a French word to describe parts of the most English of cities, but *quartier* is one of those invaluable, because untranslatable, words. It means more than district, because it implies a unity of character, whereas a district can have a mixture of characters, or none at all. It means more than area, for the same reason. 'Quarters' simply won't do, with its unmistakable military overtones. So *quartiers* it has to be.

Perhaps the most famous of all the *quartiers* is Soho, that square mile or so of wickedness broadly bounded on the west by Regent Street, on the south by Coventry Street and Leicester Square, on the east by Charing Cross Road and Tottenham Court Road, and on the north by Mortimer Street and Goodge Street, although not everybody would agree with those boundaries.

The name is usually said to be derived from the hunting

cry of 'So-ho' which echoed round the area when it was still open fields. As a derivation it is as good as any other, although one wonders why, therefore, it didn't get called Tally-ho. If it has a centre at all it could very fittingly be Soho Square, which was laid out in 1681 by Gregory King, and originally named after him. It is a rum sort of square, with its fake Tudor house slap in the middle, a house which, on inspection, turns out to be merely a cladding for the shed where the square's gardener keeps his tools. The statue of Charles II, by the Danish sculptor Caius Gabriel Cibber (pronounced Sibber), is a remarkable tribute to the ravages London's atmosphere could effect. The Portland stone it is made of, like all limestone, is soluble in dilute acid, which is exactly what London's rain became after it had passed through the air of the smokiest of cities: not for nothing was London known as The Smoke. Not now, of course; the Clean Air Acts have seen to that. The effect of the acidic rain on the Merrie Monarch is plain to see. A ravaged countenance which makes him look anything but merry; hair, or at any rate a wig, which appears to be suffering from an advanced dose of smallpox; and a general feeling that it won't be long now before the poor old thing crumbles away altogether. In view of its overall impression of decay, it seems fitting that Cibber's two other most famous statues are named 'Melancholy' and 'Raving Madness'.

The nearest underground station to Soho Square is Tottenham Court Road (Northern and Central lines), which is located at the junction with Oxford Street, opposite Centre Point, and thus has the distinction of standing on two of London's scruffiest streets and being stared at by London's most infamous building. Do not, on any account, spend more time than is absolutely necessary in Oxford Street or Tottenham Court Road. They are an insult to the eye of any sensitive beholder. Their seediness is so appalling it has been known to drive many a luckless passer-by to drink. The cure does not work. No matter how many you gulp down, the two streets still look terrible.

Soho Square itself is interesting enough. The Duke of Monmouth had a house there and used the word 'Soho' as a password at the Battle of Sedgemoor in 1685. Sir Joseph

Banks, a President of the Royal Society, lived at No. 32. He travelled with Captain Cook on his famous expedition to the South Seas and, since he was a botanist, was responsible for giving Botany Bay its name. The church on the east side, at the junction with Sutton Row, is worth a look.

From the south side of Soho Square two streets run down towards Shaftesbury Avenue. They are Frith Street and Greek Street. These are the 'real' Soho to many people. What that means these days is that they house a lot of restaurants, some good, some bad, some indifferent: some pubs, none of them especially notable: and lots of strip clubs, all of them appalling. Give the latter the widest berth possible. They are of an unbelievable tattiness; the glamorous (sometimes) young (sometimes) things who disrobe for your delectation look as bored as you will soon feel; and the truth of the old proverb, 'A fool and his money are soon parted', will dawn upon you with some force if you buy any of the near-beer you will be proffered. Do not be drawn by the provocative pictures outside the clubs. They bear no relation to the contents and could probably be comfortably 'done' under the Trades Description Act.

Much the same can be said of the street running across them from Wardour Street to Charing Cross Road – Old Compton Street. It has its share of dubiousness, but it also possesses a large slice of what so many people go to Soho for – its foreignness. The whole area is a foreign enclave, a characteristic which originated after the revocation of the Edict of Nantes in 1685. You do not, of course, need me to tell you that the Edict afforded a great measure of toleration, even protection, to the Protestants in France and that its revocation led to a merciless persecution of them. Up to half a million or so escaped, to settle in other countries. One of the host countries was Britain: one of the host cities was London: one of the host areas was Soho. It soon became a magnet for immigrants, voluntary or otherwise, from other countries, which is why Soho today has Italians, French, Spaniards, Germans, Jews, Poles, and just about every nationality under the sun. The recent and sudden take-over by the Chinese of the Gerrard Street area, on the south side of Shaftesbury Avenue, is just the latest example of the

111

process. Limehouse, down by the docks, is no longer Chinatown. The Gerrard Street area is.

It is hard not to be a little excited by Soho, however often one visits it, however blasé one has become. The excitement derives, I am sure, from the racial mix. Walk along Old Compton Street and you will hear almost as many different tongues as there are different people. With the exception of the occasional murder, they all seem to live in amity with each other. I am afraid the reference to murder is true enough, for Soho is full of vice and where there is vice there is violence. There is, however, no need to be scared: unless you go flashing your money about very late at night you are as safe in Soho as anywhere in London, and much safer than in some areas.

Try walking from Charing Cross Road to Regent Street by way of Old Compton Street and Brewer Street, but take your time about it. There is plenty to see. Dirty book shops abound, but so do cigar importers, shops of gleaming copper cooking utensils, record shops, off-licences, restaurants to suit all tastes, film company offices, recording studios, pubs, cafés, international newsagents, cinemas, delicatessens selling just about everything, fishmongers in the old style, butchers, bakers, chocolate shops By Appointment, an open market, tinkers, tailors, and probably soldiers and sailors as well.

Try the French Pub in Dean Street. Don't look for the sign, though. There isn't one – not with 'French Pub' on it, anyway. It's actually called the York Minster. It became known as the French Pub when Gaston Berlemont's father took it over in 1914. During the Second World War it was the meeting place for the Free French Forces. Gaston himself serves tirelessly behind the bar, handle-bar moustaches at the ready, the ribbon of the Legion of Honour in the lapel of his invariable black jacket. Do not ask for a pint of beer. M. Berlemont has no pint glasses, for reasons best known to himself. On sunny days, the bar, which is small, is empty: everybody stands out in the street, watching Soho swirl by, and there are worse ways of spending the lunch-hour. The 'French' is a haunt of advertising types, journalists, publishers, and out-of-work actors, but don't let that put you off. Some of them are almost human. The 'French' is a good place to observe class at work. The left-hand side is for the likes of you and me; the right-hand side is for those who can afford, or whose expense accounts can afford, champagne and such-like. As you'd expect of a place with such a nickname and such a proprietor, the wines by the glass are eminently drinkable.

If you fancy an Italian meal, you've got dozens of places to choose from. Try Leoni's Quo Vadis in Dean Street: a plaque above the door tells you Karl Marx lived here. Try Bianchi's in Frith Street. If you can't find it, look for Ronnie Scott's jazz club. Bianchi's is right opposite. Downstairs is an ordinary bistro-like place. Upstairs is the place to go. The entrance is by a separate door at the side. You will find yourself in one of London's friendliest and least spoiled restaurants. Elena, who looks after the film and show business people who frequent the place, is marvellous, and apparently inexhaustible. Sit at the table beneath the plaque on the wall and you will see that you are eating in the room where John Logie Baird first demonstrated his new invention of television. He was, of course, denounced as a fake, a fraud, an impostor, and he died in poverty, but at least the Royal Television Society has had the good grace to mark the place where his pioneer work was carried out. Bianchi's is small and popular, so give Elena a ring if you want to be sure of a table. The number is 01-437 5194.

Old Compton Street ends at Wardour Street, a thoroughfare nowhere near as glamorous as you might think. If the film industry has any glamour left, it has mostly all worn off by the time it reaches Wardour Street, which is named after Henry, Lord Arundel of Wardour, wherever that might be. He was the landlord who developed the area. But if it lacks charm, it has some good things. Plenty of food shops, both sit-down and take-away; one or two good pubs, full of film types (not film *stars*: film editors, dubbing assistants and the like, mainly). Try, especially, the Intrepid Fox, named after Charles James Fox, that large Whig gentleman, by a one-time landlord, Sam House, who was a keen supporter of the statesman.

Across Wardour Street from Old Compton Street, but slightly to one side, is Brewer Street. Narrow, noisy, crowded, and colourful, it is typically Soho. Berwick Street open air market is up the alley to the right, as is Paul Raymond's Revuebar. The Windmill, which never closed, is down a street to the left. Its gorgeous, but immobile nudes – if they moved, the Lord Chancellor would have closed them down – have gone, but you can see far more nudity there now than you ever could in those days, and it most certainly moves: Vivian Van Damm would turn in his grave if he were alive.

Go north up either Lower James Street or Lower John Street (quite right: they lead to Upper James Street and Upper John Street). Golden Square has a very pleasant central garden, with plenty of seats and a statue of George II, dressed for some reason in Roman armour. Golden Square is a very popular place on a sunny lunchtime, and is presumably much pleasanter these days than when Dickens wrote about it and its royal effigy as 'this mournful statue, the guardian genius of a little wilderness of shrubs'. The George in question is the one who made a famous answer to his dying wife's request that he should marry again: 'Non, j'aurai des maîtresses' ('No, I will take mistresses'), to which the lady summoned up enough strength to reply 'Mon Dieu: cela n'empêche pas', which can be roughly translated as 'My goodness, that needn't stop you!', a fairly splendid comment, considering her condition.

Going out of Golden Square by either of the Upper streets brings you to Beak Street, a long, narrow byway invariably jammed with traffic trying desperately to get to Regent Street and usually failing. It is also jammed with tourists, for it is off Beak Street that you will find the dreaded Carnaby Street, as hideous a tourist trap as exists anywhere. Pedestrianized, paved with garishly-coloured triangles, and soaked in the sound of pop blaring from every store, Carnaby Street reminds me of nothing so much as one of the outer circles of Hell. The 'souvenirs' sold there are vulgar, pointless, and usually shoddy in the extreme. The prices are ridiculously high. No wonder the bust of our national poet looks disapprovingly along the street from his niche high up on the wall of the Shakespeare public house.

Backing away from Carnaby Street with all possible speed, carry on examining Beak Street. The first street on the north side, coming from Regent Street, is Kingly Street, a narrow way running parallel with Regent Street up to Liberty's. It has pubs, health food shops, wine bars, and back entrances to most of the Regent Street stores. On the Beak Street corner is the Cumberland Arms, universally known as the Irish Pub. In the days of the great Jack Brady, it was everything a local should be – warm, friendly, unpretentious, with good simple food and superbly kept beers, especially Guinness. Jack has been retired now, and things have changed, but something of the Brady legacy still exists. There's a Spanish restaurant a few yards further along the street, called the Barcelona, where I was once surprised to see my lunch companion fall asleep as she was talking to me, with the result that she pitched forward with her face into her paella. Kingly Court is a cul-de-sac (Crown property, actually, so watch your behaviour) containing one of those London drinking clubs that are so seductive, the Tattie Bogle. It *is*, however, a club. You will not be too welcome if you wander down its stone steps uninvited. If you *are* invited, you will enjoy it.

There's a Greek restaurant just past Carnaby Street, and if you look at the first-floor window you will see that Canaletto, the Venetian painter, lived there. He came to London in 1745, fell in love with it, stayed eleven years, and painted many pictures of it, pictures which give me immense pleasure, even though he usually manages to make London look suspiciously like Venice.

The Old Coffee House is, oddly, a pub, popular with television types from Granada TV, a few yards away in Golden Square. Like so many pubs in this area it is very busy at lunch-time. It isn't a specially notable pub but it is warm and friendly. So is the Sun and Thirteen Cantons, fifty yards further along Beak Street. The name is unusual, but logical. It was originally called simply The Sun, but it became popular with the Swiss wool merchants who congregated around Golden Square, the centre of the worsted trade in London. They made the pub their headquarters, held expatriate cantonal meetings there, and inevitably the pub came to be called by the name it bears today.

If you are left-handed, cross the road from The Sun. There you will find what is, as far as I know, the only shop in London to specialize in things left-handed. Nothing right-handed is sold in the shop. Even the front door has the knob on the left side. Only the left-handed will be able to imagine the enormous range of items in stock.

Beak Street ends where it meets Lexington Street. At the junction of Lexington Street and Broadwick Street is the John Snow, formerly The Newcastle-on-Tyne (they go in for odd pub names in Soho). It is named after Dr John Snow who, in 1854, read in his copy of *The Times* that there had been 500 deaths from cholera in ten days, and all within a couple of hundred yards of The Newcastle-on-Tyne. He questioned all the afflicted families in the great blocks of tenements surrounding Broad Street, as Broadwick Street was called in those days, and found that, without exception, every single one of those who had died had drunk water from a pump standing outside the pub. Being a practical man, and impatient of the law's delays, he stopped any further spread of the disease by the simple expedient of removing the pump handle. He later published a paper, 'On the mode of transmission of Cholera', proving the disease was water-borne, and arose from the contamination of water supplies by sewage and the like. He was, of course, derided by the medical profession, who clung tenaciously to their view that it was an air-borne disease for another twenty years or more. The site of the pump can still be seen – it was where the pink granite kerb stone stands in Broadwick Street (there is a small tablet on the pub wall to help you find it) – and the pub is full of the newspaper reports of the time. Nobody seems to know when the pub was re-named in honour of the good Doctor.

From the John Snow, it is only a short walk, past the head of Berwick Street market, to Wardour Street, and the end of this short tour of inner Soho. However, as you make your way to Old Compton Street again, don't miss Meard Street, home of a lot of ladies of the town, but mentioned here for the excellent, if rather different, reason that it is an absolute

116

little gem of early Victorian and late Georgian architecture.

Now you can turn down towards Piccadilly Circus, ready for a tour of our next *quartier* – Mayfair. If there is some reasonable doubt about the derivation of the name of Soho, there is none at all about Mayfair. The name means exactly what it says. This area was for centuries the site of the May Fair, a jamboree that lasted for up to a fortnight and attracted crowds and crooks in about equal proportions.

It was centred somewhere around where Shepherd Market (*not* Shepherd's Market, please) stands today. The land was owned by one Edward Shepherd, who leased it from the Grosvenor family. There were tightrope dancers, fat ladies, dwarfs, giants, prize fights, fire eaters, wild animals, open air theatres (under canvas if wet), and a pond where you could watch, and bet on, dogs swimming around trying to catch the ducks which had been loosed on to the surface of the pond. There was also a famous gingerbread maker called Tiddy Dol, who has given his name to a modern restaurant in Hertford Street, not more than a hundred yards from the site of the Fair.

Shepherd Market is really something. You get to it by walking along Piccadilly in the direction of Hyde Park Corner until you reach White Horse Street. Turn up that street and you are there. It has a quality all its own. You are quite clearly in modern London and yet there is an indefinable aura of the eighteenth century. The pubs are Georgian. One of them, Shepherd's, actually has a genuine eighteenth-century sedan chair converted into a telephone kiosk. As befits Mayfair, the sedan chair is rather special. It is claimed to be one of only three extant royal sedans, and belonged to George II's son, the Duke of Cumberland. It was this gallant gentleman who, by his cruelties after the defeat of Bonny Prince Charlie's forces at Culloden in 1745, earned himself the endearing title of 'The Butcher'. The pub is eighteenth century, although its rebuilt version is perhaps a shade too self-consciously so. The upstairs dining-room is good, splendid to look at, and maybe just a touch pricey. You'll find it at the point where Shepherd Market right-angles round into Hertford Street.

There is only one word for Mayfair, and that is 'elegant'.

117

The feeling which occasionally overcomes me – that nobody in the area has ever actually dirtied their hands with work – is perhaps an unfair one, but it is certainly hard to associate the *quartier*'s habitués with something as crude as manual labour. The houses are gracious, usually terraced, and always beautifully maintained. The Rolls-Royces invariably have dove-grey-uniformed chauffeurs who either sit haughtily inside them awaiting their employer – surely no less a person than a duke – or flick with feather dusters at imaginary specks of dust on the glistening exteriors. Enormous American cars, about the length of a cricket pitch, undulate past on their way to the United States Embassy in Grosvenor Square. Ladies in mink coats teeter along with toy poodles on the end of gold leads. The men are smooth, with silver wings of hair above their ears. They always seem to be carrying their hats, and brandishing rapier-thin rolled umbrellas. If the word weren't so vulgar, one would think that Mayfair exudes one thing only – money.

It is nevertheless a very pleasant area to wander around. There is somehow less traffic in Mayfair: the pace of life is slower. With the constant spread of offices into the area, I suppose the rat-race is as real here as in other parts of London, but it doesn't give that impression.

Strictly speaking, Mayfair is the *quartier* bounded by Regent Street on the east, Oxford Street on the north, Park Lane in the west, and Piccadilly on the south, although common usage tends to restrict the name to the more south-westerly part, from, say, New Bond Street to Park Lane on an east–west line and Piccadilly to Brook Street on a north–south line. Not that it matters. There is no sudden change of character outside those boundaries: North Audley Street and Park Street are both to the north of Brook Street, but nobody would dream of denying them their location in Mayfair. It is only at the northern end of the area, where Oxford Street intrudes its undoubted feeling of vulgar trade, that one can quite definitely say 'This is *not* Mayfair'. Mayfair doesn't go in for trade. Which is not to say there isn't trade there. There is. After all, the aristocracy have got to eat, so there have to be food shops, like the absolutely splendid butcher's shop in Mount Street, just opposite the

Connaught Hotel. This is a butcher's in the old style. White tiled slabs, much-eroded chopping-block, blue-and-white striped aprons and straw boaters for the staff, and a feeling that it wouldn't be surprising to see a real-life duchess come in and order a few chops 'to be sent round'.

Mayfair's history is interesting, and irretrievably bound up with the Grosvenor family, now the Dukes of Westminster. In 1677, Sir Thomas Grosvenor married a young lady from Cheshire. She was just twelve years old – they must have matured early in those days – and she brought with her as dowry a thousand or so apparently worthless acres to the north and south of what we now call Piccadilly. Low lying, marshy and misty, they cannot have looked to have a great potential.

The heiress gave Thomas Grosvenor some sons. Then she went mad, he died, and the sons did neither. Instead they nursed the land through the period of development, westward along Piccadilly, which began in the first quarter of the eighteenth century and reached its climax around 1750. The two areas of land the heiress had brought as her dowry are now known as Mayfair and Belgravia. It is no wonder that the Grosvenors became the richest family in England. Some people have all the luck. If I had married a girl of twelve, they would have put me in prison.

The May Fair itself lasted until the beginning of the nineteenth century, but its days were numbered long before that. Land which could be used for fashionable and highly profitable building was hardly likely to be kept vacant just for the sake of an annual fair. Furthermore, as the development of the area proceeded, the aristocracy moved in, and they were not willing to put up with the rowdyism the Fair inevitably provoked. On the corner of Piccadilly and Brick Street, another of Mayfair's mysterious little byways, lived the 6th Earl of Coventry. His stately home actually backed on to the Shepherd Market area. His Lordship did not like what he saw of the May Fair and he brought strong pressure to bear to have it suppressed. So, in 1809, the May Fair had its last fling. After which the area was ripe for development, and developed it was. Building had already run the length of Piccadilly (named, incidentally, after the piccadills, or fancy neckwear, made by one Higgins in the Haymarket. He built himself a house on the westerly road and called it Piccadilly Hall) and had turned up what is now called Park Lane, but was then merely a narrow way running up to the Tyburn Gallows, and therefore known as Tyburn Lane. The site of the May Fair, in other words, was more or less surrounded with new development. What the developers today call in-filling was inevitable. The fortunes of the Grosvenor family, already considerable, now became gigantic. They still are: extremely clever financial management has ensured that the State has never yet got its thieving hand too far into the Grosvenor till.

Since Mayfair is laid out on a more or less grid-iron pattern, with some slight deviations to the west of Berkeley Square, there is really only one way to get hold of its elusive, but undoubtedly attractive, air of extremely well-groomed good breeding. That is to walk back and forward, and up and down its grid-iron. It won't take you long: the *quartier* isn't all that big. A good place to start is Bond Street. Strolling up the gentle slope from Piccadilly immediately shows you what wealth there is in the area. The shop windows tend not to be too full of goodies – just a modest diamond bracelet here and there – and very seldom have any price tags in sight. If you have to ask how much things are in Old and New Bond Street, then you can't afford them.

Turn left at Grafton Street. Turn left again – you have no option: the street right-angles to the left – and then take the sharp right turn to Hay Hill. The slope is surprisingly steep. It is, in fact, the left bank of the Tyburn brook which ran along the bottom, before winding its way across Piccadilly – the dip is still there for you to see – through Green Park and the gardens of Buckingham Palace, on its way to the Thames.

Berkeley Square stands on the site of the gardens of Berkeley House, the home of Lord Berkeley of Stratton. It was laid out in 1698. Diagonally across the square, on the west side, is Clive House, the home of Clive of India, now the headquarters of the Moral Rearmament Movement. At the north-west corner of the Square is Mount Street. The name is an indication of how rural the area was until at least the middle of the seventeenth century. The Lord Protector of the Commonwealth, Oliver Cromwell himself, decided that London needed an outer ring of defences against possible attack. He therefore threw up a string of defensive mounds, or mounts, to guard the approaches to the City. The one guarding the approach from the west was erected somewhere along the line of the present-day Mount Street. Mound Street: Mount Street.

The walk along Mount Street is pleasant enough. You pass the butcher's shop already referred to. The Connaught Hotel, that haven of expensive tranquillity and excellent food, is across the way. A little further on is Scott's restaurant, once a famous Piccadilly Circus landmark, now as comfortable in its new surroundings as though it had been there from the start.

Don't go all the way to Park Lane. The traffic there is endless and ear-splitting. Instead turn up Park Street, wander in through the entrance of the Grosvenor House Hotel if you want to see how the other half lives, and then turn right into the Square. The United States Embassy dominates everything. I happen to like Saarinen's building, but am still convinced it is out of place among Mayfair's elegant understatements. It was finished in 1961, capped by its 35-foot wing-span golden eagle. The Embassy, by the way, is the only American one in the world not owned freehold by the United States Government. Although they only pay the Grosvenor Estates a ground rent of £1 a year, they still wanted the freehold and they asked whether Grosvenor would be willing to sell it to them. The Estate considered the request and then wrote to Washington, saying 'Certainly, but on one condition. That you give us back the thousand or so acres of Florida which you confiscated at the end of the War of Independence.' As that particular plot included the whole of the Cape Kennedy space launching site, the US Government realized they had lost that particular poker game, and still pay their £1 a year leasehold rent on Grosvenor Square.

The statue of Franklin D. Roosevelt in the gardens had already been there thirteen years when the Embassy was opened. The statue, by Sir William Reid Dick, was unveiled by the President's widow, Eleanor, on 12 April 1948, the third anniversary of his death. It was paid for by public subscription. Only the British were allowed to subscribe and subscriptions were limited to 5s. (25p) per person. The necessary £50,000 was raised within twenty-four hours.

Grosvenor Square was the real start of the development of the family fortunes. Thomas's eldest son, Sir Richard, started laying out its six acres in 1695. It was finished by 1725, at which time it was the largest and one of the first of the squares for which London is still famous, despite the attempts of developers, including the infamous University of London, to ruin them.

Turn out of the Square to the north. Brook Street is famous for Claridge's, an hotel which always gives the impression of being an extremely lavish private house. But it should be famous for something else – its name. It is called Brook Street because it runs down to the valley of the Tyburn brook. Take a look at Brooks Mews at the back of Claridge's and see how steep the slope really is. Carry on down Davies Street to Berkeley Square again, cross to the west side and leave by way of Hill Street. Any of the left-hand turnings will lead you down towards Shepherd Market. Take a jar of refreshment in one of the bottle-glass windowed pubs in the area – the Bunch of Grapes will do very well, as will the Red Lion in Waverton Street – and you will be ready for our next *quartier*, which is really two for the price of one.

Kensington and Chelsea have always had different characters. Kensington always felt itself aristocratic, Chelsea artistic. Now they are one – the Royal Borough of Kensington and Chelsea, one of only three Royal Boroughs in the country – the others are Kingston upon Thames, where Saxon kings were crowned, and Windsor. Kensington got its honour in 1901, having previously asked Queen Victoria if she could do something to mark her long association with the Borough – she was born in Kensington Palace. She died before she could act, but her son knew what she had intended to do and he therefore conferred the honour himself. When Chelsea and Kensington were combined in 1964, the Royal title naturally extended to them both.

We're back in Grosvenor territory again. A map of 1815 shows their land as a triangle whose apex is at Hyde Park Corner, whose base is the Thames, along Chelsea reach, and whose sides are Grosvenor Place and Vauxhall Bridge Road on the east, and Sloane Street down to Chelsea Hospital on the west. What it would be worth today is anybody's guess. A good way would be to think of any number you like and add as many noughts as you wish. Next to it on the west was Cadogan land. The second Earl of Cadogan married a Miss Elizabeth Sloane. As a wedding present he received two-thirds of the estate left by his father-in-law, Sir Hans Sloane. Some wedding present! It included all the land between Sloane Street and Brompton Road, as far down as the Thames. The Cadogan–Sloane alliance is today remembered by nine streets, two squares and a crescent, named after the Sloanes; and four streets, two squares and a Thames pier, named after the Cadogans.

The Cadogan and Grosvenor lands, although extensive enough, are only a tiny part of the Royal Borough, but they are quite enough to be going on with. Even today the difference between Kensington and its neighbouring Chelsea is as marked as ever. As usual, the best way to sense that difference is on foot. It isn't far to walk from Shepherd Market, where last we paused to allow me to indulge in the above digression, so get yourself across the lunatic Roman chariot race around Hyde Park Corner. There is only one way to do that safely and that is by the underpasses. Be careful to read the direction signs carefully. It would be possible to starve to death in those catacombs were you not to keep your eyes open and your wits about you.

Although you may only just have had a drink at one of the Shepherd Market pubs, the strain of negotiating the catacombs may have made you feel in need of another. Even if you don't touch the stuff, please do not miss the Grenadier in Wilton Row. It must be one of London's most charming hostelries. The Duke of Wellington is said to have drunk there. It has a ghost. It has excellent food, open fires, and good beer. It is tucked away in a quiet mews; you get to it up some hollowed stone steps; the counter is as old as you'll find in London, the walls are covered with prints giving the history of the place, and the whole pub is so small and cosy that entering it is like putting on a comfortable pair of old slippers. Do not miss it, although you very well may. To find it, turn off Knightsbridge into Wilton Place, turn left into Wilton Crescent, and then hairpin back along Wilton Row. The mews are delightful, the sensation that you have travelled far from modern London, both in space and time, is completely overwhelming.

From now on the whole of Knightsbridge is yours, but as it is shopping country you had better keep a tight hold on your wallet or your handbag: money has a mysterious way of disappearing in Knightsbridge. Harrods alone is worth a whole day. In fact, it needs it if you are to see all that this wonderful store has to offer. Provided you don't buy anything, it is the cheapest and most fascinating day out London has to offer. The present building dates back to the turn of the century and is well-nigh unbelievable. They say they can get you anything in the world if you are prepared to pay for it. I have sometimes had the feeling that everything in the world is already there. The store's motto is 'Omnia, Omnibus, Ubique' ('Everything, for everyone, everywhere'), as apt a slogan as ever you'll find. The site covers 4½ acres, there are some fifteen acres of floor space, and there is a staff of more than five thousand. If you can't find what you want at Harrods then in all probability it doesn't exist.

When you leave the place, assuming you've done it thoroughly, you won't want to do anything else apart from lie down for an hour or two. When you have recovered your strength, remember that there are hundreds more stores, boutiques, galleries, craft shops and the rest strung along Brompton Road and down Sloane Street. Try going along Brompton Road to Beauchamp Place (pronounced Beecham). This leads you through to Pont Street. The derivation of the name is simple. It is the French word for bridge, and that's just what it was: a bridge over the Westbourne, yet another of London's lost rivers, now safely tucked away under ground. This is real Cadogan country – Places, Squares, Crescents, Gardens, everywhere. Turn down Sloane Street to Sloane Square. The change is almost immediately apparent. Leading out of the west side of the square is King's Road – the King's Road, as Londoners will insist on saying. Its function is almost exactly the same as that of the famous old pleasure gardens like Ranelagh and Vauxhall: it is there so that people can look and be looked at.

Much of the bizarre quality which has overwhelmed the King's Road over the last decade or so is ugly in the extreme. Shoddiness is everywhere. King's Road may once have been a genteel thoroughfare – it was, after all, originally a private road constructed for the use of King Charles II – but today it is nothing of the sort. In many ways it resembles a very long Carnaby Street, which is an idea so horrible as to be almost beyond contemplation. The young people who frequent it do not seem to be much troubled by the need to earn a living. Whether that is because they have private means or live off public money I cannot say. I suppose they are enjoying themselves in their own way, although the need to keep up with every little change in fashion, and to be seen to be doing so, must surely be somewhat exhausting. Nevertheless, the King's Road is worth a look at if only to prove the truth of the Lancashire saying that 'There's nowt so queer as folk'.

I have always found the Fulham Road healthier. I do not know why this is: Fulham is not notorious for its therapeutic qualities. But, in a curious way, just as Fulham Football Club was always more down to earth than Chelsea Football Club, so are the roads. The King's Road has never accepted that there is such a thing as death. For the King's Road, life is a great joke which will go on forever. Well, so it is, and so it will, but not in quite the way the King's Road-ites think.

Amble back, if that is your wont, up the Fulham Road towards South Kensington and thence, by Walton Street, to Beauchamp Place and Pont Street. But before you get back to their relative splendours, look at the area around South Kensington Underground station. Everybody who lives there, everybody who goes there, everybody who knows it, always calls it South Ken. In a way, this proves there *is* such a thing as a collective folk wisdom, because South Ken is not, could not be, and never will be, South Kensington. There is something raffish about South Ken. It is as though it has been specially designed to act as a transition passage between the *adagio* of Kensington and the *scherzo* of Chelsea.

If South Ken's curious hybridity baffles you, ignore it. Make your way, probably by Thurloe Square, to the Cromwell Road (that intrusive London 'the' again). On your left lies museum land. London's museums are about the best in the world, deserve a chapter to themselves, and are going to get it. So turn right, past the Victoria and Albert, to where Brompton Road comes in from the right. Cross over to the north side of the street. As you come within sight of Harrods you will see, first, the Brompton Oratory, where so many of the famous have trodden the dusty way to matrimony. Then, after Brompton Square, you will find yourself able to slide up to Montpelier Square by way of Cheval Place, where Lord Lew Grade, in his penthouse, keeps his nightly watch on the television ratings. Push through Trevor Place to Knightsbridge, but try to keep your eyes closed. That way you will be spared the sight of Sir Basil Spence's brick monstrosity, the Knightsbridge barracks. I do not think I will ever be able to forgive Sir Basil. I am one of the greatest admirers of his Coventry Cathedral, a superb solution to the problem posed by a shattered medieval building and the modern idea of how we should build a church today. But Knightsbridge Barracks are awful. One can only assume that Sir Basil got less sensitive as he got older.

Knightsbridge is so called because there was once a bridge here over the Westbourne, as it made its way to the Thames. The bridge was originally known as the Cnichtebrugge, 'the bridge of the serving boy'. There is another, equally unlikely, suggested derivation: the bridge belonged to the knights who were going off to the wars and traditionally were blessed there by the Bishops of London who came up from their palace at Fulham. The Bishops, presumably, went back to the safety of their palace while the knights went off and got themselves killed.

If you turn left along Knightsbridge, which immediately becomes Kensington Road, there's nothing very much in front of you for some distance. Then ahead, and looking rather like a Gothic rocket, you will see the Albert Memorial pointing earnestly skywards. Do not flinch, but go bravely forward.

There is, these days, a school, largely led by Sir John

Betjeman, which holds that the Albert Memorial, because it is Victorian, is therefore good. You will have to make your own mind up. I have already made mine up: I think it is terrible. It is overloaded with detail. It lacks balance. It is top-heavy. It looks as if it is going to fall over, and it looks as though it deserves to. But don't miss it. The experience is unique. Climb up the steps and examine it in detail. All that intricate carving! The four lower groups represent Africa (a camel), America (a bison), Asia (an elephant) and Europe (a bull). The hundreds of figures represent just about everybody, from all ages. It was designed by Sir George Gilbert Scott and was built between 1863 and 1872 as a memorial to Prince Albert, Queen Victoria's consort, who died of typhoid – the Windsor Castle drains were notorious – in 1861. Do not think that, as he stands there so piously, he is holding the Bible. Closer inspection will reveal that it is in fact the catalogue of the Great Exhibition of 1851 in his hand. An extraordinary piece of work, and quite unique, thank God.

The Albert Hall, on the other side of Kensington Gore, which is what the road is now called, is too well-known to need description, at least as far as the interior is concerned: the televising of the Proms has seen to that. From outside it looks like nothing so much as a slightly collapsed soufflé, and a big one at that, since it is 735 feet in circumference and can seat 8,000 people. Built in 1871 and named after the dead Prince, himself a musician, it has a place in people's hearts quite unmerited by its architectural quality.

You have lots of choices now. On the north side of The Gore are Kensington Gardens, well worth a visit. Ahead of you is Kensington High Street, with shops to tempt you to empty that purse even further. Or you can turn left down Palace Gate and Gloucester Road, turning left again at, say, Old Brompton Road and making your way back towards Hyde Park Corner. Be warned, though. It is quite a walk and at the end of the day it may be too tiring and not rewarding enough. Perhaps, on the whole, you'd be better off getting on the Underground at Kensington High Street station and making your weary way back to wherever you are staying.

There is one other *quartier* I would have liked to

recommend to you – Bloomsbury, but after what the University of London, that supposed guardian of our culture, has done to it, I am very loath. There is still something to be seen that gives the feeling of a Bloomsbury full of gracious squares and lovely elegant terraces. Tavistock Square; what is left of Bedford Square and Russell Square; Gordon Square; Woburn Walk, off Upper Woburn Place (an absolute gem this). But not, definitely not, any of that shambles surrounding Malet Street. What I would like to do to the people who have ruined Bloomsbury is so horrible that I cannot possibly put it down in print.

There are many more *quartiers* in London, even in Central London, but one can't deal with them all. As you wander around you will surely come to feel that atmosphere, that sense of character, that feeling of *place*, which is the true sign of a *quartier*, in parts of London I haven't touched on. You may come to prefer them to those I have described. They, after all, are merely my own favourites, favourites which have grown on me over the years. That doesn't always happen, of course. When I first knew Earls Court, twenty years ago, I liked its friendliness. These days I would go a long way to avoid its filth, squalor, noise and brashness. Conversely, though, some areas are coming out of such a state and may acquire their own charm in time. I hope you will find them.

Victoriana

There is no need to look very far if you want to see Victorian London: it is still very much a Victorian city. Of its three million or so 'dwelling units', as the bureaucrats insist on calling what once were known as homes, at least half must have been built in the reign of the Old Queen. Many such houses have been pulled down since the war, and many were blown up during it: a lot of them deserved either or both fates, since they were no longer fit to live in. But the laurel and privet-wreathed areas of Pooter-land, which is Holloway and Tufnell Park; areas like Islington, Camden Town, Highbury, Hackney, Paddington, Bayswater and the Bush, on the north side of the river; Peckham, Brixton, Kennington, Battersea, Clapham and Balham on the south; these still have a lot of fine old Victorian houses, many of them now split up into flats and bed-sitters, of course, but still good to look at when they are properly maintained, which, sadly, isn't frequently enough.

To most people, however, the phrase 'Victorian London' means dark gloomy alleys, rat-ridden tenements, over-crowded hovels, streets full of filth and peopled with the dregs of the underworld. I strongly suspect it is all the fault of Charles Dickens. No man, with the possible exception of the incomparable Henry Mayhew, drew a more vivid picture of the dark side of the London of his day. It is true that some of this still remains. Wander round the deserted wharves of Bermondsey on a misty November evening, and see if you can manage it without once looking nervously over your shoulder. Try Wapping High Street on the same sort of night. Travel further east to Narrow Street, in Limehouse, and shudder.

Not that you need go so far out. Running up from the Strand to Maiden Lane is Exchange Court, down which Victorian actor-manager William Terriss walked to his death by stabbing, that December night in 1897 (see p.172). The court, with its paving, its gaslights, its narrowness, its garbage put out for the descendants of what the Victorians used to call 'the night soil men', will really make you believe you are in Victorian London, even though the traffic of the Strand is roaring away only a few yards from you. If, after walking up the few yards from the Strand to Maiden Lane, you feel in need of a little sustenance to steady your nerve, there, almost in front of you is one of the most Victorian restaurants in London, Rules. Not so long ago it was threatened under the Covent Garden Development Scheme. Once in Rules you will definitely feel you have gone back in time. Dickens ate and drank here: so did Thackeray and a host of other names from the nineteenth century. The place hasn't changed much since their day. The staff look Victorian, and give you the sort of service that age was famous for. Electricity has replaced gas, but the chandeliers, the panelling, the pictures, the alcoves, and the splendid English food – the roast beef has always been remarkable – definitely remind one of an age long gone.

Perhaps, after you leave Rules, you might like to wander around what is left of Covent Garden. A walk along Floral Street, which runs south-west from the Opera House, will get you feeling more and more nineteenth century until you reach Rose Street, which is positively antique. Slip down a covered alleyway, by the side of the Lamb and Flag pub. Read the notice inscribed on the roof of that alleyway, about how the poet Dryden was attacked and left for dead just there, remember that the pub's nickname has long been 'The Bucket of Blood', and dodge quickly inside for a nerve-strengthener. Once again the impression, as with Rules, is that time has slipped back.

If it's still dark and desperate Victorian gloom you are after, I suggest that you get on the District line to Whitechapel or Aldgate East stations, remembering as you do so that you are now heading for Jack the Ripper land.

If you alight at Aldgate East, which is marginally preferable for a tour of the Ripper sites, just across Whitechapel High Street you will see Gunthorpe Street (or you will if they haven't knocked it down by the time you read this, for the whole area is undergoing redevelopment). Gunthorpe Street used to be called George Yard, and it was here, in the early hours of 7 August 1888 that the body of Martha Turner, a prostitute, was found on the stairs of George Yard Buildings. She had been stabbed no less than thirty-nine times, with both a bayonet and some sort of surgical instrument. No one was ever arrested, the 'work' showed no special medical skill, and so it is not possible to say whether this really was the first of Jack the Ripper's victims.

It was another three weeks before the batch of murders which made Jack the Ripper one of the most famous names in the history of crime definitely began: 'definitely' in the sense that forensic examination of the bodies convinced the experts they were the work of one man, whereas there is still doubt about whether Martha Turner's murder was by the same killer.

At 3.15 a.m. on Friday 31 August the body of Mary Anne, or Polly, Nicholls, was found in what is now called Durward Street, immediately to the north of Whitechapel Tube station. It was lying at the entrance to Old Stable Yard, now no longer there, although some of the little old houses still are, and give a good idea of what Whitechapel was like in 1888. When they took the body to the mortuary they discovered a lot of unpleasant things about it: for one thing, her throat had been cut from ear to ear, and for another her abdomen had been so severely slashed that she had virtually been disembowelled.

Eight days later, another prostitute, Annie Chapman, met her death in Hanbury Street, which runs from Commercial Street in the west almost to Durward Street in the east. In her case, too, the head had been almost severed and the body cut open: the kidneys and ovaries had been removed. There were two odd things about this killing: two of Annie Chapman's front teeth had been removed, which repeated something about the Polly Nicholls murder which had not been noticed before. And secondly, and most bizarrely, some coins and two brass rings were laid out at her feet. Whoever killed her knew what he was doing, because he must have been very swift and very cool. There were more than a dozen people sleeping in 29 Hanbury Street, outside which the body was found, yet nobody heard a scream or any suspicious noise of any kind. There is another point to substantiate the murderer's coolness. Annie Chapman was seen alive about 5 a.m. The body was found at 6 a.m. and by that time the sun had been up for about half an hour (there was no British Summer Time until 1916). As the murder took place down a little alley by the side of 29 Hanbury Street, the possibility of discovery must have been very high, yet the murderer still went on calmly – almost professionally – with the work of the dissection of his victim.

By now the newspaper boys were running all over London shouting 'Special! Special!', for those were the days when any event of importance merited a 'Special Edition'. More was to come. Three weeks later, a letter arrived at a news agency, signed by 'Jack the Ripper'. Whether it was genuine or not, the name caught on. Just two days after the letter was received, that is to say on 30 September 1888, *two* murders were committed in Whitechapel. At 1 a.m. that day a hawker drove his horse and cart into a yard off Berner Street, itself off the Commercial Road. He found the body of Elizabeth Stride. She, too, had had her throat cut, but the work of disembowelling was not complete. It may be that the noise of the horse's hooves and the rattle of the wheels of the cart alarmed the killer before he could finish his work.

Just 45 minutes later a policeman passed through a yard joining Mitre Square to Duke Place, across Houndsditch from Aldgate Station (Circle line). There he found the body of Catherine Eddowes, a prostitute who had been released from Bishopsgate Police Station at 1 a.m.: she had been taken in there for drunkenness. Catherine Eddowes's body had suffered the usual treatment – throat slit and body disembowelled. 'Jack the Ripper' sent another letter to the news agency, written in red ink, and posted only hours after the murders, in which he 'apologized' for the fact that an interruption had stopped him from doing the jobs properly: he had intended to cut off the victims' ears and send them to the police. (Eddowes's ears had been, in fact, partly severed.)

The panic in Whitechapel can be imagined. The area was full of narrow streets, dimly lit, little back alleys and yards, usually unlit, and of prostitutes who used them to ply their trade, since few of them had 'a place of their own'. Teams of 'vigilantes' patrolled the streets at night and had some effect. There were no further murders, and the panic began to die down. Until, on 9 November, a rent collector called at the home of Mary Kelly, in Millers Court, Duval Street, off Commercial Street, no more than 400 yards east of Liverpool Street station. What the rent collector saw when he looked through the window probably stayed with him for the rest of his life. Mary Kelly's body was lying on the bed. Her head had been near-severed. Her heart had been taken out and was lying on the pillow. She had been disembowelled, and her entrails had been draped around a picture hanging on the wall.

There were three more murders in the area in the next two years or so, all showing some similarities with the Ripper murders. Some 'experts' say they were definitely by him: others, equally 'expert', say they were not. Nobody was ever arrested for the killings, although various suspects, some rather more likely than others, have been named. The theories as to the murderer's identity are as ingenious as they are different. It is, however, quite certain – and I admit that this is not the most shattering statement ever made – that the murders happened, and that they all took place in Whitechapel.

You will find little of the original area left these days. The Blitz and redevelopment have changed the face of Whitechapel considerably. But not completely. Hanbury Street is still there (Annie Chapman), Gunthorpe Street is still there (Martha Turner), Durward Street is still there (Polly Nicholls), and so are Mitre Square and Dukes Place (Catherine Eddowes). If you go to Whites Row, off Commercial Street, and literally within yards of Middlesex Street and its famous Petticoat Lane market, you will be within a few feet of where Mary Kelly was cut to pieces. There is no point in going to the places in broad daylight, except for the sake of saying you have been there. Go when the sun has gone down, and mist is settling over the streets. (Remember how dimly lit those streets were in 1888, seek out the few remaining houses – Hanbury and Durward Streets were particularly good in that respect until only a short time ago – and you might begin to get just an inkling of how terrified Whitechapel was when Jack the Ripper stalked the area. And if the experience inspires you to start formulating theories of your own, you'll have a lot of preliminary reading to do: the bibliography is enormous. You could do worse than start with *Encyclopedia of Murder* by Colin Wilson and Pat Pitman (Pan Books, 1964). Be warned, though: they list eight books and a lot more articles which set out to prove who the Ripper was. You could be in for some splendid winter evenings of reading by the light of a single flickering candle, nervously glancing at the window from time to time.

Is that someone trying the latch . . . ?

After all that horror, you deserve something a little more peaceful. Why not try the capital's railway stations? The 'surface' ones are all Victorian and have about them a charm rarely equalled anywhere in the city. With the exception of Waterloo and London Bridge, the main line termini are all north of the river; an excellent underground network connects them, so that, north or south, you can easily see all of them in a day and do precious little walking while you're about it. 'Underground' is, of course, something of a misnomer: there are many stretches where, possibly to your surprise, you will find yourself in the open

134

air, and not all that far below the surface either. Didn't Sherlock Holmes once solve a mystery by working out, after a few minutes with a map, where the body found on the roof of an underground carriage must have been dropped from to have been carried to where it was found? The house where the man died must clearly have overlooked one of the 'open-air' sections of the underground. Elementary, my dear Watson.

To take the termini in the chronological order of their construction would be tedious and rather pointless since some, Euston being a notable example, have been almost totally reconstructed. Others remain in much the same state as their great Victorian builders left them and, in some people's opinion, are all the better for that.

The two classics are St Pancras and King's Cross. Stand opposite St Pancras, on the other side of the Euston Road, and look at its incredible Gothic façade. Then pan your gaze to the right, to King's Cross, with its severe modern façade. It is easy to see which is the earlier construction, isn't it? In fact it isn't easy. King's Cross, the modern looking one, is twenty years older than St Pancras, the antique one.

The reason isn't far to seek. It came from a well-developed sense of economy, which seems odd when you consider St Pancras's wealth of ornamental detail. But hear me out. Sir George Gilbert Scott, the architect, had been invited to submit a design for the new Foreign Office in Downing Street /Parliament Street (not Downing Street/Whitehall: the latter becomes Parliament Street at the Cenotaph). Scott was very fond of the Victorian Gothic style then much in fashion – think of the Houses of Parliament, the Law Courts in the Strand, the Public Record Office in Chancery Lane, and the huge Prudential building in Holborn, not to mention the Albert Memorial. Lord Palmerston, who was Prime Minister at the time, and crusty with it, didn't like the new-fangled Gothic style, and indicated his disapproval rather strongly. In fact, when Scott had earlier submitted a design for the India Office, Palmerston had forced him to do it in the Italian Renaissance style. This time Scott's design was so complicated, and so disliked by the Prime Minister, that Scott had two goes at it: the first one, a modification into a Venetian palazzo style, merely caused Palmerston to growl 'A regular mongrel affair' and reject it once again. Scott bowed to the Old Man, designed him something he liked, and saved a vast amount of his Foreign Office Gothic for a design for the façade of St Pancras station and its attached hotel.

That is why the later of the two station, St Pancras and King's Cross, looks far more ancient. But behind the façade you will see just how modern the engineering design of the station itself is, as compared with the architectural design of the façade. The engineer, W.H. Barlow, who doesn't even rate a mention in *Chambers Biographical Dictionary*, while Scott gets the full treatment, designed one of the most staggering pieces of railway engineering this country has seen, and certainly the most staggering seen up to the time of the station's construction at the end of the 1860s. One huge unsupported semi-cylindrical roof, the arch leaping across 240 feet. If you compare that with Lewis Cubitt's more modern-looking design for King's Cross you will find that, to cover the same width, he could only manage two unsupported spans of 120 feet each. Clearly the science of structural engineering had moved on from Cubitt's time to Barlow's.

But there is much more to commend St Pancras than its great arch. There is the façade itself. Seen through the autumn mists of a London which had no Clean Air Acts – seen, say, from the heights of Pentonville Road, as in John O'Connor's wonderfully romantic painting, now in the London Museum – it must have looked like a fairy castle. You can still see something resembling John O'Connor's vision if you climb up Pentonville Road about as far as Penton Street any twilight, and look back. Very little in the view, apart from the intrusive tower blocks in the distance, has changed since that picture was painted in 1884.

If we go back to the station itself, it pays not to have to catch a train. That way you will have time to stand and stare: you will have plenty to stare at. Take the ticket office at the western end of the vast station concourse. It is all in linenfold oak panelling: *all of it*. The cost of the ticket hall alone would give a modern railway architect a heart attack of fairly massive proportions. Nothing is skimped. The workmanship is perfect and has stood the test of time – more than

136

a century of it. It is reminiscent of one of those medieval cathedrals where a man might put years of skilled craftsmanship into making, say, roof bosses which were so high up he knew – for he did *not* know there were going to be telescopes, field glasses, and Long-Tom camera lenses – that no man would ever be able to see what he had made. It made no difference: he worked for the glory of God and his own pride in his craft. The parallel isn't altogether far-fetched. The impression one gets in the St Pancras ticket hall *is* of a church, a church where the highest standards of skill were employed for the highest possible reason.

The 'I am in a cathedral' feeling is even more pronounced if you go into the St Pancras Hotel. It is, of course, a hotel no more, having been converted into railway offices back in 1935. Decay was thereafter inevitable, as a few sharp-eyed moments under the portico at the west end of the façade will show you. But if you can persuade British Rail to let you into the place you will see again an incredible amount of decoration and ornamentation, little of which ever stood a chance of being noticed by the hotel patrons, however high in the air they held their noses. The hotel had 600 bedrooms. As you walk through it now you can almost hear the Palm Court orchestra playing. As you climb the great staircase you can almost hear the swish of the crinolines and see the bows the gentlemen gave the passing ladies. The staircase, by the way, and it is a wry comment on what time has wrought, has been put to little use in recent years, except by railway clerks, engineers, surveyors, and their secretaries, rushing up and down it to their offices, strung along the 150-yard long corridors. Little use to match its grandeur – apart from once when a film producer, making *The Three Musketeers*, wanted a staircase for the inevitable sword-fight. This was the one they used. I don't know whether Gilbert Scott or, even more, W.H. Barlow, who were forward-looking men, would have approved. I approve, though. It is nice to think of the old hotel, once so magnificent, having a final glamorous fling, so long after it must have thought its great days had passed for ever.

You can wander around St Pancras for a long time and keep on being surprised. One extremely unpleasant surprise is the ghastly tea bar, apparently made of plastic Lego, and red plastic Lego at that, which seems to have been designed deliberately to ruin the impressiveness of the great concourse. So give it a miss and turn into the Shires Bar, one of the station's best surprises. Four sorts of real beer, plus all the other varieties of drinks that cheer and do inebriate, a lunch bar with the cheapest and best salads, patés, and the like, and all this with a pool table as well. No wonder it fills up at lunch-time wⁱᵗʰ railway staff who are very clearly in the know. Well, so are you now, so give it a try and I guarantee you won't be disappointed.

One final point: it occurs to me you may be wondering who in Hell, or perhaps I should say who in Heaven, St Pancras was? Well, he was actually one of our smallest saints, which is rather odd in view of the size of the station. He died in AD 303, aged just fourteen, shortly after he had been baptized, which was a rotten piece of luck. The Emperor Diocletian, whose anti-Christian purge was responsible for Pancras's death, then resigned the emperorship and took up gardening and philosophy, something St Pancras may have wished he had taken up a little earlier. If you want to know what St Pancras is alleged to have looked like, all you have to do is look at the King's Cross end of the station roof. There, right on the peak, is the little fellow, all gilt and haloed, but you will need a pair of field-glasses to make him out as he looks down at the millions of us rushing to use the station named after him.

King's Cross is a much less exuberant station than St Pancras. The whole style of the place is as restrained and simple as Lewis Cubitt's frontage. But there is one remaining bit of the days of railway glamour. That is the departure each morning, at 10 a.m., of the Flying Scotsman. There are few more enjoyable ways of getting to, say, Newcastle from London than by this romantically-named train. For one thing, it leaves on time; for another thing it runs to time; and for a third thing the service is still old-fashionedly splendid. Ten o'clock out of the centre of London, 1.30 in the centre of Newcastle – 280 miles in 3½ hours, an average speed of eighty mph from start to stop. Try achieving that on M1. And on the way, lunch in a dining-car that still has individual movable dining chairs, served by a staff who still seem to believe they are working for a railway company with an identity and a record of service, rather than for an anonymous nationalized industry.

Euston, just west along the Euston Road, is the earliest of the genuine main-line terminals. It was built in 1837 for the London and Midland Railway, running from England's biggest city to its second biggest city, Birmingham. The old station was a gem – a huge waiting hall, the famous Euston Doric arch in front of the station, and the incredibly grand but comfortable Euston Hotel just across Euston Square. The Great Hall always made me think I was in the first-class ballroom of the *Titanic*, it was so stately. It has disappeared just as finally as that ill-fated ship, at the end of what the *Architectural Review* called a 'long drawn out history of bureaucratic dilatoriness and evasion', a history in which the British Transport Commission, the London County Council, and the Government of the day were all equally involved and all equally to blame. It is especially ironic that the Euston Arch is now seen to have been demolished quite unnecessarily. As the magnificent entrance to the first railway terminus in the world to be built in a country's capital, it had a special place in history and the hearts of Londoners. It had, apparently, no place at all in the hearts, if any, of the three groups mentioned above, groups supposed to be its guardians but who, in fact, connived at its destruction.

And what have we got now? An absolute nothing. A huge characterless concourse in which, at first, British Rail refused to put any seats, in case it encouraged undesirables to doss there – try standing two hours, waiting for a train, with nowhere to take the weight off your feet. The result was inevitable: the undesirables dossed on the floor, spreading out their belongings on their own specially-picked pitches. The architecture, if it can be called that, is appalling and not even efficient. The concourse, being too big to keep clean, is constantly a mass of paper, beer cans and vomit stains: the taxi rank, being underground, is so thick with diesel fumes that bronchitics go there at risk of their lives. The station, in a word, is a mess. Avoid it if you can.

Marylebone and Paddington are much more attractive,

which is probably why British Rail decided, not so long ago, that they would like to demolish them. As a result of what they had done to Euston, however, the uproar, not just from railway enthusiasts, but from all sorts of people who cared about London's industrial archaeological legacy – for that is what the stations are part of – was so great that British Rail backed hastily into their running shed. There is not the slightest reason to suppose, however, that they aren't still working on some evil plot to pull both termini down when they think nobody is looking. So beware, and be quick: they may have disappeared before you get a chance to inspect them.

Of the two, I personally prefer Paddington. The Great Western Hotel alone is worth the money. It is a splendid place. People coming up from the West Country still stay there, as once one could do at Euston and St Pancras. To have lunch or dinner there is to experience what it must have been like in the old days, when one of the Great Western Railway's steam monsters, always immaculate in their company livery, would have brought you up from Cornwall or be waiting to run you out to Bristol.

Paddington has a real claim to be considered Victorian. The young Queen herself used it as early as 1842 to travel from Windsor to London, boarding the train at Slough, in those days a pleasant place. She wrote to her constant correspondent, Uncle Leopold of the Belgians, to tell him she was 'quite charmed' with the trip. Her husband-to-be, Prince Albert, had taken his life in his hands and travelled on the railway in 1839. If the Royals could do it, so could their subjects. The Railway Age, already booming, now took off.

In 1842 the Queen's train ran into little more than a siding. The present great station wasn't built until 1854 by that wonderful railway engineer, Isambard Kingdom Brunel – he just had to be wonderful, surely, to live up to a name like that? When Euston was built it was called 'The Eighth Wonder of the World'. Paddington received much the same veneration. The painter W. P. Frith devoted one whole year of his working life to painting Paddington. The picture is called 'The Railway Station' and can be seen in the Royal Holloway College. The crowds who flocked to view it were quick to spot the resemblance to the inside of a cathedral: the great arch; the intricate wrought-iron; the globe lights hanging down from the roof, the stained-glass feel of the whole place. Frith, who was no slouch when it came to making money, knew he was on to a good thing with the painting. He sold it for more than £5,000, and most of Victorian England thought the money well spent, for was it not a religious painting, really, and was it not, therefore, a Good Thing?

Marylebone was the last of the main-line termini to be built in London (not *re*-built, of course). It has always been quieter than the others: in fact, it is so quiet these days (being no longer 'main line'), that I can think of few better places for a nice, uninterrupted sleep. It was, in fact, only just Victorian, since it was not opened until 1899, and the way it opened was prophetic of the way it was going to carry on. On the inaugural day the first train out carried five paying passengers. The busiest train that day carried forty-four.

It hasn't changed since. As A.G. Macdonell described it in *England, their England*, it is a place 'where the porters go on tiptoe, where the barrows are rubber-tyred and the trains sidle mysteriously in and out with only the faintest of toots on their whistles, so as not to disturb the signalmen'. It is still the same today. For how much longer, though? That is the question. Just in case British Rail pull a fast one and demolish it, which they would dearly like to do, go and see it as soon as you can.

While you are there, look across at Marylebone's hotel, opened the same year as the station and destined never to make a penny profit. It had far too many rooms – some 700 – and was equipped with huge dining- and lounging-salons, great staircases, and the sort of decoration I have already described in talking about the St Pancras Hotel. Not even the existence of a specially built cycle-track *on the roof* (!) could bring in enough paying customers. It was taken over by the Government in both world wars, was bought by the LNER railway from Frederick Hotels who administered it (the Great Central line into Marylebone ran out of money and a consortium of City financiers had to be assembled to provide the cash to build what was considered to be the essential terminus hotel), and then passed into the ownership of the British Transport Commission when the railways were nationalized. It is now the headquarters of the British Railways Board and is no longer called the Great Central Hotel (although you can still see the GCR initials in the wrought-iron railings): instead, it is now prosaically known as 222 Marylebone Road. How are the mighty fallen!

The other main-line termini do not have the magic, *for me*, that those on the King's Cross–Marylebone axis have, perhaps because throughout my life I have used the latter far more than I have the others. I must, however, confess to a little shudder of delight when I read the foreign names inscribed over Victoria, Waterloo and Liverpool Street: shades of the Orient Express and the Trans-Siberian railway! Shades of Agatha Christie and E. Phillips Oppenheim! I seem to remember that the late Peter Fleming's book *Travels in Tartary* started with him sitting in his first-class carriage, tapping away at his typewriter (which must have got on the other passengers' nerves), and watching London slipping away as he set out to travel to those distant lands. And all by train. These days we'd do it by air in a matter of hours, and get little sense of having travelled and even less sense of the countries we had passed over.

Mention of Liverpool Street reminds me that if it, and its splendid Great Eastern Hotel, attract you, make sure you go and see them soon. For years now, British Rail have been rubbing their hands with glee at the thought of the site value of Liverpool Street and Broad Street. Broad Street is already virtually derelict, most of its roof gone, forests of weeds growing between the unused platforms, and a distinct, almost tangible, feeling that British Rail are saying to themselves 'If we let it rot a little bit more, there's no hope we'll ever be able to restore it, so we'll be able to demolish it and make millions out of the site.'

The two western bays of Liverpool Street and its Gothic block are 'listed' as buildings worth preserving, but the sword still hangs over the rest of the complex, including the hotel. There was an inquiry in 1976, after which things cooled down somewhat, but you never know: the fire might suddenly burst out again, and all that will be left are the ashes of one of the great sights of Victorian London.

There is one other great class of Victoriana, of course. The churches. Inevitably, in London, the Wren churches and those roughly contemporary with them get the most attention, but people like Sir John Betjeman and Professor Niklaus Pevsner have demonstrated that there is much beauty in the churches built to cater for the nineteenth-century's great population explosion. The sad fact is that, these days, most of the churches are not wanted. The nation seems to have lost interest in religion. The churches are vast, expensive to heat, and cripplingly so to maintain. So what is to be done with them? Conservationists might say 'Keep them', to which the Church Commissioners (for it is mainly Anglican churches which are in this situation) are surely entitled to reply 'And who's going to pay for their upkeep?'.

Therefore, before it is too late (how many times already have I uttered that Cassandra-like phrase?), arm yourself with the works of Betjeman and Pevsner, and go and see their top recommendations before Time bears them away, as it has already borne away those who used to attend them.

Finally, if you want a church visit more than a little out of the ordinary, go to Tufnell Park, an area which is itself a monument to Victoriana, in the shape of its housing. Take the tube to the Tufnell Park station, turn along Tufnell Park Road, and you will come to St George's church, as was. It is now the St George's theatre. The church happened to be octagonal, as was Shakespeare's Globe. It also happened to have almost the same dimensions. A splendid conversion has been carried out. The old church pews, now cushioned, provide the best back-supports in any London theatre. Sitting there, you can watch Shakespeare acted on an apron stage the same size as Shakespeare's, in productions based on the idea that the words of the poet are more important than the ideas of a director trying to make a name for himself by the originality of his interpretation of the works. And in the interval you can look around you and enjoy the architecture (or you can ignore it and use the refreshment facilities), secure in the knowlege that you are looking at Victoriana which is being fruitfully used, rather than allowed to crumble away into a pile of rusty nothingness.

The Victorian Age was a great age. Derided by people

whose stature, compared with the Victorians, was minuscule, the age is at last coming back into its own. It may be too late. It may be that we have begun to re-appreciate its qualities just in the nick of time. So make sure you sample it before it is gone for ever.

Statuary

When the Irishman was asked if there were any leprechauns about, he is reported to have replied 'Leprechauns? Sure, an' the streets is paved with them.' You could say much the same about London and its statues: the streets is paved with them. And the parks. And the walls. And the buildings. And even the bridges.

Nobody knows how many statues there are in London, and that means however you define London. Whether you talk about the City proper, or employ the wider usage, which includes the West End, Westminster, Chelsea, and sich-like, as that well-known Londoner Mrs Sairey Gamp would say, the statues are numberless to Man. Counting them, or trying to, would be as pointless as trying to count the grains of sand on the shore. So this chapter can and will do no more than point out one or two of the better-known, or less-known, or funnier, or sadder, statues in what, for shorthand's sake, we can call

Central London. Even with those limited terms of reference there's plenty to be going at: far too much, but whoever really meant it when they complained about being spoiled for choice?

The initial problem is the usual one: where to start? This time the answer is easy. It is the answer with which this book began: start by the river. To be precise, start by the steps at the Big Ben end of Westminster Bridge.

The magnificent group of Queen Boadicea, or Boudicca, as modern historians call her and I refuse to, is by Thomas Thornycroft, one of a famous family of sculptors – father, mother, brothers, and sister all carved away like mad. What they did with the chippings, the Lord only knows. Probably paved the way from Westminster back to where Boadicea had come from, which was East Anglia, where she was queen of the Iceni. She died in AD 62, but not until after she had shown the Romans just what a native revolt could mean. After the death of her husband, Prasutagas, she was made joint heir with the Emperor Nero to all their tribal lands. It doesn't sound an ideal arrangement, and it wasn't. It resulted in insults, degradation, and humiliation. Nero's procurator seized Boadicea's palace and estates, his tax collectors tried to wring even more out of her people, and when the royal family objected, Boadicea was flogged and her daughters were raped. Enough is enough. The Iceni rose in revolt, and Imperial Rome suffered its worst blood-letting ever in Britain. Colchester was razed to the ground, and then Boadicea and her warriors marched on London. The capital suffered the same fate as Colchester. Excavations in the area once bounded by the city wall still turn up a layer of black ash, some ten to twenty feet below the modern surface. It is the ashes of Roman London. That done, Boadicea turned north to St Albans – Verulam, as it was then. That went the same way. Some 70,000 inhabitants of the three towns perished in the onslaught. But revenge was waiting. The general Suetonius caught Boadicea and her army somewhere in the Midlands. The Britons were no match for the Romans; they were slaughtered and Boadicea took poison.

So why is her statue there, a monument to a rebel, facing, even menacing, the seat of lawful government? Presumably because another way of looking at her story is to say that she was a native of this land, revolting against a foreign

146

occupying power, and is therefore part of our rough island story. Be that as it may, Thornycroft's group, put there in 1902, is pretty impressive. He was, however, clearly a better sculptor than he was a charioteer. Boadicea is riding to eternity with not so much as a single rein to control her galloping steeds.

If you now walk down the steps to the Victoria Embankment and stroll northwards, with the river on your right, you are walking on what was once water. This was the foreshore of the Thames, reclaimed by Sir Joseph Bazalgette when he built his great intercepting sewer to stop crude sewage pouring into the Thames. The sewer lies beneath your feet. Having built the retaining wall, Bazalgette then constructed, on top of the reclaimed land, the gardens you see ahead of you.

It seems that when the Victorians saw an open space they felt an irresistible urge to build a statue on it. The Victoria Embankment Gardens are a fine example of this. Mind you, they had a lot of people to build statues to: they were a very great people. But the first statue you'll see isn't Victorian at all. It is very recent, being a memorial to Hugh Montague, the first Viscount Trenchard, who died in 1956 and is still referred to as the Father of the Royal Air Force, since he was its first general officer commanding and its first Air Marshal. The statue, by William Macmillan, has Trenchard with his back to the Defence building behind him. This was once the Air Ministry, tout court, and they say that when the Air Force was incorporated in the Ministry of Defence, and the building became the Ministry of Defence (Air), the statue, which until then had faced the building, became so disgusted that, overnight, it turned its back on the old building for ever. I cannot vouch for the truth of this tale.

The next statue ahead is that of General Charles George Gordon, of Khartoum fame. A peculiar man, who seemed to combine Bible-reading with self-flagellation, he was nevertheless a brave and experienced soldier. On the underside of the plinth he stands on are listed all the places he served in. Amid so many exotic names 'Gravesend' seems slightly bathetic. The sculptor, Hamo Thornycroft – one of the Thornycrofts already referred to – seems to have known about the two sides of Gordon's nature, since he shows him with a cane under his arm and a Bible in his hand. The statue was commissioned after Gordon's death at the hands of the forces of the Mahdi during the siege of Khartoum. The column which should have relieved him arrived late, Gordon was killed, the Government was blamed, and the General became a national hero. Recent biographies have suggested that his end was due as much to his own death-wish as to the actions of the Mahdi, but then the first task of modern historians seems always to be the debunking of recent heroes. Gordon's statue can go on standing in Victoria Embankment Gardens, secure in the knowledge that it is a tribute to a very brave man.

A little farther on, on the Embankment wall, we are back to the Royal Air Force. This memorial, which was designed by Sir Reginald Blomfield and Sir William Reid Dick, was put up in 1932. There is very little that can be said about this memorial, and I don't intend saying it.

To be quite frank, this walk through the near-paradise gardens of Victoria Embankment owes as much to the flowers as it does to the figures, since not many of them are all that distinguished. But one in particular has always struck me as magnificent in its arrogance. Up towards the Charing Cross dungeon, where the road goes under the railway and the dregs of society find themselves huddled in the small hours, is what must be the biggest statue in this whole pleasant stretch. In the middle of a circular plot, which rises in a flat cone from the circumference to the centre, is a pedestal. On the pedestal there is a plinth. On the plinth is a figure decidedly larger than life-sized. And on the pedestal, this word appears: 'Outram'. Nothing else. Not one word of explanation. The implication is quite clear. Outram must have thought himself, or have been thought by society, to be so famous that his reputation would be imperishable. I have news for him. Like most reputations, it wasn't. But if you are interested enough to know who was this unforgettable giant of a man, the man to whom this giant of a statue has been erected, I will tell you. He was General Sir James Outram, who went with Sir Henry Havelock to the relief of Lucknow. One dictionary of biography says that he will always be remembered for 'his expedition up the Gumtri'. I have a feeling there's a misprint there. If not, the Goons should have heard of him. He would have made a wonderful companion for Col. Grytpyppe-Thynne.

Pass under Charing Cross railway bridge. In the next section of the Gardens is a wonderfully bizarre coupling of statues. Robert Burns, as the world knows, was fond of a dram or eight. His statue by Sir John Steel, stands, for some reason, next to that of Sir Wilfrid Lawson, by David McGill. Since Lawson was a temperance enthusiast (why is total abstinence so often called 'temperance', I wonder?) and his statue is surrounded by four figures called Temperance, Peace, Fortitude and Charity, that is perhaps why Burns is depicted with his eyes closed, as if the very sight of all that moral rectitude was too much for him. Either that, or he is in a drunken sleep.

A much more appropriate coupling appears in the Gardens. Near Charing Cross pier there is a medallion to Sir William Schwenck Gilbert. A little further along is a bust to his colleague, Sir Arthur Sullivan, with the inscription 'Is life a boon?', a line of Fairfax's in *Yeoman of the Guard*. Both medallion and bust are most suitably placed, since this particular stretch of the Gardens runs along the foot of the Savoy. It was in the Savoy Theatre, from 1881 onwards, that Gilbert and Sullivan presented most, and certainly the finest, of their comic operas. The British, or particularly the English, have never really given these two brilliant men their proper due. Gilbert's words, and Sullivan's music, are frequently as good as, and often much better than, contemporary Continental operettas, but you wouldn't think so to judge by some English reaction. If it's foreign music it must be better music seems to be the thinking. Rubbish! Lie back and think of Britten.

The Victoria Embankment Gardens statuary does not, as a rule, go in for undue modesty. The statues are usually larger than life, the achievements of the subjects are usually billed as only a little less than world shattering, and we are generally invited to agree with the sentiment that the millennium is a damn sight nearer as a result of their efforts. It is, therefore, nice to find that the man who was responsible for the Gardens, Sir Joseph Bazalgette, whose tremendous idea of an intercepting sewer which simultaneously cleaned up the Thames and created the land on which these gardens and the Embankment road could be built, has perhaps the smallest of all the memorials the Gardens contain. You will find, with some difficulty, a bronze mural set into the wall at the bottom of Northumberland Avenue. Perhaps the thinking is that, as with Sir Christopher Wren and St Paul's, if you want his memorial, look around you: 'Si monumentum requiris, circumspice.'

If you now walk up Northumberland Avenue to Trafalgar Square, a left incline at the top brings you to the famous equestrian statue of King Charles I. Its history is a little more exciting than that of most other London statues. It was cast in 1633, and erected soon afterwards. During the Commonwealth which followed Charles's execution, it was taken down and sold to a brazier with the appropriate name of Rivett. The idea was that it should be melted down. As the ingenious Rivett made a small fortune out of selling knives supposedly made from the metal, Cromwell's supporters had good reason to suppose their instructions had been obeyed, even though they may not have liked the idea of relics of the king being put on sale and bought so eagerly. It turned out that Rivett had been deceiving both the purchasers of his knives and the Cromwellians. He had hidden the statue in his garden – it must have been a big garden, or else he had dug a very deep hole in it – with the result that he was able to produce it at the Restoration in 1660. This inspired Edmund Waller, the turncoat poet, to write:

> That the First Charles does here in triumph ride:
> See his son reign, where he a martyr died;
> And people pay that reverence, as they pass
> (Which then he wanted) to the sacred brass;
> Is not the effect of gratitude alone
> To which we owe the statue and the stone.
> But heaven this lasting monument has wrought,
> That mortals may eternally be taught,
> Rebellion, though successful, is but vain:
> And kings, so killed, rise conquerors again.
> This truth the royal image does proclaim,
> Loud as the trumpet of surviving fame.

Not a word, you will see, about the resourcefulness of the ingenious Rivett. But then poets are notoriously disinclined to be factually accurate.

Just in front of the King Charles statue, at which, by the way, members of the Royal Stuart Society lay wreaths each year on 30 January, the anniversary of the king's execution, there is a plaque telling us that here stood the last Eleanor Cross. The Eleanor in question was the wife of Edward I; she died in Nottinghamshire in 1290. Her devoted husband brought the body back to London, later building a cross at each spot where the cortége had rested overnight. The Charing cross marked her last resting place before the final short trip down to Westminster. The Cromwellians had a go at this one, too, smashing it as an idolatrous object. These days it would be called vandalism, and psychiatrists would be called in to investigate the reasons for their behaviour. The cross now standing in front of Charing Cross station is a replica, designed in 1863 by Edward Middleton Barry, the son of the man who built the Houses of Parliament after the disastrous fire of 1834. The sculptor was Thomas Earp: I find it mildly interesting that the cross was commissioned by the London, Chatham and Dover Railway Company, whose connection with Eleanor of Castile can only have been marginal.

It would require more than perversity to ignore one other statue in Trafalgar Square: it would require stone blindness. Horatio, Viscount Nelson, Duke of Bronte (and I bet you didn't know that) stands 17 ft 4½ in. high, on a fluted column of Devon granite so tall that the pigeons who perch on the admiral's hat are 184 ft 10 in. above ground level. The statue's sculptor was Edward Hodges Baily; the Corinthian column was the work of William Railton; and the bronze lions are by Sir Edwin Landseer, as well known for them as he is for 'The Monarch of the Glen'. It is a fascinating insight into the British love of urgency to reflect that, although the Battle of Trafalgar took place on 21 October 1805, the statue wasn't hauled into place until 1843, and the Landseer lions weren't coaxed into position for another twenty-three years. Mañana is another day. And, again typically British, the lions, the column, and the statue were all condemned at the time for their general ugliness, lack of taste, and, in the case of the statue, what *The Spectator* magazine called 'a daring disregard of personal resemblance'. The whole edifice is now probably the best-known statue in the world, and, yes, I have heard of the Statue of Liberty.

Before you leave Trafalgar Square, take a look at the busts of the three admirals set in the wall of the terrace overlooking the Square in front of the National Gallery. One of them, that of Lord Cunningham, C-in-C Mediterranean during the Second World War, promoted to First Sea Lord in 1943, is naturally a recent one – actually 1967, and by Franta Belsky. The other two – John Rushworth, Earl Jellicoe (by William Macmillan) and Lord Beatty (by Sir Charles Wheeler) – are reminders of the First World War, in which Jellicoe's name is associated with the Battle of Jutland in 1916, and Beatty's with the surrender of the German Grand Fleet at Scapa Flow in 1918. Since neither admiral was particularly fond of the other it is perhaps appropriate that they seem to be deliberately looking in opposite directions. The story that they have been slowly turning further and further away from each other as the years go by is probably no more true than the story, mentioned earlier, of the behaviour of Lord Trenchard's statue in Victoria Embankment Gardens.

Two more Trafalgar Square statues: the first is considered a success, the second a disaster. In front of the National Gallery is an equestrian statue of James II, a king not normally thought of as particularly heroic, although he did sterling work during the Fire of London, fetching and carrying with the best. It is as well he is mounted on a horse, for he has done quite a bit of moving about since he was first carved. Erected initially in Priory Gardens, he was then shifted to the middle of Whitehall. Tiring of this location, His Majesty then galloped off to the forecourt of the Admiralty, and finally he came to rest on his present site. The sculptor was Grinling Gibbons, in the time he could spare from decorating such great houses as Chatsworth, Burghley and Petworth. I am not quite sure why James is dressed as a Roman, except that it was the fashion of the time to depict celebrities wrapped round in completely unsuitable accoutrements. Since it has been described as the finest outdoor statue in London, I suppose neither the shade of the king nor his creator are very much bothered.

Only a few yards away, on an island in front of the National Portrait Gallery, is a statue of Nurse Edith Cavell, who was shot in 1915 by the Germans for alleged spying and for her work in procuring the escape through Belgium of many First World War British prisoners. The famous words 'Patriotism is not enough' were added four years after Queen Alexandra unveiled the statue in 1920. It could apply to the inspiration for the design as well: the *Dictionary of National Biography* describes it as 'one of Frampton's most conspicuous failures', the Frampton in question being Sir George Frampton, whose other perhaps less conspicuous failures include the Peter Pan memorial in Kensington Gardens, of which more later.

From the Cavell island in St Martin's Place it is only a few yards, by way of Irving Street (note the statue of Sir Henry Irving, the first theatrical knight, on your way), to Leicester Square. Leicester Square, particularly at night and at weekends, is a disgrace to any capital city, with its drunks, meths drinkers, pimps, whores, garishly vulgar advertising on the cinemas, and as graceless a collection of litter as can be found in any public place in London. It is therefore ironic, if not downright tragic, that Leicester Square is the place where we honour five of the greatest names in British history: Shakespeare (a copy of the bust in Westminster Abbey); Sir Joshua Reynolds; William Hogarth; Sir Isaac Newton; and William Hunter, the famous physiologist and brother of the even more famous John Hunter, the founder of modern surgery. None of the statues is of any great power, but in an odd way they all gain dignity from a comparison with the squalor of their surroundings.

If you think you can stand some more squalor, walk along Coventry Street to Piccadilly Circus. The Circus is appalling. What was once called the hub of the Empire now resembles nothing more than the hub of a rusting and broken bicycle wheel. Entirely surrounded by railings apparently chosen specially for their ugliness, it is a jumble of traffic; of pedestrians; of drug addicts waiting for midnight so they can rush into Boot's all-night chemist for their first fix of the day; of litter; of all the detritus of a modern city. In the centre is a statue which once vied with the Nelson Column for the title of the best-known statue in the world. For film producers and directors it was the one picture which said, without the need for super-ed sub-titles, 'This is London'. I refer, of course, to the statue known to just about everybody as 'Eros'. In fact, its real name is the Shaftesbury Memorial, after the 7th Earl of Shaftesbury, the famous philanthropist. There is a story, which I rather like, that the statue, intended to represent the angel of Christian charity, is also a neat visual pun on the good Earl's name – the archer is about to bury the shaft somewhere. Be that as it may, Sir Alfred Gilbert's figure is world famous as Eros, and deservedly so. It is a miracle of balance and grace. Not that you'll get much chance to appreciate its virtues. Cut off from everybody, except those who choose to climb the railings and sit on the steps of the statue, eating their sandwiches and leaving the paper to flutter about, or, even more depressingly, just sit there doing nothing at all, poor Eros doesn't stand a chance. The intrusiveness of those ghastly guard rails makes any calm examination of Gilbert's work almost impossible. For years we have been told of plans to 'redevelop' Piccadilly Circus. For years we have been told that such plans would destroy the Circus's essential character. Looking at it now, in all its horror, aren't we entitled to ask – what essential character? Isn't Gilbert's famous and lovely statue worthy of a better setting than the one it has at present? I am not suggesting it should be moved. I am suggesting that something should be done about the Circus and done soon, before every single one of the millions of tourists who visit the city every year goes back home to tell the family that London is the lousiest, most squalid place ever seen. At present, I do not see how we could answer such a charge.

Working on the assumption that you will now be in need of something a little more satisfying aesthetically, I suggest you stroll down Haymarket (not *the* Haymarket, please: men have been hanged for less), to Pall Mall. Here at least some elegance has been preserved.

For example: at the bottom of Haymarket, turn right.

154

Within seconds you will come to the bottom of Lower Regent Street. Ahead of you is the declining club-land of Pall Mall. To your left – and to your right – is an assemblage of statuary the like of which you have never seen before.

First, look to the left. That is not Nelson's Column. It is a column on which stands a Duke of York. No. Let us not be mealy-mouthed. It is *the* Duke of York. Of course you know the one:

> The grand old Duke of York,
> He had ten thousand men,
> He marched them up to the top of the hill,
> And he marched them down again.
> And when they were up, they were up,
> And when they were down, they were down,
> And when they were only half way up,
> They were neither up nor down.

You must admit he looks splendid on top of that column – the column on top of the St James's Steps, leading down from Pall Mall to *The* Mall, and across the green grass of the park to the winkle-picker towers of Whitehall.

There is only one slight snag. So bad was the Duke's reputation at one time that, when the statue was hoicked up to the top of its column, a lot of the wits of the town said he had only been put there to escape his creditors: when he wasn't leading his troops – either up or down – he was apparently trying to escape being dunned by importunate plebs and bourgeoisie, to whom he had given his Royal patronage and who now had the effrontery to demand payment for the services he had so encouragingly asked them to supply him with. This, by the way, was not the Duke of York who helped his brother, King Charles II, to fight the Great Fire of London, and then went on to become the short-reigning James II. This was a much later one. He was born in 1763, the second son of George III. Nobody could say he was brilliant, but it is quite definitely posible to say that, without him, the Battle of Waterloo would not have been won, because he pushed through a lot of much-needed Army reforms. That meant he bequeathed to Wellington (wrong word: he didn't die until twelve years after Waterloo, but I'm sure you know what I mean) a splendidly-trained force for the Iron Duke to use whichever way he wished.

Here are some quite useless bits of information. The statue of the Duke is thirteen feet high and weighs around seven tons. It is carved out of Aberdeen granite, that mottled igneous rock bespecked with long lozenges ('phenocrysts') of pinkish felspar: hence the general colour of the rock and the column.

The only way to get up to His Grace is by means of a spiral staircase of 169 steps. Do not worry. The public have no access to it. The monument cost £30,000 and was paid for by a voluntary/compulsory deduction of one day's pay from every officer and other rank in the Army. They called him 'The Soldiers' Friend'. He either was, or they were being sarcastic.

Come back away from the Duke of York Steps and look at what there is to see in the rectangle which has, as its two axes, Lower Regent Street and Pall Mall. There is not much point in suggesting that you should start at any particular point. The assembled statuaries are there, ranged all around you. Let me remind you of what they are, and you can choose for yourself what you want to see and which way you go about seeing it.

If size is your criterion, you have no option. You will *have* to start with the Guards Monument. It dates from 1859, and it commemorates the 22,162 guardsmen who died in the Crimean War. The official wording is 'fell' in that war; but as at least half of them died from diseases contracted after they had been brought into the hospitals, or diseases which, contracted before they entered the hospitals, could nevertheless not be treated once they *were* inside, I personally prefer the word 'died', which is what they did anyway.

What about Captain Robert Falcon Scott, Scott of the Antarctic? He is there, too. The statue was presented by brother officers of the Royal Navy in 1915, just three years after Scott's attempt to get to the South Pole before anybody else. Unfortunately, the Norwegian Amundsen beat him to it, and Scott and his companions died on the way back. He is shown in the statue dressed for the expedition, with ski-sticks in his hands. I would be the first to admire his courage,

156

since I do not think there is any consideration which would make me do what Scott did. I would also be the first to say that, as far as fact can be established, the death of Scott and his companions was to some extent due to Scott's own inelasticity of mind and his refusal to consider any opinions other than his own. I could, however, be wrong. I hope I am.

Perhaps the Scott-ian highmindedness is too much for you. Then what about Florence Nightingale? Her motives must have been pure? Not if modern biographers are to be believed. But who the hell believes *them*? If most modern biographers had done one-tenth as much as the people they seem to be pillorying, I would read a few more of their books.

The serried ranks of renown are so deep here that you will have some difficulty in choosing your favourite statuary hero or heroine or, come to that, your favourite anti-hero or anti-heroine. I would like to offer you two I have always liked.

You will see, if you do but seek, a statue to Sir John Burgoyne, a soldier of some repute. Why I like him is that he was a brave man; he was with Wellington in the Peninsular War and fought at the sieges of Badajoz and Ciudad Rodrigo. Tiring of the Iberian Peninsula, he then moved on to the Crimean Peninsula, where he seems to have sentenced fewer British troops to death by lunatic orders than some of his colleagues. I also like the fact that this man was the natural, i.e. illegitimate, son of Gentleman Johnny Burgoyne, whom G.B.S. portrays so sympathetically in *The Devil's Disciple*, and the opera singer Susan Caulfield. Anybody who can be the brave, uncomplaining, bastard son of a British general and an opera singer has got me on his side from the start. The statue, by the way, is by Sir Joseph Edgar Boehm.

The other Pall Mall-ish statue I like is that of George Nathaniel Curzon, first Marquis Curzon of Kedleston. A typical working-class boy – born in Kedleston Hall, Derbyshire; educated at Eton; and then just failed to take a first in Classics at Oxford – he nevertheless managed to become a Fellow of All Souls. This may have turned him into, or perhaps he already was, the most pompous man in Britain.

I particularly like three stories about him. The first tells how, visiting troops in Flanders in the First World War, he saw a group of them sitting in a trench, eating a can of plum and apple jam. Using a word popular at the time, a word synonymous with 'celebration', he said to them 'Ah, having a little beano, are we?'. The reason the weary soldiery looked at him in bewilderment is because he pronounced it in the Italian way, 'Bay-ahno'. When he saw a group of officers and men swimming together in the nude, enjoying their first bathe for months, he is reported to have been surprised that, without their uniforms, you couldn't tell the officers from the men. And the third story is the famous one about the bus. He had been arguing in his club about omnibuses. Somebody suggested that, since he had never been on a bus in his life, he knew nothing about them. George Nathaniel Curzon snorted, leapt up, went out, flagged down a bus with his umbrella, and said to the conductor: 'Take me to the Foreign Office.'

Although he was made Viceroy of India when he was only thirty-nine, and subsequently became Foreign Secretary, he remained, to the end of his life, severely shaken by the fact that he was passed over for the Prime Ministership when Bonar Law died in 1923. His parliamentary manner was likened to 'Divinity addressing black beetles', and his belief in his own infallibility probably surpassed that of the Pope. He was, however, an enormously talented and energetic statesman, and deserves his statue.

If you now walk along Pall Mall you will find, on the right-hand side, a street leading up to St James's Square. In the centre of the square is a statue of William III. He it was who took over after the expulsion of James II; he it was who died when his horse tripped over a molehill in Hampton Court. That is why Jacobite supporters (those who adhered to the exiled Stuarts, James Edward, the Old Pretender, and Charles Edward, the Young Pretender, Bonny Prince Charlie), used to raise their glasses to the mole that killed him, and toast 'the little gentleman in black velvet', and that is also why the statue is shown with a molehill under the horse's hooves.

I do not know how your hooves are feeling after all this walking, but if you are still in the mood for more, make your way up to Piccadilly and turn west towards Hyde Park Corner. Opposite Apsley House, known as Number

One, London, because it was the first house inside the Hyde Park turnpike gate, is a statue to the man who used to live there. the Duke of Wellington, the Iron Duke, victor of Waterloo. He is on his famous horse, Copenhagen, a horse so famous that, when it died, it was buried with full military honours.

The nearby statue of David leaning on Goliath's sword is in honour of the men of the Machine Gun Corps who died in the First World War. The inscription is horrifyingly frank and seems to be glorifying slaughter: 'Saul has slain his thousands but David his tens of thousands.'

Negotiate the insane traffic of Hyde Park Corner by means of the underpass and go into Hyde Park. Over on the left you will see a huge bronze statue known as Achilles. This was intended as a tribute to the Iron Duke and was erected in 1822, seven years after Waterloo. It cost £10,000 and was paid for by contributions from the women of England. When it was unveiled they were shocked – or delighted, I know not which – at its larger-than-life nakedness, and a fig leaf had to be added before it was considered fit for ladies to look at. The figure, by the way, is a copy of one of the horsemen on the Monte Cavallo in Rome.

Two or three more statues, all of them in or around Hyde Park and Kensington Gardens, and we are done.

Keeping to the Hyde Park grass, to avoid the fumes of the roaring traffic, make northwards to Marble Arch. This great arch has a delightfully bizarre history. It was designed by no less a person than the great John Nash himself, as the main entrance to Buckingham Palace. It was erected in 1828, when it was soon discovered that it was extremely difficult, if not impossible, to manoeuvre the state coach through it, so in 1851 it was moved to its present site. I find the idea that Nash designed it without considering the width of what had to go through it, rather comforting. Even Homer can nod.

Along the Bayswater Road now (still that intrusive 'the'), and then turn into the Park by the Victoria Gate – no, on second thoughts, why walk on hard pavements when you can walk on soft grass? So make your way through the Park, parallel with the Bayswater Road. Between you and the Serpentine you will come across the 'Rima' statue by Jacob

Epstein. It is in honour of W.H. Hudson, the famous naturalist, and is now surrounded, entirely appropriately, by a bird sanctuary. Fashion is a funny thing. Just as I cannot understand how the clubmen of old Vienna hated the new-fangled music of Mozart, equally I cannot understand how anybody could be so upset by 'Rima' that they wanted to tar and feather the statue: but they did, and several times. People are funny peculiar.

In the summer of 1978 a new and wonderful exhibition took place in Hyde Park, an outdoor exhibition of some of the work of Britain's most famous sculptor, Henry Moore. There is a campaign afoot to keep some of these sculptures on permanent exhibition here. Their strong and primitive shapes can be seen from slopes near the Serpentine. Visitors should not miss them at any cost. Incidentally, some of Henry Moore's work can also be seen in Battersea Park, and there is an interesting collection of modern sculpture sited near the Achilles statue already mentioned.

Make your way along to the ornamental gardens at the head of the Long Water, which is the name given to the northern end of that salubrious stretch called the Serpentine. When you've rested there, and it really is very pleasant (incidentally, there's a statue here, too: it is to Edward Jenner, pioneer in vaccination against smallpox. The obelisk opposite is to the memory of John Hanning Speke, who discovered the source of the Nile), you can make your way along the waterside path to one of London's most famous statues.

'Peter Pan', by Sir George Frampton, was actually commissioned by the author of the play, Sir James Barrie himself. He had it erected here by means of a private fiddle with the Commissioner of Works, and questions were asked in Parliament. The statue had, however, become so popular with children, so quickly, that the matter was allowed to drop. I find it a dreadfully sticky piece of *art nouveau*, but Frampton didn't make it with me in mind. If you want to see just how popular it is with children, look at the ears of the rabbits – polished smooth by the stroking of millions of little hands.

Incidentally, while you are in Kensington Gardens, and

while we are on the subject of children, you might as well walk across to the north-west corner and look at the Elfin Oak. It was originally carved from a tree trunk in 1930 but suffered some wear and tear, not all of it fair, over the years. It is now refurbished. A plaque says the fairies did it, but I, and a lot of other people, have a shrewd suspicion that they got a deal of help from the comedian and scriptwriter, Spike Milligan, whose devotion to causes such as this is an indication of the essential kindness of the man. You'll find the Elfin Oak by the side of the Broad Walk, which is useful, because that's where we're going now to our last statue.

Go right down to the bottom of Broad Walk and turn left, i.e. east. Make your way along the Flower Walk, always a pleasant stroll. You will pass the Albert Memorial, which I have touched on in another chapter. I would not be surprised if (a) you felt compelled to avert your gaze, or (b) burst into wild laughter. I have, in the past, indulged in both reactions. Carry on straight ahead. As you approach the bulk of the Hyde Park Hotel, not far from Albert Gate, you will see, coming in from Knightsbridge, an opening which is flanked by more Epstein. This is his 'Family of Man'. I find it hard to imagine that there are people who cannot feel the force of this composition – compositions, really, since there is a group on either side of the road. A man, his wife, their child, and a leaping, straining hound; and very powerful, too. Look at the bottled-up energy until you feel tired, and then heave a sigh of relief, for you have finished my round of London statues.

What I have described is, of course, merely a fraction, and a very tiny fraction at that, of what London has to offer in the way of free outdoor statuary attractions. Don't just look at those I have written about. Use your eyes. Make your own selection of what pleases you. The ones I have picked are merely those in Central London, and only on the north bank of the river at that. So go ahead and draw up your own list.

Don't think, by the way, that you can only go statue-hunting in summer. See them also against bare branches, with a cap of snow on their heads: under such circumstances I will swear that each statue puts on a lugubrious expression especially to show you how miserable it is feeling. I do not believe that London's statues are static, preserved for ever in one position. I believe that, like the Stone Guest in *Don Giovanni*, they are capable of movement when the occasion demands it.

Whether they are or not, however, they are well worth looking at. American visitors might like to look at the bust of John F. Kennedy, at the point where the Euston Road becomes Marylebone Road. It is a bust where the sculptor seems to me to have failed signally to catch a likeness. South African visitors might like to look at the statue of Field-Marshal Smuts in Parliament Square. Lovers of Dickens might like to walk a couple of hundred yards farther along Marylebone Road from the Kennedy bust and see the mural carving in the porchway of Ferguson House. Visitors from...

You see. I could go on for ever. You must make your own decision about what else you would like to see. I have brought you to Hyde Park Corner after a tour that is probably far too long for you to have done in one day. It is up to you now to get back to your hotel or boarding house, get your feet up with a relaxing drink, and plan for tomorrow. Good luck and enjoy yourselves.

Ghosts

I've never been too sure about ghosts myself. Spirits I can believe in. What I can't believe in are their clothes. Ghostly doublet and hose, ghostly armour, ghostly stockings, even, I suppose, ghostly knickers and underpants. No, that I find hard to accept. This is, however, not a difficulty that worries a lot of other people. They believe in their ghosts and the clothes they see them in. As some of the believers happen to be friends of mine, to be well educated, to have fine minds, and to be not unduly credulous, I am forced to the conclusion that there may be something in it, even if I can't see it. After all, a blind man can't see things, but they undoubtedly exist.

I'm glad to have found that particular get-out, because it is an undoubted fact that London is just about the most haunted town in the world, and I don't see how it could be if there weren't such things as ghosts. I suppose one should have expected it anyway. As one of the oldest continuously-occupied centres of civilization, the place where deeds most dirty have been performed, where the sense of history is so strong it is sometimes almost tangible, London is clearly an odds-on favourite to be a spectral centre.

The George, opposite the Law Courts, is the pub whose half-timbered superstructure looks old but isn't, since the pub was rebuilt in the 1930s. But it was built on the site of a very much older establishment. One hot day, early for a Fleet Street appointment, I called in its cool depths for a beer. The landlord came over to me and, since I had just made a series of tv films about the ghosts of London, said 'You should have given our ghost a mention.' I explained that I didn't know they had one, and would he tell me all about it. He did, starting by saying that he himself had never seen it. 'But my wife has. Down in the cellar. And now she refuses ever to go down there again.' He explained that one day, just before morning opening, she went down to bring up a bottle or two of something they were short of in the bar. After a couple of minutes she came rushing back up, trembling with fear, and gasping that never again would she go down there. The landlord tried to calm her down, gave her a medicinal brandy, and asked her what she had seen. 'A man, standing in the far corner, under the barrel vaulting, just staring at me. He never moved and he never said anything. He just stared.' Her husband asked her what the man looked like. She had no hesitation: 'He was dressed like a Cavalier, pointed beard, ruff, and hat with a large feather.' The landlord wondered if anybody had slipped in while the doors had been opened to let in the fresh morning air, so he went down to have a look for himself. He saw nothing, though he did admit that he felt shivery. 'But whether that is because it was so cool in the cellar, or because of my imagination after what the wife had said, I don't know. Anyway, I saw nothing, and I actually went over to the corner where he'd been standing.' That corner, by the way, is now out under the street as a result of the widening of the Strand over the years.

I listened to the story politely, and then he sprung the twist on me.

164

'Three months ago, we were having the place redecorated. The painting gang arrived about nine o'clock in the morning, led by a Cockney foreman about six foot two or three and as broad as a barndoor. We talked about what had to be done, he set the men on their various jobs, and then announced that he would whitewash the cellar himself. He went up and down several times collecting his stuff together, and about half past ten he started work. About twenty minutes later – it would be exactly the same time my wife had seen it – he came rushing upstairs and said "You play fair with me, guv, and I'll play fair with you. Weren't you man enough to tell me?"' The landlord asked him what was the matter and he replied 'That feller down there. He just stared at me, didn't say anything, just stared.' The landlord remembered his wife's earlier phrase and said 'What did he look like?' The foreman thought for only a second. 'Historical. You know, like them Roundheads and Cavaliers. Anyway I'm going.' And he did. He rang up his employers, told them he had to leave the job for personal reasons, and went away in a panic, never to come back.

Well, naturally, after a story like that, you'd want to investigate, wouldn't you? So I did. The landlord took me down into the cellar and left me there, and I concentrated like mad, and actually went and stood where the ghost had appeared. I saw, and felt, exactly nothing. Perhaps it was the wrong time of the day. But I never pass The George now without looking at my watch and, if it is about quarter of an hour before opening time, wondering whether a Cavalier is standing in the cellar. Never moving. Never saying anything. Just staring.

About ten minutes' walk from The George, up Ludgate Hill, is Amen Court, a quiet place with a lovely name. (Do you know why? The fact that you get to it by way of Ave Maria Lane, and that opposite, on the other side of Ludgate Hill, is Creed Lane may give you a clue. They were all places where religious processions from St Paul's paused to say the appropriate words, the Creed in Creed Lane, the Ave Maria in the lane of that name and the Amen at the corner of this quiet oasis in the shadow of the great cathedral.) Jack Hallam, in his book *Ghosts of London*, (Wolfe, 1975), says it is haunted by a black shape, which might have been a dog or a cat. It usually appeared just at the time of the executions taking place outside the Newgate Prison which used to be on the other side of that great old stone wall which marks the boundary of Amen Court. Hallam tells of a clergyman who saw such a shape crawling along the top of that wall in 1948. He could not tell whether it was a cat or a dog. A cat seems more likely, since dogs aren't noted for walking along wall tops, and some clergymen have been known to be short-sighted.

The tradition of a sinister black shape crawling around the area goes back at least to the seventeenth century, so it seemed worth while to take a tv film crew to Amen Court in 1975 and see what happened. I started to tell the story with the wall in the background and then moved to a tree springing from the lawn, chosen because it had a gallows-like shape of branches that made a nice, spooky shot. Close-up on the branches, my doom-laden voice recounting the grisly details, zoom back to reveal me in front of the tree, and a slight shiver down the spine as I got to the black shape. Everything worked perfectly first time off. Better than we had expected – in fact much better. For when I got to the words 'a sinister black shape' a huge black cat came from nowhere, slid into the centre of the shot just in front of me, crouched, bared its teeth at both the camera and me, spat ferociously at us, and disappeared as alarmingly as it had appeared. I'm not saying it was a ghost: I'm not saying it wasn't. I'm merely saying that it doesn't do to take these stories of hauntings too lightly.

One who did take them lightly lived only a few yards away, in Dean's Court on the other side of Ludgate Hill. He was the Very Rev. Martin Sullivan, Dean of St Paul's until his retirement in September 1977. The Dean, a lovely, earthy little New Zealander, had often been told his deanery, a splendid eighteenth-century building, was haunted, but it didn't worry him. The strange creaks, he told me, were because the building was so old: the bumps in the night were because the central heating was getting on a bit, too. But he confessed to being slightly baffled by a toilet-roll holder, which seemed deliberately to go wonky when anybody else looked at it, but which was always in order again by the time they called the Dean to fix it. 'Baffling' the Dean said, in his New Zealand accent. 'But since I can't conceive of a haunted toilet-roll holder, I can only put it down to my *flyming* lack of skill at do-it-yourself.'

Just down from the deanery is the old church of St Andrew-by-the-Wardrobe, so called because the king's ceremonial costumes were kept in Wardrobe Court until the Great Fire. St Andrew's has a most peculiar ghost. It is a bell named Gabriel, and it now rests in the church vestibule. According to Hallam, it once hung in the belfry of the village church of Avenbury in Herefordshire, where it would ring, with nobody pulling it, whenever the rector of the parish died. This was clearly a habit-forming practice, because when Gabriel came to London in 1937, and was hung in the St Andrew belfry, he twice rang out over the City rooftops of his own accord. On each occasion they found that the rector of Avenbury – which is 150 miles from London – had died that very day. It could have been the strain of haunting at such a distance that caused Gabriel to crack, which is why he now rests inside the church door, presumably to haunt no more.

One snag about this story is that the Post Office Gazetteer doesn't record any Herefordshire village called Avenbury (there is one, though: near Bromyard: population 303). It doesn't matter. St Andrew-by-the-Wardrobe is a very lovely church and Wardrobe Court is one of those places where you feel you have slipped back through the centuries. Cobbled stones, plane trees, ancient windows, and a total absence of noise, although you are, in fact, only 100 yards from the traffic of Ludgate Hill to the north and literally only ten yards from Queen Victoria Street to the south. So enjoy the silence, and if you do hear the cracked tones of Gabriel ringing out above you, you will know there are more mysteries in heaven and earth, Horatio, than are dreamt of in your philosophy, as Hamlet said on a somewhat similar occasion.

Walk down the steps of St Andrew-by-the-Wardrobe and you will be in Queen Victoria Street. As it is a very ugly street you will wish to be soon rid of it. You can do that very easily by crossing over and getting yourself on to Upper Thames Street, which runs parallel with the river. The whole area hereabouts smells of trade. Not trade as business, but trade

167

as trade. Here is the vintners' quarter. Here is the fur traders' quarter (they've been there since the days of the charter for the Hudson Bay Company, so let's have a bit of respect); and other trades too smelly to mention. The one thing you won't smell there is garlic, which is odd, since our next stop is Garlick Hill. Obviously, some centuries ago this was a hill once covered with that beautiful white flower, the wild garlic (did you know that, far from being a beastly foreign herb, garlic was once known as 'the English vegetable'?).

At the bottom of Garlick Hill stands the church of St James, with the full name of St James's Garlickhythe, hythe merely meaning a quay. Here you are in for a treat, because this is a place where, although there may be no ghost, there most certainly is a body. He's called Jimmy and he is a mummy.

Nobody knows just how old Jimmy is. The church was built in the early fourteenth century, so he could date from that era himself. They found him when they were doing some work in the churchyard; they put him in a glass-fronted coffin in the vestibule of the church; and they attached a sombre cautionary verse to him:

> Stop stranger, stop as you pass by.
> As you are now, so once was I.
> As I am now, you soon will be.
> So pray prepare to follow me.

While not exactly handsome, Jimmy looks mild enough, which makes it odd that he should want to go haunting the place. He only seems to have started the practice since a bomb fell on the church in the Second World War, perhaps giving him a nasty turn. He is said to have been seen in the nave, and on one occasion, Hallam reports, an American boy, touring the church in the company of his mother and younger brother, looked up and saw a dried-up corpse standing at the head of the stairs leading from the vestibule. The boy is said to have noted that it was wrapped in a shroud and had its hands folded 'mummy-like' across its chest. It isn't reported whether Old Jimmy was still in his cupboard at the time. If he was, then presumably he wasn't doing the haunting; that may mean St James Garlickhythe has two ghosts, which seems a trifle greedy, even for so old a church.

When I filmed Jimmy Garlickhythe in 1975 the minister told me that he had never seen any hauntings, except being haunted by tourists who came to look at the old boy. So many, in fact, that they were going to put him underground once more. But I'm sure that, if you ask, they'll let you see him down in the crypt. If not, spare the time to look at the church. It is a beauty by Sir Christopher Wren, who built it after the fourteenth-century original had been destroyed in the Great Fire. Damaged during the Blitz, it has now been completely, and superbly, restored. And if you do happen to see the ghost of Old Jimmy – or any other mummy, come to that – you might like to show your gratitude by dropping a coin or two in the box placed there to help the upkeep of this lovely church.

The two Thames Streets, Upper and Lower, make a bee-line for the Tower of London. If it's ghosts you are after, this is the place for you. You've got your pick of hundreds. As the scene of executions for many centuries, you can hardly move without bumping into (well, walking through) one. I doubt, though, whether you'll see any. Very few ever have during daytime, even though, with about 15,000 people a day passing through, you might have thought there would have been one or two among them sensitive enough to make a sighting. But the Tower of London ghosts only seem to appear after dusk, when the Tower is locked up against visitors. Why this should be so, when other London ghosts pop up at any time of day or night, has never been explained.

I do not recommend, however, that you therefore make fun of the Tower ghosts. The inhabitants of the place have always taken a strong line with those who offend. They have incarcerated them, decapitated them, and even bitten them. Bitten? Yes. The story is told that in the 1930s a Nazi Minister was being taken round on tour. When he heard the old saying that the British Empire would never disappear until the ravens left the Tower, he laughed and said 'In Germany we have eagles'. Whereupon one of the ravens bit him. A thought occurs to me: the ravens are still there, but whatever happened to the British Empire?

Lady Jane Grey seems to be the favourite Tower ghost.

169

Quite a lot of people say they have seen her, although one or two didn't actually recognize her at the time, and had to be told who she was by that splendid man, my old friend James Wentworth Day, in a letter to the London *Evening News* at the end of August 1970. Jack Hallam tells two separate and fairly recent stories about sentries on duty in the Tower at night seeing her. One of them actually had his attention drawn to her by the stones she threw at the top of his sentry-box from the battlements above. As it happened to be 3 a.m. on the morning of 12 February 1957, the 403rd anniversary of the execution of Lady Jane Grey, Mr Hallam naturally assumed it was her ghost – 'a strange white apparition with no shape' which was seen at the same time by another soldier on sentry-go. That ghosts can do strange things to people is shown by the second incident, quoted by Hallam from Col. E. H. Carkeet James's book *His Majesty's Tower of London*. It concerns an officer 'in the pink of condition and stone sober' who had an unnerving experience at the Bloody Tower gate, so unnerving, in fact, that 'a few seconds' later he found himself on the steps of his mess, soaked in sweat and remembering nothing of his terrified sprint. The Colonel tells us the officer was training for the Olympic Games. It seems an unnecessary piece of information. The mess steps are 300 yards from the Bloody Tower gate. Anybody who can cover that distance in a 'few seconds' is clearly no mean athlete.

But if Lady Jane Grey is not to your taste, try some others: Anne Boleyn; Margaret, Countess of Salisbury; a procession of phantoms carrying a stretcher, with a headless man on it, the head being neatly tucked underneath his arm. Other soldiers have seen the ghost of a bear (the Royal menagerie used to be kept in the Tower); a long-dead Duke of Northumberland; Catherine Howard, Henry VIII's fifth wife; Guy Fawkes; My Lords Essex, Hastings, and Dudley; and the Little Princes in the Tower, who disappeared so mysteriously in the reign of Richard III. You can hardly deny there is something there for everybody's taste.

But let me remind you that precious few ever show themselves in daylight. Maybe it's because they are all very English ghosts and the tourists who throng the Tower are mainly very foreign. But whatever the reason, you can't help enjoying a visit to the Tower of London, ghosts or no ghosts. So try it and see what happens. And if you do encounter anything a bit spooky, let me know, will you?

Since all that history can be a bit dusty, you might find you need a drink or two to wash the dust away. I have just the place for you: a haunted pub and not all that far from the Tower, either. It is the Nag's Head, in Hackney Road, roughly midway between Shoreditch and Bethnal Green tube stations. This is a biggish pub, which goes in for a lot of pop music, and rather loud with it, so you may want to wear earplugs or else want to give this particular spectre a miss. But if the noise doesn't put you off you may see something to shorten your breath and make your hackles stand on end, and I'm not talking about the very attractive landlady. The pub is haunted by the ghost of an old woman, probably unable to sleep because of the music. She wears a long grey skirt and a black shawl over her head and is said to have frightened a cellarman out of his mind when he turned round and found her looking over his shoulder. Filming there in 1975, I felt no awareness of a presence, although the cellars are spooky enough, since this is the oldest building in Hackney. I was standing outside in Hackney Road, delivering a short speech to camera when, at the precise moment I got to the words 'Old woman' etc., a shrivelled old creature wearing a long grey skirt and a black shawl came shuffling across the shot, and cursed us all roundly. As I've said before, it doesn't do to be too sceptical about London's ghosts: some of them could be listening to you with malice aforethought.

Perhaps while we're in the East End we should investigate the Vicar of Ratcliff Wharf. No, on second thoughts, not just yet. It might have an unfortunate effect on you. So let us catch the underground back to Central London. The most convenient station is Covent Garden because there'll you'll get two ghosts for the price of one. The first one couldn't be handier: it's actually the station itself that's haunted. Jack Hallam, in his invaluable if slightly unsceptical book, tells us the ghost is that of William Terriss. It is certainly true that this star of Victorian stage was murdered one night in 1897 as he made his way to the Adelphi Theatre. The murderer was a fellow actor – with colleagues like that, who needs enemies? – who was arrested for the crime, found to be guilty but insane, and went to Broadmoor.

The reason Terriss haunts the station, rather than the theatre outside the stage door of which he was stabbed to death, is apparently because he used to travel from his Putney home to Covent Garden station every night, alight there, and stroll through the narrow alleys of the area down to the Adelphi Theatre in the Strand. Why a ghost should haunt a draughty underground station rather than the comparative warmth of a successful West End theatre is something we shall never know until we meet the late Mr Terriss and ask him. In any case, he does dodge into the theatre from time to time: he was seen there in the sixties. Mostly, however, he reserves his manifestations for Covent Garden station. There he has been seen many times, always dressed in the same grey suit, white gloves, and a curly-brimmed hat. The suit must be in need of a pressing by now, the gloves in need of a scrubbing, and the hat in need of a brushing. But maybe ghostly clothes never get dirty.

Once you've had your fill of Covent Garden station, which could be quite quickly, it is no more than a couple of minutes' walk to our next theatrical ghost. The Theatre Royal, Drury Lane, must be one of the most famous theatres in the world. It is also one of the most haunted. The reports on its ghost go back many years and come from many sorts of people: what other ghost can claim to have been seen by the entire cast of a musical, Ivor Novello's *The Dancing Years*? That was in 1939. He is known as the Man in Grey, and is the ghost of an eighteenth-century dandy who was stabbed to death in a brawl over a girl the manager of the theatre had taken a fancy to. His body was then walled up in the theatre to avoid the consequences of the murder. At least that is the theory. And, certainly, a body with a knife between its ribs was discovered when the theatre was being altered in the nineteenth century. This young gentleman wears a long grey riding cloak, knee-breeches and buckled shoes, a curled wig and a three-cornered hat, and he seems to be very friendly, since he makes a habit of turning up on the first nights of what later prove to be long-running shows. If you want to meet him, choose your first night, and book the first seat in the fourth row of the upper circle. As that is his seat, you may have company.

I think you are now in the right mood for my old friend, the Vicar of Ratcliff Wharf. This is a wharf down in Limehouse, off Narrow Street, a street which runs parallel with the Thames just before it makes that great sweep south to enfold the Isle of Dogs. The Vicar is an eighteenth-century ghost: his dress makes that clear. In his gaiters, his black coat, his white neck-stock, his flat clerical hat, his long hair, his crouch and his old walking stick, he is obviously a figure from a bygone age. Jack Hallam's theory, based on a study of the reports in *Man, Myth, and Magic* (a part-work produced by Phoebus Publishing Co. Ltd) is that he is the ghost of a vicar who used, with the help of buxom serving wenches, to lure sailors newly come ashore to a fairly sticky end, the object of the exercise being to get his hands on their doubtless bulging paying-off purses. There are many accounts of his appearances – and disappearances when approached – and all of them took place in broad daylight. Every one of them is given chapter and verse, including the names, ages and occupations of those who saw him. He is, without doubt, a really well-substantiated ghost. So much so that when I was filming his story in 1975 the manager of the wharf told me that his son, a lecturer in psychology in an American university, had written to say that accounts of him had begun to appear in learned journals in the States devoted to the study of the supernatural and allied subjects. The evidence for his existence is overwhelming, and the detailed accounts of the witnesses, and what they saw, must make all doubters pause.

I have to admit that while I was filming at Ratcliff Wharf I saw and felt nothing at all. This could be due to the fact that the whole story, from start to finish, biographies of ghost and witnesses alike, was invented by a friend of mine one wet afternoon when the deadline for his article in *Man, Myth and Magic* was drawing perilously near and he didn't seem to have an idea in his head. Two or three pints of good beer provided the necessary inspiration, and the Vicar of Ratcliff

Wharf, and his witnesses, were soon immortalized in print. The odd thing is that, since the story first appeared, several people who had never read the story nor knew of its existence have seen the Vicar and have described him in exactly the same style as his inventor did when, desperate in a pub in Fitzrovia, he sat down to fill a magazine page which would otherwise have been embarrassingly empty. As I've said several times already in this chapter: don't be too sceptical. One of these days you might be in for a shock.

Showplaces

London Museum – National Postal Museum
British Museum – Victoria and Albert Museum
Natural History Museum – Geological Museum
Science Museum – Imperial War Museum
Pollock's Toy Museum – Geffrye Museum
Bethnal Green Museum – Jewish Museum
National Maritime Museum
Sir John Soane's Museum – Wallace Collection
Horniman Museum – Courtauld Institute Galleries

Showplaces, not showpieces. London has lots of showpieces, many of which I've been talking about in this book.
So far its showplaces have hardly been mentioned. They are
the places where things can be seen: the museums and the
galleries, of which London has more than its fair share. But
who, visiting London, is going to complain about that?

All the museums and galleries have their own individual
guide-books, which are cheap, lightweight, and absolutely
essential if you are to get the most out of the showplace you
are visiting. The purpose of this chapter is to show you *why*
you should visit them: to put it more bluntly, why you would
be a fool not to, since this may be your only visit to London
(unlikely though that may sound).

Let us take museums. In a sense, and a very real sense,
London itself is a museum, a living museum. Much of its
past is on display in the streets, for those who have eyes to see

it. How much longer it will be is, of course, a very interesting question: I sometimes think it is a very depressing question, as those who have read so far will perhaps realize. If London *is* a museum, then it is a very curious museum, since it seems intent on destroying all the exhibits it has amassed over the twenty centuries or so of its life.

The point, though, is that this macro-museum, London, contains many of the world's very best micro-museums. So many, in fact, that once again we are faced with the old familiar question – where to start? In this case, since this is a book about London, the answer is easy. Start at the Museum of London in the Barbican.

This museum, an amalgam of the old London Museum, which used to be located in Kensington Palace, Guildhall Museum, and various other bits and pieces, is absolutely superb. You get to it by taking the underground to Barbican station, on the Circle and Metropolitan lines. There are sign-posts to the museum inside the station itself, so it's hard to get lost, but if you do, it won't take you long to find yourself again. The station will disgorge you on to Aldersgate Street. Turn right. You will soon see an overhead pedestrian way. Climb up to it, ignoring the shoddy workmanship, which means that there are pools of standing water on the staircase after every rainfall – long after – and that there are rain streaks down most of the concrete walls. There, across the concourse, is the entrance to the museum, and you'll be lucky if there aren't a lot of schoolchildren milling around it, since it has already become one of the most popular of school trips – but not *the* most, as we shall be seeing.

There is little doubt that museum display techniques have improved enormously over the last ten or fifteen years. The Museum of London, being just about the most modern of showplaces, exploits the improvements to the full. Once you have handed over your coat, hat and umbrella, you will find yourself at the beginning of a controlled walk through more than a quarter of a million years of London, or at least Thames Valley, history.

There is no need to wonder what to look at next. The museum lay-out solves that problem for you. There is no way to go except onwards and upwards, like the youth in

176

'Excelsior'. The important thing – and it is something I am going to be emphasizing often in this chapter – is to take it easy. There is so much to see that to rush through the museum is not only a waste of your time; it is also a waste of the time of the people who clearly thought very hard about the layout and the display.

Each visitor will have his or her own preference among the thousands of exhibits, but there are three things in particular you should make every effort to study at length. One is 'The Fire Experience'. This is a valiant attempt to give you the feeling of what it was like to be alive and a Londoner during the Great Fire of 1666. It is done in a small theatre by means of film and tape. A diorama of the London of Charles II's time glows ever more fiercely as the flames take hold. Actors' voices quote from contemporary accounts. The roar of the flames grows louder. The twin hills of London are seen in dark silhouette against a halo of fire. Old St Paul's is ablaze. So is Baynard's Castle. Gradually the City is destroyed, and ends up as acres of smouldering rubble. I am not saying you will come out of 'The Fire Experience' with your eyebrows singed, but I am positively asserting you will come out more aware of the magnitude of the catastrophe, and of the almost universal feeling Londoners had that the Fire was God's way of cleansing the City after the Great Plague of the year before, and bringing sinful man back to his senses.

'The Fire Experience' doesn't last very long, and is repeated almost continuously throughout the day. It is a popular exhibit – if exhibit is the right word – so you may find there is a queue. Don't let that put you off. The queue is never very long and is soon on the move. You will not regret whatever delay there is.

Not far from 'The Fire Experience' is one of the most magnificent models I have ever seen. It is of the old White-hall Palace, which once covered all that area we now collec-tively call Whitehall – the street itself, and the Government offices on either side, from the river, west to St James's Park, and from Parliament Square north to Scotland Yard. As the model makes clear, the Palace wasn't really a palace at all. It was more a small village, and not so small at that. It provided

Thames-side homes for the king and queen, necessarily separate, since Charles II's five officially-admitted mistresses lived there too: it contained the Great Hall, the White Hall after which the whole complex was named; the Banqueting Hall, almost the only surviving fragment – but what a fragment! – of Whitehall Palace; and it was big enough to have space for more than 2,000 rooms and offices for the huge crowd of Court hangers-on. On top of all that, there were formal gardens; the king's aviary; a tilt-yard; a tennis court for the king's own use; the Holbein Gate, named after the great painter who had lodged there at the time of Henry VIII; royal coal and wood yards; a theatre; a science laboratory; and many other things of worthy note. Not all of these existed from the beginning, of course. Whitehall Palace, like Topsy, just growed, so that by the time Charles II came to the throne in 1660 it was exactly what a foreign visitor described it as: 'ill built, and nothing but a heap of houses erected at diverse times and of different models'. What it became is beautifully shown by the model, which alone deserves an hour or so's study.

Down below the ramp leading to 'The Fire Experience', you will get a glimpse of gold. It is the Lord Mayor's Coach. Surely he doesn't keep it here when he isn't using it for his Show on the second Saturday in November? Of course he doesn't. This is merely a fibre-glass replica. Merely? It is magnificent. Full-sized, it shows what modern technology can do. You won't actually be able to sit in it, but you'll get nearer to it, and for longer, than any loyal citizen does as the procession passes on its way to the Law Courts. There the Lord Mayor is met by the Lord Chief Justice, to present himself as a right worthy citizen and Her Majesty's most loyal servant, something which I am sure the Lord Chief Justice, who might have been dining with him the night before, has never really doubted. You will find some difficulty in getting within arm's length – actual touching is forbidden – of the coach, because it is almost invariably surrounded by wide-eyed children staring at it unbelievingly. This should be no disadvantage, as you will certainly be bigger than they are and can therefore look over their heads at this wonderful piece of work.

178

There is so much more in the Museum of London that I could go on for ever. You will be glad to learn that I am not proposing to do that. I am just proposing to urge you, once more, to go there. Do not, however, go on Mondays: it is closed. On the other weekdays it is open from 10 a.m. to 6 p.m. and from 2 p.m. to 6 p.m. on Sundays. It is closed on Bank Holidays, which seems odd, as well as Christmas Eve, Christmas Day, and Boxing Day. If you can date and time your visit so that London schoolchildren are all slaving over their books (if, indeed, schoolchildren ever do that today), you will be doing yourself a lot of good. Concentration on the objects laid out for your edification and delight becomes a trifle hard when you are surrounded by a horde of youngsters saying 'Miss, Miss, Sir, Sir, what's this?'. If it does happen that way, pull philosophy to your aid and reflect that it is largely for the education of children such as these that the museum is designed. From which you will gather that the Museum of London is not usually shrouded in the sepulchral hush which used to be the rule when you and I were young. And a good thing too.

London's other main museums are far from the Barbican, but if postage stamps are your passion you will be able to indulge yourself only a few hundred yards away from the Museum of London. Go down Aldersgate's continuation, St Martin-le-Grand. On the right is Angel Street. At the head of this street is the National Postal Museum, where more than 350,000 stamps are on display, or so they tell me; I haven't counted them. If you are a philatelist you will not have needed me to tell you this; if you are not, then the exhibition may turn you into one. On the other hand, the overwhelming number of stamps on display may turn you off them for life, but that is a risk you will have to take and something you must make up your own mind about.

The nearest great museum is a brisk half-hour's walk away, but the exercise will do you good, and you pass a lot of interesting places on the way. Turn south out of the National Postal Museum (if you haven't been in there, it doesn't matter: the route is just the same) and then turn right (west) along Newgate Street, past the Old Bailey, with its shuddering memories of the frightful Newgate Prison, along Holborn

Viaduct across what was once (still is, come to that) the valley of the River Fleet, past the great red cliff of the *Daily Mirror* building, past Staple Inn, a real glimpse of what Old London was like, and along High Holborn. At Holborn tube station turn right (north) up Southampton Row. On the left-hand side is Great Russell Street. Three hundred yards along, on your right-hand side, is the finest museum in the world – the British Museum and British Library.

There is some division of opinion as to whether the British Museum is the biggest in the world, but precisely because it is the *British* Museum I am going to assert that it *is*. It certainly feels like it when you walk round it.

That is the trouble. People will try and walk round it. Do not fall into this trap yourself. Make a decision about what you want to see, and go and see it. Then go back to your hotel or boarding-house and think over what you have seen. If you do not follow this advice, if you insist on cramming in everything in one visit, you will suffer from severe mental, cultural, aesthetic and intellectual indigestion, and serve you right.

There is no problem at all in deciding which bit of the museum you want to do on any one day. Just inside the door and to the left is a plan of the building, with its various sections clearly labelled. May I suggest a 'taster' for you? Having turned to the left as you pass through the door under the portico, go along the long hall where all manner of postcards, pictures, models, replicas and the like are on display. Buy a copy of the Summary Guide to the museum. Do not lose it: it will be your staff to lean upon for many a long day to come.

Continue along the same direction – westerly, if it is of any interest. Which reminds me: a compass would be no bad thing; I do not know of anybody actually getting lost and starving to death in this tremendous complex, but who knows what they might find in a mummy case one of these fine days?

Towards the end of your westerly walk you will come across the Assyrian Section. Do not be afraid you will miss it. Not even a blind man could miss the enormous lion at the entrance to the Assyrian Hall. It is quite magnificent. The whole impression of the Assyrian Hall is one of barbarousness, of tremendous power, of irresistible force. And yet it is all so human. Come up out of the Assyrian Basement into the Assyrian Hall again and there in front of you is a face, a huge face. It is at least 2,500 years old, maybe much more. It is from Nineveh. It is staggering. The impression that it is going to open, slowly, those hooded eyes; that those full, sensual lips are going to smile, slowly; and that the nostrils of its bulbous nose are going to twitch, slowly, as part of the smile, is so strong that I find myself standing in front of it, actually waiting for it to happen. You can see what effect the Assyrian Section might have on you? So take care you don't spoil it by going off and sampling another section – say the Egyptian one or the Greek one. Save those for another day. One day for each.

In the Egyptian Section you can see mummy cases of exquisite lacquering, five thousand years old at least. The faces are coldly beautiful. Are they sneering, are they supercilious, or are they simply above the ordinary things of our lives? They are certainly not *of* this day and age, and yet, equally certainly, they are *for* this day and age. They have something to say to us. What it is I do not know, but that they do have something to say is certain.

Walk along their ranks, in that sort of bewildered trance, and you will be brought suddenly back to earth by a thing stupendous. There, in the middle of the aisle, is the Rosetta Stone, that infinity-to-one chance discovery, the stone which, by virtue of the fact that it is inscribed with the same message in hieroglyph and in Greek enabled the scholar Champollion to decipher the ancient Egyptian script for the first time. There it is, the Rosetta Stone, the *real* Rosetta Stone, in the middle of the aisle, and it isn't surrounded by ropes and by notices saying 'Keep Off'. It is there for anybody to peer at, to pore over, and to ponder about the miracle that enabled us to learn all we know about Egyptian life up to six thousand years ago. The British Museum is truly a wonderful place.

And you will still have seen only the tiniest part of its treasures. Go back another day and make for the Greek Section. Greek carving is a lovesome thing, God wot. The British Museum has some of its most wonderful work. The

Elgin Marbles may have been stolen from Greece by Lord Elgin in 1816; they may be the subject of acrimonious exchanges between Greek and British governments; but they are meltingly beautiful. They are, of course, taken from the frieze of the Parthenon, from the Erechtheum, and from other buildings in that noble cluster at the top of the Acropolis. They are housed in the Duveen Gallery, specially built for them from a benefaction by the dealer and connoisseur, Joseph Duveen. I can swear they move, so exquisite is the carving. Draperies sway slightly in the breeze. Surely those limbs are stretching, those lips about to speak? The glory that was Greece is nowhere better demonstrated than in the British Museum. Nor is it all on a large scale. Look at the Portland Vase, standing alone in its glass case. Walk slowly round it, time and time again. Look at the delicacy of it all. How can so fragile a thing have come down the ages unscathed?

It is sights like these, and thoughts like these, which make me feel the need, once again, to say that, despite the temptation to go on cramming more and more in, like a greedy child with a bag of sweets, not happy until they all have gone, and then very unhappy afterwards, you really should ration yourself. Do not dull one set of impressions by overlaying them with another on the same day. Give the first set time to digest. It is a hard discipline if you are only in London on a short visit, but it is worth the effort. Even if you don't see everything – or a thousandth of everything – what you *do* see will remain in your mind unclouded, to give you joy for ever.

Among your remaining visits to the British Museum should be one to the Roman Section, where there is a bust to Julius Classicanus, who lived and died in London, where he was buried. He it was who asked Nero to send out a pacifying Governor to Britain, not a vengeful one, after Boadicea's rebellion: Nero agreed. There is also a head of the Emperor Hadrian which was found in the Thames, and an aristocratic fellow he looks, too.

The other absolute must is the Reading Room. You won't be allowed in, unless you have a Reader's Ticket, for which you have to apply to the Director, and he won't grant you one unless you are a bona fide scholar. You may very well be, but not on this visit, you aren't, so – no ticket. Nevertheless you can look in at the enormous room – the dome is wider than that of St Peter's in Rome – and you can imagine all the great ones who have worked here: Karl Marx sat in Row G; Lenin used the place; Swinburne, characteristically, fainted here. There are also the mute inglorious Miltons, the village Hampdens, those born to waste their sweetness on the desert air with schemes little, if anything short of lunacy: they, too, found the Reading Room their Heaven on earth.

However you arrange your visits to the British Museum you will need to know that it is open each day from 10 a.m. to 5 p.m., Sunday 2.30 p.m. to 6 p.m., and that includes Easter Saturday and Monday, as well as the spring and summer Bank Holidays. It is closed only on Good Friday, Christmas Eve, Christmas Day, Boxing Day and New Year's Day. And it is free. All those wonderful things free! You could spend a lifetime in there, warm, dry, and unaware of the world. Some people have done.

Enough of Bloomsbury. There is yet another museum area waiting, and that one even greater, at least in extent, than the British Museum. The area, all 87 acres of it, is within a few yards of South Kensington Underground station (Circle, District, and Piccadilly lines). As you come up the steps to ground level, turn right out of the station arcade and hairpin back – that is to say, turn north – to Cromwell Road. Ahead of you, on either side of Exhibition Road, is the most varied load of delights the mind of man can ever have dreamed of.

As you stand on the south side of Cromwell Road, at the bottom of Exhibition Road, there, opposite you on the right, is the Victoria and Albert Museum. This is probably the most unfortunately-named of all museums. To a lot of minds its title suggests a stuffy, narrow, unartistic era. The fact that the Victorian Age was probably the greatest century, in just about every field of endeavour, that this country has known seems somehow to get overlooked. Nevertheless, the impression remains. Lytton Strachey has a lot to answer for.

Even if the name does happen to put you off, don't

bother. Just *go* to the Victoria and Albert, but don't go on Fridays, because it is closed, at least at the time of writing. The reasons are said to be economic, and they could very well be, but it is a pity all the same. Other museums seem to have escaped cuts like this: why is the V & A singled out?

On the assumption, however, that it is not Friday, you are in for a treat. More than a treat, more like a treatment. Because you will certainly be in need of treatment if you try and take in too much of this treasure-house at one go. You will come out feeling as though you have been struck between the eyes by a fourteen-pound hammer. But you cannot come out before you have gone in, so let us adventure.

The V & A, as seen from the south side of Cromwell Road, looks to be favourite for the label of 'London's Ugliest Building', although there are, of course, many other highly-qualified contenders for that particular title. Not being a Paris, I shall make no judgement. I shall merely tell you that apart from Fridays, Good Friday, Christmas Eve, Christmas Day, Boxing Day and New Year, the museum is open every single day of the year from 10 a.m. to 5.50 p.m., Sundays 2.30 p.m. to 5.50 p.m., and admission is free. Another free treasure-house! Would we care more, or go more often, if we had to pay? I don't know, but a recent attempt to charge admission to our galleries and museums did result in a considerable drop in attendance. The British clearly are not too keen on paying for culture. Anyway, we don't have to pay these days, so go right in, up the steps, past the tablets commemorating the two stages in which the museum was built. The first was laid in 1899 by Queen Victoria (in the sixty-second year of her reign!) to mark the completion of the museum inaugurated by her dear Prince Albert all those years before: hence the present title of the museum (it was formerly known as the South Kensington museum). The tablet on the right-hand side of the door was laid by the son of Victoria and Albert, King Edward VII, in 1908, the ninth year of his reign, to mark the completion of the additions. In view of Edward's well-known tastes, I am pretty sure, even without looking into it, that that was the only time he ever darkened the museum's doors.

Inside you are faced with about 150 rooms, so, if you want

to do them all, I advise you to follow the example of George Bernard Shaw in his days as an art critic, and fit yourself out in a pair of walking boots. The museum is actually devoted to the 'Fine and Applied Arts', which results in a division into two appropriate parts. That was the original scheme and it has lasted until the present day. Since the arrival on the scene of Dr Roy Strong, formerly at the National Portrait Gallery, things have taken a turn for the livelier. Dr Strong is strong – the pun is unavoidable – on presentation. A thin, bespectacled man, with a depressed-looking moustache, he gives the impression of being effete and ineffectual. He is most decidedly neither. He bubbles with ideas, and his energy is exhausting. This personal note is included simply because what he *is* shows itself in what he has *done*. The V & A now is very different from the pre-Strong version.

Do not go a step until you have bought the short guide to the museum and its contents. Only then will you be in a position to proceed profitably. If the caution about trying to take in too much at once applies to the British Museum, it applies equally, or even more so, to the V & A. This is not because of the shock to the system which the clash of cultures displayed in the BM can give you, but because in the V & A the sheer weight of just about everything in the world becomes insupportable. Everything in the world *is* displayed there: if it isn't, then all I can say is that it feels as if it is. After all, the V & A covers more than ten acres, which is about the same area as five Wembley football pitches! You see what I meant about walking boots?

Broadly, the two divisions are concerned with (a) primary collections, as they are called, of masterpieces of all the arts brought together by period, nationality or style, as the official wording has it; and (b) study collections, which are arranged on the basis of the materials they employ, such as pottery, woodwork and so on. The division helps to make some sense of the enormous amount of work on display. Help is most certainly needed. You must make your own choice, with the help of the guide, but here are a few of the things you can choose from.

First and foremost, I suppose, are the Raphael cartoons, which the artist did for Pope Leo X in the year 1516. They came to the V & A from Hampton Court in 1865, braced upright in a stout wooden framework and drawn by eight stout horses. Then there is the Great Bed of Ware, which both Shakespeare and Ben Jonson mentioned. Measuring about 11 feet square, that probably required even stouter horses to drag it here. In contrast, the V & A contains the world's finest collection of portrait miniatures, the name of Nicholas Hilliard featuring strongly. There is a shattering collection of Italian Renaissance masterpieces, including Donatello's 'Ascension, with Christ giving the keys to St Peter'. Just about every other period of art is covered, naturally only by the best examples. In the study collections, you can see three rooms from old London houses, each furnished exactly as it was in its time. You can see glasswork, bronzework, ironwork, gold and silver work, furniture and furnishings, from all ages and all countries. You can see. . . but the list is endless. The guide will help; the catalogue requires a furniture van to transport it. The injunction not to try and take it in all at once is really unnecessary: it is quite impossible.

When you have left the V & A, utterly exhausted – and proud, I hope, to belong to the race, the human race, which has developed the myriad skills necessary to produce all that – you can then stun yourself with the thought that there are another seventy acres or so to go at, and all of them right there in front of you. That is clearly the point at which you will feel the need for rest and refreshment. Take it while you can.

Immediately across Exhibition Road, with an enormously long Cromwell Road frontage, is the Natural History Museum, properly called the British Museum (Natural History Section). You will feel shattered even before you go in here if you spend too long looking at Alfred Waterhouse's façade. Cleaned in the late seventies, it now presents millions of square feet of pale cream stone at you, 'decorated' with trillions of blue tiles. The windows appear to be Norman – at least they are arched; there are gables along the roof line; the chimneys twist and coil as though designed by some demented Elizabethan architect (to add to the effect, they are in cream and blue as well!); and there is a massive, positively horrendous, main entrance in Romanesque style, the arch a dazzling mass of zig-zags, the supporting columns a dizzying mass of spirals. It is the sort of portal which should carry a government health warning: 'This doorway can damage your eyesight.'

Inside there should be another sign saying 'The contents of this museum can enlarge your mind'. The entrance hall alone is boggling. As well as hundreds of children – there are *always* hundreds of children in the Natural History Museum – there are enormous stuffed elephants, rhinoceroses and hippopotami. If they are life-sized I don't ever want to meet them in the bush, whatever that might be.

What most people want to see in the Natural History Museum are fossils, especially dinosaurs; the enormous, 90 feet long, cast of the biggest creature on earth, the blue whale; the tremendous collection of birds and their eggs; and the Meteorite Room. They are all easily got at; they are all equally stunning. To stand and look up at the enormous carcass of the blue whale is to experience feelings of awe that never quite crystallize into something as firm as thought. To look at the three little jars of 'krill', its main food – creatures about the size of stunted shrimps placed below it for comparison – is to realize that not only are there more things in Heaven and earth than are dreamt of in your philosophy, Horatio, but that there are more things in Heaven and earth than could have been dreamt of in anybody's philosophy, had we not seen it with our own eyes.

To get to the dinosaurs, take the first hall to the right as you enter the building. The whole theory of evolution and natural selection is laid out in that hall as clearly as this complicated subject is capable of. Since, in fact, the theory depends on only a few simple principles (it is the details which cause the complications) it is possible for even the least knowledgeable person to gain something from this display, provided they are interested, that is: 'no profit grows, where is no pleasure ta'en.' By this time you will have moved slowly along the brilliantly-lit cases and absorbed what the captions are saying, but you may have forgotten that it is the dinosaurs you are after. Once you have seen them you will never forget again.

Undoubtedly the star attraction is dear old diplodocus, a beast of very little brain. Himself (and herself, too, I suppose) about eighty feet long from nose to tail, the old grey matter was about the size of a walnut. No wonder they died out. Tyrannosaurus rex looks an unfriendly creature, posed against the wall. He was. In fact, he was probably the most unfriendly creature the earth has ever seen. The dinosaur footprints next to T. rex I find quite fascinating. First, they give me the feeling that whatever it was only very recently passed by this way. Secondly, I'd like to know what sort of 'whatever' it was. Thirdly, the explanatory notes indulge in a touch of dry academic humour. Read them and you will see what I mean.

The dinosaurs are in a hall which runs off, at right angles, from the hall which I personally find the most fascinating in the whole museum. This is because I know and love the little West Dorset town of Lyme Regis, a perhaps-obscure statement which I hope will become clear in a moment. It was at Lyme Regis that a twelve-year-old girl, Mary Anning, the daughter of a local carpenter (who, alas, died before he could know of his daughter's triumphs), discovered the fossil skeleton of a 'fish lizard', an ichthyosaur, and instantly became world-famous. Not content, she then went on to discover the first plesiosaur, *Plesiosaurus dolichodeirus*. That's it, up on the wall there; below and to the right is a drawing of Mary herself, with her little dog, Tray (artistic licence – Tray must have been dead many years before that 'likeness' was taken). Then, and still only twenty-nine years old, she went and discovered the first ever pterosaur to be found in Britain. That, too, is in this gallery. Not bad for a young, uneducated, orphaned child from an insignificant South Coast town. All those finds, and the thousands of others she made, came from the black, slippery cliffs between Lyme Regis and Charmouth. It is still a fossil hunter's delight. I know, because I've tried it myself. Now you can perhaps see why I have a particularly soft spot for this gallery.

The Meteorite Room is upstairs. To get to it you climb up the great steps from the entrance hall, wend your way back along the balcony, in the general direction of Cromwell Road, and turn into the geological section. This isn't really the geological section; it's more the mineralogical section.

Case after case of all the beautiful minerals the various earth-processes have produced. You might be seduced enough by them to forget that your target is at the end of the room. To help you remember, it is clearly labelled 'Meteorites'. I find it oddly pleasant that the room is actually called the 'Meteorite Pavilion'. Pavilioned in splendour . . .

When you consider that everything on display has actually fallen from the skies (thus proving that what comes down doesn't necessarily have to go up first), it is a wonder that nobody got hurt. This is even more the case when you notice – how can you miss it? – that one of the exhibits weighs 3½ tons. Meteorites are really still very much a mystery, and the display, with proper scientific open-mindedness, is the first to admit it. Do yourself the favour, after you have studied the exhibits, of keeping the same sort of open mind. They came from outer space . . . but where, when, how, why?

There is one other major exhibit in the Natural History Museum which you mustn't miss. It is the brand-new Hall of Human Biology. One thing I particularly like about this lay-out is that it reinforces what I have been saying all along – don't try and cram too much in at once. The notice at the start says that it is a large exhibit, and you shouldn't do it all in one go. If that is true of a single exhibit, how much truer is it of a whole museum?

This is an entirely new form of display. It is very much do-it-yourself. You are invited to press buttons and see what happens. You are tempted to sit in tiny viewing theatres, tucked away in shrouded corners, to press the appropriate control, and to see and hear what the pictures and the voices say. You are asked to go through a tiny maze and remember what you pass: there is a check list at the end to show you that your powers of observation aren't quite as good as you thought they were. Done in bright red plastic, and various other modern materials, it is hard, shiny, and maybe a trifle gimmicky. But it is also fascinating. There is very little about the human body, both physical and mental, that isn't covered in this splendid display. One slight snag: it is all very well for the notice to urge you not to try and do it all at once. If you break off halfway through, it is as hard to get out as it would be if you tried to leave the Hampton Court maze after only a few minutes. Apart from that, it is an intriguing idea, and a must for schoolchildren. All those buttons to press. All those lights flashing. Bursts of pop music. Wonderful. And if you get a little weary of the children, you will be glad to know that there is a decent little cafeteria on the first floor, and on the ground floor there are rest spaces, reserved for adults only. Somebody has clearly been very thoughtful.

All the above merely skims the surface of what the Natural History Museum has to offer, but it will be enough to be going on with. So leave the museum, through that incredible main entrance, and turn left along Cromwell Road. Turn up Exhibition Road and there you will find the Geological Museum. It sounds as though it is for geological buffs only, and it is true that you will get more out of it if you have at least a smattering of the subject. However, museums are not just for the experts: they are the people who don't need them. Museums are quite definitely for laymen, so don't be frightened. Plunge in, and learn something about the earth we live on.

I think there are two exhibits you will find especially interesting. First, on the ground floor, is 'The Story of Our Earth'. It tells the incredible story very well, from its beginnings (although ideas about how *that* happened are still the subject of fierce arguments among geologists, astronomers and the like) right up to the present day. The time-scale involved makes a lot of our present little local difficulties look rather trivial.

The other exhibit, on the first floor, is a very clever model of the structure of the South East of England, showing the succesion of rocks and how they have been bent, broken, arched, and worn away over the millennia. The least this exhibit will do is make you buy one of the explanatory booklets on sale, after which every train or car journey you make will be all that much more interesting. I must declare an interest here: as a keen amateur geologist in my earlier days, I find it a subject that makes every trip, whether on wheel or on foot, much more enthralling. And how nice to be able to answer those childish questions: 'Daddy, why are those mountains there? Daddy, why is that river all twisty and bendy? Daddy, why has the soil suddenly gone red?'.

Once you have explained why, in your masterful way, your offspring will look at you in a new light. And all because you spent an hour or two in the Geological Museum.

Further up Exhibition Road is a museum where your child, if it is a typical modern child, will be able to answer *your* questions. The Science Museum, and if ever a museum was popular with children, it is this one. For boys particularly (is one allowed to make that distinction any more, I wonder?) it is little short of Paradise. There is Stephenson's 'Rocket', and one or two of its competitors; there is a replica of the Wright Brothers' plane, with which they made history at Kitty Hawk on 17 December 1903; there are wonderful models of ships, planes, trains, and cars. Press a button and you're down a coal mine. Press another and something equally fascinating will happen. The galleries, like the caverns through which Alph, the sacred river, ran, are measureless to man; but for the modern-minded, or those who have consistently failed to get the number they have been dialling, Gallery 66 is a must, since it is a history of telecommunications. If your kitchen stove has just blown up as a consequence of being converted to North Sea gas, the gallery showing the history of the gas industry from William Murdoch onwards might be some consolation. Since it also includes a description of how they drill for gas and oil in the North Sea, you will come away from the exhibit a thoroughly modern Willie, well up in all the latest exploratory techniques. The diorama of the history of transport is one that never fails to attract the children – and the grown-ups. It will make you eager to leave for home and your toy railway.

By now, you may have had enough of South Kensington, although there is still much more further up the street. I don't blame you, although I shall be surprised if you don't feel compelled to come back time and time again. But we must now look elsewhere because, believe it or not, there are dozens more London museums we haven't even mentioned. Obviously we can't visit them all in one trip to London – not even in many trips – but if I tell you of one or two I have enjoyed, perhaps you might feel tempted to have a look for yourself.

The Imperial War Museum is a particularly fascinating

place. You get to it by the Bakerloo line to Lambeth North, or Elephant and Castle (it is just about midway between these two stations). The museum is set in the grounds of the Geraldine Mary Harmsworth Park, which lies between the fork formed by Lambeth Road and St George's Road. It is *not* a museum for the glorification of war. It is merely a museum of the history of war – and not all war: merely the most recent big ones. If it also shows that men are capable of supreme heroism in war, then so much the better for men (or worse, depending on which way you look at it). It is a nice irony that the building it is housed in was once the Bethlehem Hospital, commonly known as Bedlam. That a museum of war should be housed in a former lunatic asylum seems entirely appropriate. Do go and see it, however, whether or not you yourself ever got caught up in the last (do I mean latest?) madness. Admission is free and the museum is open every day of the year except Good Fridays, Christmas Eve, Christmas Day, Boxing Day and New Year's Day. Weekday hours 10 a.m. to 5.50 p.m., Sundays 2.00 p.m. to 5.50 p.m. Lovers of irony might like to note that a museum devoted to war is also open on Easter Sunday, a day devoted to the Prince of Peace.

In complete contrast, what about my next selection? Pollock's Toy Museum. It is in Whitfield Street, not far from the Post Office Tower. The nearest Underground station is Goodge Street (Northern line). Although small, the museum has been a favourite for about a century. It doesn't just concentrate on the toy theatre, which is its main *raison d'être*, but has a fine collection of dolls from all over the world, and a most attractive display of the successive attempts to make moving pictures, a long endeavour finally ending in the cinema, something which probably put paid to toy theatres for ever. It is open from Monday to Saturday, from 10 a.m. to 5 p.m., and is closed at Easter and at Christmas as well as on Bank Holidays. There is an admission charge – 20 pence (at the moment of writing), half price for the under *17s* (!).

The Geffrye Museum is too often ignored. This is probably because it is out east. Not very far east though: only Kingsland Road, Shoreditch. The simplest way to get there is probably by underground to Liverpool Street (Circle, Metropolitan and Central lines) and then walk or go by any one of a series of buses (22, 22a, 48, 97, 149, 243A). If you don't want the bother of changing your method of transport and are lucky enough to be staying near a 67 or 243 bus route, then you are made, since both of them pass the door. Although I said the Geffrye is virtually ignored, I meant by tourists. It is extremely popular with schools and study groups which come from all over to look at rooms dating from the beginning of the seventeenth century, each furnished according to the taste of the time. It is in a singularly appropriate location, since Shoreditch and Hoxton were, and to some extent still are, the centre of the furniture industry. The museum, which is free, is most attractively housed in what was once a group of eighteenth-century almshouses, built with a legacy from Sir Robert Geffrye, Master of the Ironmongers' Company and a former Lord Mayor of London.

If you are interested in the history of the theatre, by the way, and particularly the theatre of Shakespeare's time, you might as well take advantage of the area once you have finished with the Geffrye. Turn left out of the museum and walk down towards Shoreditch High Street. The church at the near end of the street was built in the middle of the eighteenth century but stands on the site of a thirteenth-century foundation. In the yard of that older church were buried James Burbage and his son Richard, both of them colleagues of Shakespeare, who wrote for them and acted with them. Richard was Will's first Shylock. You will find a tablet to father and son Burbage in the north wall, put there in 1913 by the London Shakespeare League. And if you walk for about five minutes down Shoreditch High Street you will find, just to the right (west) of the High Street, a thorough-fare called Curtain Road. Appropriate name, Curtain. For it was here, in 1576, that James Burbage built England's first-ever theatre. Not unnaturally, with no predecessors, it was simply called '*The* Theatre'. It was so successful that it soon attracted competition. In 1577, one Henry Laneman or Lanman, Gent., built another theatre only a couple of hundred yards away. He called his theatre 'The Curtain'.

Hence the name of the road. Sensibly enough, they pooled forces after a while, so that when Richard Burbage, Will Shakespeare, Will Kemp and the others, migrated from Southwark after falling out with Richard Alleyn, they played both theatres. Where The Curtain was exactly we shall never know, but on the wall of Nos 86 and 88 Curtain Road, you can see a tablet commemorating England's first, *The* Theatre.

All of which has taken us some way from museums, but no matter. We can soon get back to the subject. Not that there is much more to tell. Well, in fact there is, but no room here to do it. Let me end, then, with a brief list of some other show-places and give you some idea of what they specialize in to help decide if they interest you or not.

The Bethnal Green Museum, for example, in Cambridge Heath Road, almost opposite the Old Ford Road junction (by underground to Bethnal Green, Central line), has a wonderful collection of dolls' houses, toys and games, mostly from the eighteenth and nineteenth centuries; a costume collection; and fine examples of silk (nearby Spitalfields was where the Huguenot refugees settled and carried on their silk trade). Usual opening, times, closed Easter and Christmas etc. Open Bank Holidays.

The Jewish Museum is on the corner of Upper Woburn Place and Endsleigh Place. It isn't open on Saturdays, of course, nor on Jewish Holy days. Monday to Thursday 2.30 p.m. to 5 p.m., Fridays and Sundays 10.30 a.m. to 12.45 p.m. Oddly enough, it is closed on Christmas Day, as well as Good Friday, Easter Sunday and Monday. It contains all sorts of Jewish artefacts – rams' horns, an Ark of the Covenant, and lots of scrolls.

At Greenwich is the National Maritime Museum and much else. The museum is in Greenwich Park. There you can see the uniform in which Nelson was killed at Trafalgar, as well as model ships and real figureheads by the score. If seamanship and navigation turn you on, there is a print room, a library, and a collection of nautical instruments, such as sextants and chronometers, including the very first, the one designed by John Harrison of Pontefract which won him first prize in a government competition in the 1760s. Whether or not you are particularly mad about the sea, surely even *you* would like to see the world's largest ship-in-a-bottle? Of course you would. It's here. Don't forget that the museum is also a library, with more than 20,000 volumes, and an art gallery, with the greatest British painters all represented. So throw caution to the winds, even if you get sea-sick on a boating pond, and take the Thames steamer from Westminster or Tower Piers, and arrive at Greenwich the proper way – by water. After the museum, there is always the Naval College and its wonderful Great Hall. When you have seen all that, there is still the *Cutty Sark*, itself most definitely a museum, even though it is one of the most famous ships ever built. There is so much more to see in Greenwich that the whole place can be considered as a museum, and it is one you *can* do in a day because there is plenty of walking, green spaces, and fascinating streets to wander through, so that indigestion is unlikely. You can also do that intriguing thing: you can stand astride the Greenwich meridian so that one leg is in the Western, and the other is in the Eastern, hemisphere. Childish, but strangely satisfying. Most of Greenwich's attractions are open for the usual times and closed on the usual days. Some are free, some are not: none is expensive.

Two more places, often ignored by the tourists: first, the Sir John Soane's Museum in Lincoln's Inn Fields, which is very much a case of *multum in parvo*: a lot in a little. You'll find all sorts of things here, including Hogarth's famous 'Rake's Progress', and his masterpiece of political cynicism, 'The Election'. Since the house is very much as Sir John left it (and designed it, too, for he was his own architect) you might also find a strong eighteenth-century feeling. The second largely-ignored gem is the Wallace Collection in Hertford House, Manchester Square (nearest underground stations: Bond Street or Marble Arch, both on the Central line). The collection, which by deed can neither be added to nor subtracted from, is a tremendous display of eighteenth-century taste. It is named after Sir Richard Wallace. He inherited it from his supposed father, the Marquis of Hertford, after whom the house is named. And the Marquis of Hertford was a descendant of the Duke of Manchester, after whom the square is named. Clear now? Whether or not you are, please visit the collection. When I tell you the pictures include several Rembrandts, and works by Van Dyck, Velázquez, Rubens, Reynolds and Gainsborough, as well as Watteau and Fragonard, you will see that if you do not visit the Wallace Collection, you will be missing a great deal. Entrance is free and Hertford House is closed only on Good Fridays, Christmas Day etc., and is open at the sort of times we should be accustomed to by now.

I said *two* more showplaces to finish with, but I've suddenly thought of a couple more. One is a museum, a few miles from the City but easily got at by train, and a fascinating hotchpotch. The other is an art gallery, right in the centre of the area we are especially concentrating on throughout this book, and a very high priority 'must' for anybody especially interested in modern art.

The museum is the Horniman Museum, London Road, Forest Hill, which you can get to by train from London Bridge or by a whole string of buses (12, 12a, 63, 176, 176a, 185, and P4). The museum was built in 1902 in the *art nouveau* style, architect Harrison Townsend, and was presented to the people of London by Mr F. J. Horniman, who I assume, but I'm not certain of it, to be a member of the famous tea family.

Fascinating hotchpotch, I said, and so it is. How else can you describe a collection which covers musical instruments, early tools, an aquarium, a real-live beehive under glass, so that in summer you can see the colony at their never-ending work, and a collection devoted to magic and religion? Go and see for yourself: if you feel knocked out by it all, you can always go and rest yourself in nearby Dulwich Park.

The art gallery is in Central London, at Woburn Square in the heart of Bloomsbury. The location is appropriate, since the gallery houses a collection of all the art treasures bequeathed to London University over the years. It is particularly interesting to those whose taste is for Impressionism and after. There are paintings by Cézanne, Manet, Renoir, Seurat (he of the dots) and Van Gogh, and there is also the Roger Fry Collection, the work of the artist-critic who was such an important part of the vastly over-written-about Bloomsbury Set. Incidentally, Woburn

Square has a habit of not being shown in 'A to Zs'. Don't worry. Just head for Russell Square (nearest Tube station has the same name). Woburn Square runs out of the north-western corner of the square towards Gordon Square, but it does it by way of Thornhaugh Street, and they're doing so much redevelopment in that area that you may be pushed to find your way through the confusion. Persevere: the Courtauld – the Courtauld Institute Galleries, to give it its proper name – is well worth it. Open 10 a.m. to 5 p.m., Sundays 2 p.m. to 5 p.m., closed Good Friday and Christmas Day.

By now, the more knowing of you will be howling 'But what about the most famous galleries of all?'. Well, what about them? Do you really need me to tell you about the National Gallery, the National Portrait Gallery, and the Tate Gallery? Of course you don't. Do not, however, just because I haven't mentioned them, think they are not worth a visit. *They are worth hundreds of visits.* Go there (Trafalgar Square underground for the National and the National Portrait: Pimlico for the Tate); buy as many of the catalogues as you can afford or carry, and start the slow walk round. The usual warning applies. Do not try and 'do' each one in one visit. Go many times, choosing one section each visit, and feast your eyes and your mind until you feel drunk with delight. That way pleasure lies. Much good do it unto your gentle heart.

INDEX

209